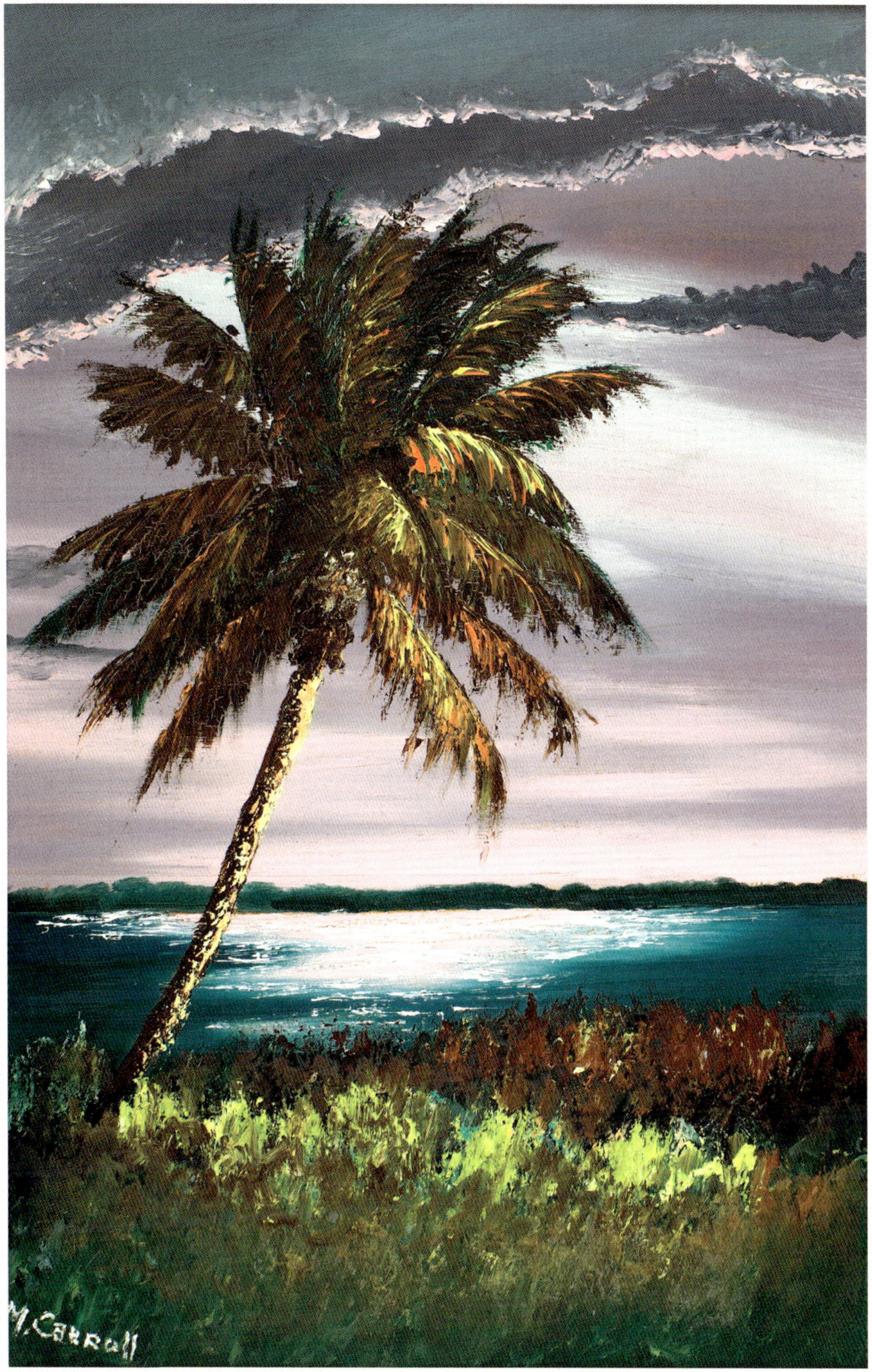

I0446107

Mary Ann Carroll

UNIVERSITY PRESS OF FLORIDA

Florida A&M University, Tallahassee
Florida Atlantic University, Boca Raton
Florida Gulf Coast University, Ft. Myers
Florida International University, Miami
Florida State University, Tallahassee
New College of Florida, Sarasota
University of Central Florida, Orlando
University of Florida, Gainesville
University of North Florida, Jacksonville
University of South Florida, Tampa
University of West Florida, Pensacola

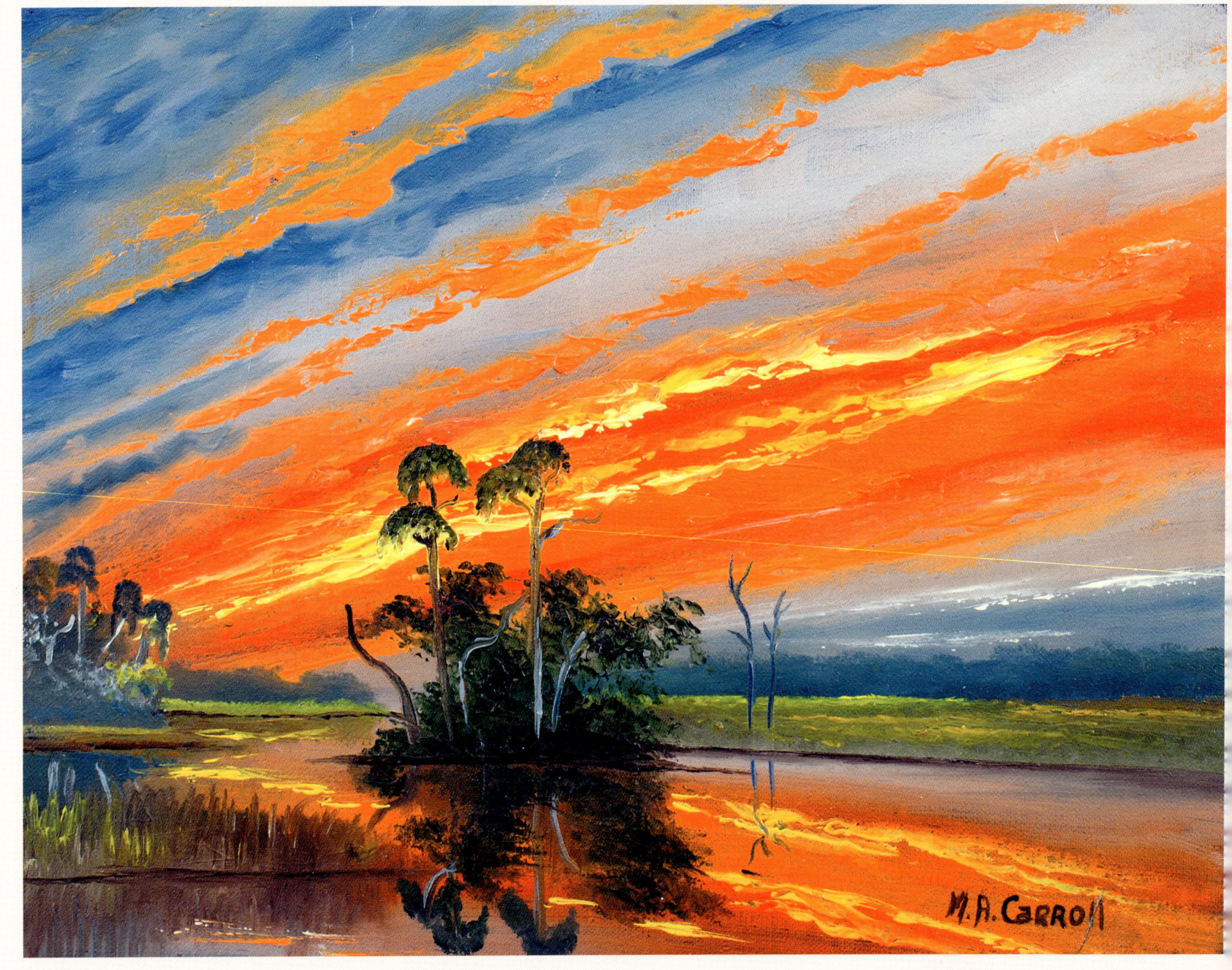

Mary Ann Carroll

FIRST LADY OF THE HIGHWAYMEN

GARY MONROE

Foreword by Virginia Lynn Moylan

University Press of Florida

Gainesville · Tallahassee · Tampa · Boca Raton

Pensacola · Orlando · Miami · Jacksonville · Ft. Myers · Sarasota

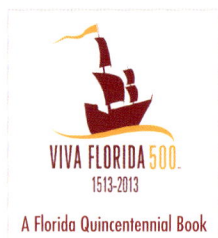

A Florida Quincentennial Book

First cloth printing, 2014
First paperback printing, 2024

29 28 27 26 25 24   6 5 4 3 2 1

Monroe, Gary, author.
Mary Ann Carroll : first lady of the Highwaymen / Gary Monroe ; foreword by Virginia Lynn Moylan.
pages cm
ISBN 978-0-8130-4969-4 (cloth) | ISBN 978-0-8130-8088-8 (pbk.)
1. Carroll, Mary Ann, 1940– 2. Florida Highwaymen. 3. Landscape painting, American—Florida—20th century. 4. African American painting—Florida—20th century. I. Moylan, Virginia Lynn. II. Title.
ND237.C2825M66 2014
759.13—dc23
2014003464

The University Press of Florida is the scholarly publishing agency for the State University System of Florida, comprising Florida A&M University, Florida Atlantic University, Florida Gulf Coast University, Florida International University, Florida State University, New College of Florida, University of Central Florida, University of Florida, University of North Florida, University of South Florida, and University of West Florida.

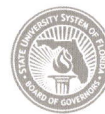

University Press of Florida
2046 NE Waldo Road
Suite 2100
Gainesville, FL 32609
http://upress.ufl.edu

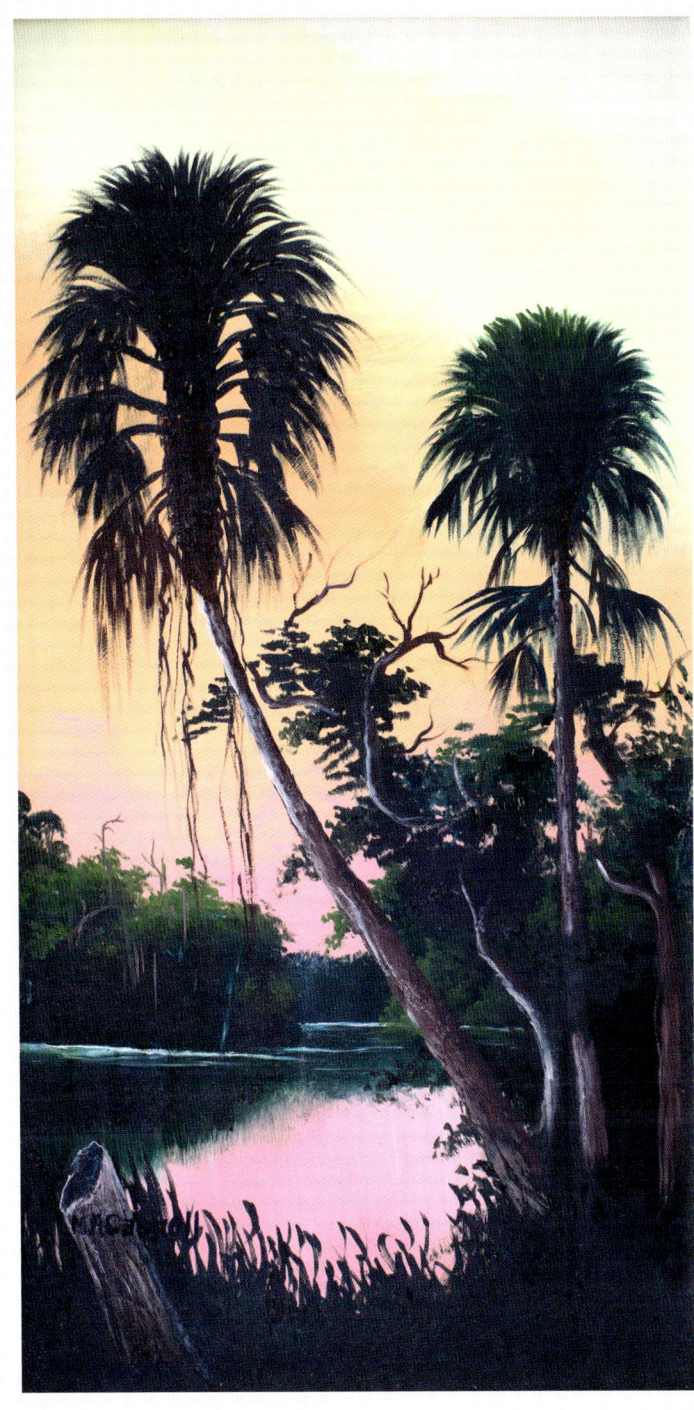

Contents

Foreword

The American poet Ralph Waldo Emerson advised, "Do not go where the path may lead, go instead where there is no path and leave a trail." So goes the life of Fort Pierce artist Mary Ann Carroll, the only female member of Florida's illustrious group of African American landscape painters known as the Highwaymen. Carroll's achievements are all the more impressive considering that she blazed her trail during a time when black visual artists were nearly invisible and Jim Crow laws reigned supreme in the South.

Carroll, the daughter of migrant laborers, began painting in earnest in the late 1950s. By then the New Negro movement of the Harlem Renaissance era had faded, and the Black Arts movement, sparked by the Black Power movement in the 1960s, had yet to emerge.

Paradoxically, although both of these movements were preoccupied with issues of visual culture, they chiefly focused their energies on literature, music, and the performing arts.

Nowhere was this artistic slight more obviously displayed than in the famed Black Arts movement mural titled *Wall of Respect*, painted on a building on Chicago's South Side in 1967 by members of the Organization of Black American Culture (OBAC). The organization was founded in Chicago that same year by a group of African American writers, scientists, educators, historians, and artists, ostensibly "to organize and coordinate an artistic cadre in support of the 1960s bare-bones struggle for freedom, justice, and equality of opportunity for African Americans in the United States." Viewing cultural expression as a "useful weapon in the struggle for black liberation," the group's visual artists designed the mural to honor positive African American role models. Ironically, although the mural featured a pantheon of more than fifty black heroes including political and religious leaders, musicians, actors, and writers, no visual artists were featured in this celebratory vision.

During the 1950s and 1960s, few black artists—and even fewer black women—were accepted into the mainstream of American art. Regardless of talent or prestigious degree, almost without exception, art galleries in both the North and South prohibited black artists from exhibiting their work or participating in competitions. Harlem Renaissance artist Lois Mailou Jones, who graduated from the School of the Museum of Fine Arts in Boston, had to exhibit her watercolors and textile designs in Paris, where there was no race prejudice. When recognition from the States finally came in 1938, it was bittersweet. Believing she was white—after a white friend from France entered her painting *Indian Shops, Gay Head, Massachusetts* into a contest—the Corcoran Gallery in Washington, D.C., presented Jones with her first major award. Fearing that she would be disqualified if her race were discovered, Jones had her award sent to her by mail. Sadly, twenty years later, little had changed. (In 1990 the Corcoran Gallery exhibited her work, threw her an eighty-ninth birthday celebration, and apologized for their previous racial policies.)

Despite this cultural vacuum, Mary Ann Carroll emerged from a firmament of African American female artists as one of the few black women to achieve success in the deeply segregated South. In this rare accomplishment she followed a path similar to that of the iconic Florida writer Zora Neale Hurston, who resided in Fort Pierce during the last years of her life. While Hurston was masterfully sowing metaphors, Carroll was capturing the unique beauty of the Florida landscape.

Carroll pursued her art during a turbulent period in the history of race relations. In the late 1950s the South was still reeling from the crisis that followed several historic Supreme Court decisions concerning civil rights. The upheaval began in 1944 with *Smith v. Allwright*, when the Court declared the South's practice of excluding blacks from voting in primary elections unconstitutional. The Ku Klux Klan responded with a rampage of cross-burning terrorism to discourage potential black voters from exercising their constitutional rights. Black citizens who dared to vote despite the consequences risked loss of employment and retaliatory violence.

Florida NAACP secretary Harry T. Moore defied white resistance by forming the Progressive Voters League to facilitate a statewide drive to register black voters. As a result of his courageous efforts, by 1950 the number of black voters in Florida had risen to 116,145, a nearly sixfold increase from 1944. Sadly, a year later on Christmas Eve in 1951, Moore and his wife became the first NAACP activists to be killed in the civil rights movement, when the Ku Klux Klan detonated a bomb under their Mims, Florida, home.

That same year, NAACP attorney Thurgood Marshall won three cases before the Supreme Court, including one that struck down segregation in higher education. And in 1954 Marshall won another historic victory with the Court's landmark decision in *Brown v. Board of Education of Topeka, Kansas*, which declared segregation in public schools, and in effect all public places, to be unconstitutional. These victories, combined with President Harry Truman's proposals for civil rights legislation, ignited a firestorm in Dixie, where American apartheid was a way of life.

This oppressive social structure left black women in the double bind of sexism and racism. Those women whose families could not afford higher education and training were relegated to low-paying, labor-intensive work. Since Fort Pierce was chiefly an agricultural center, Carroll's choices were effectively limited to menial domestic work, picking vegetables in the fields, or working in the packing houses. Faced with sole responsibility for supporting her seven children, she moved beyond the sweat and toil of the fields, finely honed her artistic skill, and broke through the social, cultural, and economic barriers to become one of Florida's most successful and celebrated landscape painters.

Mary Ann Carroll's remarkable life story, conveyed here with clarity and pathos, is one of uncommon courage and fortitude, talent and determination, and an ever-present and unshakeable faith. In the wake of her groundbreaking achievements, she has given present and future generations of female artists of every race a living legacy, not only of the beauty and vitality of the Florida landscape, but of the vital role of women in shaping our society and adding spice and grit to its creative genius.

Virginia Lynn Moylan
West Palm Beach, Florida, 2013

Preface

Mary Ann Carroll is a difficult interview, and because of this she seems almost two-dimensional at times. I cannot say she is enigmatic; rather, I suspect, she is careful not to reveal too much. Two ingrained factors may contribute to this: she's a seasoned salesperson, and she is cautious among white people. In fact, these attributes are second nature to her now and were likely honed while she sold her paintings during the civil rights era, in the thick of racial discord, to a white clientele.

Mary Ann was the first Highwayperson I met fifteen years ago as I began research on *The Highwaymen: Florida's African-American Landscape Painters*, and we simply hit it off. Back then, black Fort Pierce was an unwelcoming and dangerous place, and one devoid of white people. Run-down and blighted, its central area, Avenue D, had become a haven for drugs and prostitution; the streets were unsafe at night. But despite its very bad reputation then, I never had any difficulties. The only time I kept my eyes on the rearview mirror was when I had gone there to visit Highwayman Livingston "Castro" Roberts and was surveilled by an unmarked police car. Castro lived in a duplex apartment behind which other artists and friends hung out, some working on their cars while he often painted beside them.

Mary Ann recognized my intentions and introduced me to other Highwaymen, some of whom were either hard to locate or not interested in meeting me. This was well before they attained celebrity status. Few were even painting at this point. Most, in fact, had ceased painting at least a decade before. Mary Ann explained that there was little trust toward white people and that some of the artists were receiving SSI (Supplemental Security Income), which they didn't want to jeopardize by talking to a middle-aged, pasty-skinned white guy getting out of a nice car with a clipboard in hand (my description, not hers). Nevertheless, she was welcoming, agreeing to accompany me around the area.

It took months to meet the artists and break the ice, and I couldn't have done it without Mary Ann. We became friends in the process. I'm likely closer to her than any other Caucasian, and because of this I was happy and honored to write this book. I guarantee readers that Mary Ann is a multifaceted individual. However, I must confess that I feel I haven't captured the whole Mary Ann, although she may say that I have.

If Mary Ann seems not to be fully forthcoming, it is perhaps because she measures her life by biblical standards; her religious devotion is her road map, and she answers to a much higher authority than any of us. Maybe she is simply reticent, but more than likely she just does not want to revisit difficult times. I did get the feeling that she is afraid to unleash some old emotions. She says she has a temper. For sure, she had to be plenty angry some of the time because of what she must have seen and the way she and other African Americans must have been treated. She is a guarded person, I guess. It is almost as if she would think less of herself if she did open up. Perhaps she is just a wise businesswoman and lets bygones be bygones, not wanting to sully sales by recalling old grievances. Then again, her lack of verbosity might simply be a matter of possessing the two wise traits of discretion and restraint.

After reading my books about each of them, one might know less about Mary Ann than about Al Black, but then so many details of Al's life can readily be found on the streets and in court records. Readers of my books might feel that they know more about Harold Newton or Alfred Hair than about Mary Ann. Both of those Highwaymen, however, led large lives and were dead by the time I wrote about them, so maybe people were more likely to talk about them. The Highwaymen that I queried about Mary Ann had little to say, but merely spoke of her in the sort of taken-for-granted familiar way that one speaks of old friends. I gleaned no revelations or scandals.

Modernists, such as Mary Ann, are naturally transparent in their creations. Maybe, I thought, her ego dissolved into her paintings. After all, through an explication of her paintings we might get a glimpse into who Mary Ann really is. But there is no turmoil in her artwork, no resentment toward society, no bitterness toward anyone. Nothing scratches at the surface of Highwaymen paintings. Highwaymen art was, at one time, a ticket of sorts into another world, another dimension perhaps, given the civil divide during her heyday. In that bifurcated world, Mary Ann had feet in both the black and white sections. Although she enjoyed respect in both areas, it seemed to cause her as much inner strife, owing to her social conscience, as it offered contentment.

After years of association with the Highwaymen, I was taken aback by an exchange I recently had regarding how the Highwaymen cohort was regarded by their fellow African Americans. Highwayman Willie Daniels explained that the Highwaymen's apparently free-wheeling, romantic lifestyle—painting, driving nice cars, drinking beer during work hours—created envy and sometimes resentment among black laborers sweating in the groves and produce fields. In addition, Mary Ann felt she was resented by black women who saw her as a possible rival. Whether their recollections were accurate appraisals or just hyperbole is not the point. The artists were, in fact, admired and envied. But her memory of the way it was speaks volumes about who she is.

Although Mary Ann Carroll has given and given back, she seemingly still carries a heavy burden. Her attitudes and convictions led her on an unimaginable trajectory, a life without a road map, a life, as she says, of survival and struggle. It took daring, she told me, to survive. Hers has been a life of harsh travail, extreme perseverance, and outstanding achievement. My friend and editor Margie Miller said to me, "Mary Ann could be such a wonderful example for young women, but then she really owes the world nothing." Indeed, she has already paid her dues.

Gary Monroe
DeLand, Florida, 2013

A Note on the Paintings

Gallerist Lisa Stone (www.lisastonearts.com) oversaw the photography of the plates for this book, and photographer John Michael Bullock (www.johnmichaelbullock.com) made the digital files of the paintings. It is thanks to them, and the capable folks at the University Press of Florida, that the reproductions look so good.

Rather than rely on any one person or institution to provide illustrations for the books that I write, I reach out to curators and collectors to yield a diverse, insightful, and, ultimately, encompassing body of work. Otherwise I'd be treating the artists, and in this case Mary Ann Carroll, unjustly. The collectors' understandings have enhanced mine and facilitated my telling the story fully and engagingly.

The paintings in this book belong to the following people and institutions.

Cheryl Anacker

Michael Bowers

Omar and Elizabeth Castillo

Andrew and Jennifer Denick

Samuel Gaines

Don and Dianne George

Jack Harris

Larry Helmuth

Mark and Renee Hill

Tim and Eileen Jacobs

John Jetson

Scott and Candy Kaplan

Rich Kerchner

Dan Lambert

Roger and Pattama Lightle

Frank and Nancy Mannino

Gary and Teresa Monroe

Henry and Florence Parish

Earl and Christy Powell

Arnie Redfern

Matt and Crystal Samuel

Scott and Annie Schlesinger

Stan Shirah

Todd and Lisa South

Jasen and Maria Torres

James and Donna Wagner

Mark and Susan Weedman

Eric Wieler

South Florida State College Museum
of Florida Art and Culture

The Highwaywoman

I asked God for two things—wisdom and strength—and he gave me both.
MARY ANN CARROLL

Today, with the resurgent popularity of the Highwaymen's art and the attention that they have received, Mary Ann Carroll stands alone. "My views were different than other people's, my dreams were different," she has said. In the world in which she grew up, black women lived in the shadows. Zora Neale Hurston, one of the country's greatest writers, was isolated, working as a substitute teacher in the same Fort Pierce where Mary Ann came of age. There Hurston died, penniless and nearly forgotten, in 1960. Although she had a loyal support network of people who had recognized her genius, she was living in the County Welfare Home and was laid to rest in an unmarked gravesite that became unkempt and neglected until it was identified by author Alice Walker in 1973. Such was the plight of a black woman at this time, in this place. Such was the societal atmosphere when Mary Ann was a young woman.

Being black was a strike against you, a stigma; so was being a woman. But Mary Ann Carroll, as she assesses her past, says, "I have never seen it as a man's world or a woman's world. What I saw was survival." And survival meant struggle, perhaps the defining word of Mary Ann's life. Survival in a white man's world was challenging, to be sure. Social norms of the time were dismissive of, if not downright hostile toward, black ambition and enterprise. But Mary Ann, along with twenty-five other fledgling African American artists later dubbed the Highwaymen, would prosper under the pervasiveness of de facto segregation. Ultimately their paintings would cross race and class lines, creating Florida iconography. With tenacity and youth on their side, they saw opportunity in the face of Jim Crow laws and their aftermath. As Mary Ann puts it, "Why should I go and clean somebody's house for five dollars a day when I can paint and make two paintings in a day and make fifty dollars?" She was the only one of the group to see being a maid as an employment option, because all of the other artists were men.

During their early days, long before the Highwaymen were formally recognized, a shared identity emerged from their images that expressed something elemental about Florida and the experience of its land. Underlying this lasting visual testament to the Sunshine State's natural beauty is a collective yearning for the wild landscapes of our imaginations. When *The Highwaymen: Florida's African American*

Landscape Painters was published in 2001, reviewer Mark Derr in the *New York Times* opined that "these colorful landscapes . . . shaped the state's popular image as much as oranges and alligators." Florida's iconic palm trees and shimmering waters are staples in these paintings, reinforcing the romantic images of Florida that many people already held dear.

The incredible journey of the Highwaymen began in 1953, when a young and undefined Harold Newton returned from Georgia to Gifford, the African American community neighboring affluent Vero Beach on Florida's east coast. He had sketched and painted some during his teens, but now he wanted to become a professional artist and began to hone his skills. Soon Newton was selling his Florida landscape paintings door-to-door, from one professional office and private home to the next. In his column in the *Vero Beach Press Journal* of February 11, 1954, Bob Curzon wrote, "We wonder if Harold Newton, the young Negro artist, ever sleeps??? It seems that every day he shows up at the office with another painting." On July 21, 1955, the same newspaper again highlighted the "talented Negro artist, [who] has brought culture and appreciation of the arts to the courthouse. Several of the county offices now boast oils by Newton." To Newton, every individual and all businesses were potential customers.

A few years later and a few miles south, in rural Fort Pierce, high school student Alfred Hair was taking Saturday morning painting classes in the studio of the Caucasian regionalist A. E. "Bean" Backus. Hair saw and admired Newton's success but he wanted more than what Newton had accomplished. Hair had an unequivocal dream—he wanted to become a millionaire by his thirty-fifth birthday. Soon after graduating from high school, he would apply warp speed to Newton's practices. Hair knew that to achieve riches he must sell many paintings, since he could not compete with the established Backus, who enjoyed a studio and a waiting list for his canvases. Using simple math, Hair decided that he must produce ten paintings in the time that it took Backus to complete one. He would sell them before the oils had time to dry, for twenty-five dollars apiece, to earn the same amount of money.

The saga continued to unfold around Alfred Hair, whose personality and charisma attracted other would-be artists, for whom form would truly follow function. Aesthetic concerns were secondary, a means to the end of accumulating wealth. Hair could create a finished 2' × 3' painting, or two or three, in less than half an hour. In his converted back porch he could simultaneously and methodically develop twenty paintings all at once. This technique saved time, and as a function of speed, Hair developed his own frenetic style. Unconsciously eschewing the formulas employed by Newton, Backus, and other professional artists, he did not care about their majestic artistry.

Hair enlisted family and friends to paint alongside him, showing them his technique, which ignored the classical approaches and altered preexisting formulas. Mary Ann Carroll, together with the other aspiring artists, observed both Hair and Newton at work; these other painters joined the ranks and began to realize their own potentials. It was Hair's radical departure from established modes of landscape painting that shifted this paradigm into a new form, one that was inviting because of its sketchiness, defined more by suggestion than by specificity.

Harold Newton, on the other hand, provided a fairly traditional model for the growing legion of fellow artists. His virtuosic renderings transformed the land in a manner that was less pretentious and more inviting than had been the standard. Still, he followed many conventions of landscape painting. His paintings remain highly prized today, just as they were in the Highwaymen's banner years between 1960 and 1980.

Ultimately both Newton and Hair gave definition and structure to their emerging genre. These two men profoundly influenced the exotic dreamscapes that flowed from the assemblage of painters surrounding them. Most of the Highwaymen wanted to paint like Newton, but they also valued the more accessible techniques of the renegade Hair, which allowed them to paint fast and thus earn more money.

Highwaymen art became not only a new genre of landscape painting but an excellent metaphor for the Florida experience. Although the group did not set out to revitalize an established aesthetic in order to be relevant to the changing physical and social landscape, new forms resulted from their work; they were accidental iconoclasts. Their carefree fast-painting imagery reinforced the idea that their art was divine, natural, and wild—God with a tropical twist.

The majority of the Highwaymen, including Mary Ann, came from the Fort Pierce neighborhood that was called Lincoln Park, or Blacktown, where the streets were numbered and the avenues were lettered. Most of the artists had attended Lincoln Park Academy, which in the early 1960s was still a symbol of the white establishment's too-little, too-late attempt to provide the "equal" part of "separate but equal." By then their paintings had become an alternative to the work that the segregated schools prepared young African Americans to do, the kinds of work that seemed their lot in life. It was unimaginable that these young painters would leave a visual legacy of Florida that was perfectly suited for Floridians then and now. These unlikeliest of artists created an unforeseeable but enduring cultural phenomenon.

By the time Alfred Hair graduated from high school in 1961, Mary Ann had already dabbled in the visual arts. However, she would come into her own as part of the group inspired by Alfred. Despite institutional racism and individual discrimination, these artists saw opportunity through art. The paintings these young African Americans produced quickly disarmed new-to-the-state consumers as they encountered the unique Florida images; to them this new land was uncharted and yet promising.

Although twenty-six painters eventually constituted the Highwaymen collective, eight of those artists established the true range of its art. All but Alfred Hair were self-taught; they were "learning from one another's strokes," says Mary Ann. All painted views of pristine Florida, in overlapping styles. These were the scenes that awakened something perhaps dormant in the viewers' collective unconscious. These dreamy, romantic landscapes of an unspoiled Florida—moss-draped cypress trees standing in still water, bold oaks with vines dancing around their trunks, marshlands with oasis-like estuaries, storm-tossed seas and windswept beaches with bent coconut palms, tall slash pines among expanses of sawgrass, the sunny Intracoastal Waterway, blazing poinciana trees, skies with pink sunrises or crimson sunsets, river bends by moonlight, herons and egrets accentuating the natural wilds—these were the scenes that stimulated pleasant thoughts. These were the scenes that sold.

A spirited competitiveness arose among the Highwaymen, and each member's personal style developed in tandem with the shared aesthetic that evolved. Mary Ann's use of color set her apart from the rest of the group. Some of the participants were in this enterprise for the long haul, while others came and went; a few were prolific to the point of obsession. All of these artists painted fast, sold quickly, and played hard, some more than others. Hair led the pack of highly driven young men who were out to conquer, if not change, the world. They often painted in groups, through the night as the beer flowed and the barbecues flamed, while Mary Ann, the lone female, was working to nurture her family.

Myths abounded, and still do, about these painters. Contrary to the rumor of specialists painting in an assembly-line style, in truth a single artist created each painting. Furthermore, they did not steal materials from construction sites or use shoe polish as paint. The most challenging fact to verify, however, is the number of paintings that the Highwaymen produced. They kept no records and issued no receipts. Common belief today is that this itinerant group produced nearly 250,000 paintings, although the true number may be half of that. It is similarly difficult to estimate how many paintings survive, because they often changed hands, were placed in storage and lost, or were simply thrown away.

While on the road to prosperity, driving a luxury car was an intermediate goal for some of the Highwaymen. With skyrocketing sales, any one of the artists who wanted to drive a Cadillac was able to do so. Mary Ann preferred Buicks, sometimes Chryslers and Lincolns. "I always had a nice car; my credit was all right," she offers. At fifteen Mary Ann got her first car when she took over the payments on a '48 Chevrolet purchased by her uncle Lucious. When Mary Ann began driving, "everyone else was taking driver's ed," she says, while she was the only student with a car.

Her favorite car was a Chrysler with red velvet seats. "I never really liked Cadillacs," she says. It was at her suggestion that Alfred Hair bought his first Lincoln, a Mark III. He had been driving Cadillacs until Mary Ann pointed the Lincoln out to him, the one that she had her eye on; he beat her to it. "He went to the car lot and got it," she says, adding, "It was the last car he had, before he got killed" (at Eddie's Place, a Fort Pierce juke joint, in 1970).

During the early days, the artists drove to towns and cities along the coastline, usually selling their paintings out of more modest cars. The Highwaymen went to any place where there were people—residences and businesses alike—eager to sell as many paintings as possible at each stop. The number of paintings dwindled as the day wore on, but they would get back behind the wheel and drive in search of more enthralled customers until their cargo was gone.

Mary Ann sold her own paintings, but she also had others vend for her, sometimes retaining two salesmen at once during the most demanding times. She remembers having engaged the services of "quite a few" salesmen during those heady years. These men were usually employed one at a time and included Willie Johnson, Archie Hill, Freddie Moore, Billy Eckles, Clarence Banks, her brother McArthur Pullen, and even her husband James. Legendary Highwaymen-salesman-turned-painter Al Black sold for her, as he had for almost all of the other Highwaymen. "Blood [Black] was the best salesperson. He could go out at eight a.m. and come back at noon with nothing left," she recalls. "He would move five to ten paintings at such times."

Mary Ann was among the first of the artists to offer 30 percent commission to the salesmen who were peddling her paintings. This incentive caused them to hustle. They compared notes, but Al Black would never say where he went to sell his paintings. Highwayman Isaac Knight attests that Black was the consummate salesman, saying that "Al Black wasn't afraid of anything." His ambition and daring are integral to understanding the development of the Highwaymen.

The road from Fort Pierce stretches westward, through surrounding cattle pastures, citrus groves, and vegetable fields, across flatlands accentuated by occasional cypress and hardwood hammocks, to the northern rim of the River of Grass, Florida's Everglades. "At a bar in there, in the town of Okeechobee, Al sold twenty to thirty paintings. Couldn't eat or drink there, though," Knight says wryly. In this area of Florida especially, rural whites' racism and intolerance kept the black people at bay. To be sure, even the threat of terror wouldn't deter these young artists; it only increased the challenge to sell and succeed. However, it was Mary Ann who went to that intimidating area first.

↓ ↓ ↓

The story of the Highwaymen is, of course, situated within the civil rights movement; most of the young black artists lived in Fort Pierce during a transitional time and looked forward to uncertain futures. But this is not a textbook story about race. For the Highwaymen, art and capitalism were melded into a form of cultural currency that allowed them access to white communities. They sold especially fast to Florida's newcomers during the space race of the 1960s. It was a time when Americans were dreaming about the future. The Highwaymen's tropical scenes mirrored the optimism that flourished along Florida's Atlantic seaboard, primarily among upwardly mobile whites, a dominant demographic during that era. For them, the paintings were ripe with meaning. The tropical images symbolized good health and good fortune and a good life in their edenic home.

Following the cue of the hardworking Fuller Brush man, the Highwaymen realized that selling paintings instead of accepting hourly wages for mundane jobs was hugely more profitable. They unknowingly echoed Alfred Fuller's central principle: "If I had picked strawberries on an hourly wage, I would have eaten most of them, and quit early to swim in the enticing river that was never out of view." The Fuller Brush Company had made door-to-door selling socially acceptable, and now the Highwaymen utilized Fuller's model for success. Instead of a fiber suitcase like Fuller's, an artist would carry a painting in each hand, using as handles the makeshift frames of carpenter's molding trim, or lug a stack of nested paintings to possible customers, while being careful not to smudge the still-wet paint or get it on hands or clothes.

People who could not afford the works of established artists such as Backus, or did not have access to them, were quickly sold less costly versions of paradise. Taking their paintings to the doors of their would-be patrons, the Highwaymen had inadvertently created a brand-new market for art and turned many a collector into an art connoisseur. The Highwaymen were messengers then; their biographies were of no consequence. Today their signatures sell their paintings.

Early buyers of Highwaymen paintings did not concern themselves with highbrow aesthetics, avant-garde melting wristwatches, or three-eyed women. To the contrary, they bought what appealed to them. In the fertile market of affordable and original Florida art, the buyers of Highwaymen paintings probably realized that they were not acquiring fine art. That was not what mattered to them. They knew what they liked, which was art that assuaged any doubts about what tomorrow would hold and that reinforced their belief in an exciting and beautiful new world.

These settlers' destiny was here. Their children could even play outdoors year-round. In short, Florida's east coast residents were well primed to buy these paintings, images that mirrored their time and place and their aspirations.

At that time the paintings were trophies, solid evidence that their owners had arrived in paradise, or an American middle-class dreamy iteration thereof. Today, though, the paintings are viewed through the lens of our uncertain times: overcrowding, global warming, water shortages, vanishing wilds, escalating fuel prices, unaffordable colleges, failing schools, collapsing financial institutions, bad mortgages, inaccessible healthcare, social-media-inspired revolt, threats of war, violence, and terror. When their oils still glistened, the ravishing beauty of their images was unsullied by the conditions that now render them nostalgic. Back then, unspoiled land was sacred; now it is scarce.

↓ ↓ ↓

Today Mary Ann Carroll drives one of her luxury cars from her newly purchased but modest home in the quiet part of town, along the same streets she has traveled most of her life. Fort Pierce has remained largely undeveloped, and the African American community there has become more run-down in the last four decades. Today is Sunday, the Lord's day, and Mary Ann is going to church. She is going to *her* church, where she presides. There she will lead devotees in prayer and song, and she will preach.

Mary Ann has held services at various locales throughout town, and her present church is set amid one-man garages in Fort Pierce's African American neighborhood. It is housed in what looks like an old beat-up strip mall for derelict cars. In its earliest days, church attendees have to walk from the street through uncut grass, then on a cracked sidewalk through which weeds creep up. After passing through the gate of a tall chain-link security fence, the churchgoers navigate a barrier of battered and rusted vehicles. The path to the church is mazelike; the people gathering there must turn sideways as they make their way past the immobilized cars and a myriad of stacked and scattered auto parts. This place hardly seems worthy to be a station of prayer; it seems beyond salvation. But Pastor Carroll is unfazed by these surroundings, because service has always been her primary mission in life.

The church is a work in progress, and within months it is improved. Newly upholstered pews shape and define this place of worship. From the organ, Mary Ann leads the congregation in devotional songs. Next to the organ and along the back wall are a drum set and a piano. The interior is no longer dark; long fluorescent bulbs overhead illuminate the space. The bright white walls spread the light, making the church look more spacious, albeit somewhat sterile. Four ceiling fans and six standing fans ward off the heat.

Everything draws attention to the raised pulpit. It is an elaborate set, built by hand and painted white. Only the lectern is left as natural wood, but varnished to a high sheen. This ornate centerpiece is again raised, channeling eyes to the speaker. A gold-fringed purple cloth drapes the pulpit. Seats are ranged behind it in a row, and then there is another table with plastic potted plants at each side. At the front of the altar is a small table. Yet another table, with chairs at its sides, sits below at ground level on a purple rug. A large gold offering bowl is placed on a stand in front, in the center. Behind the pulpit hangs a five-

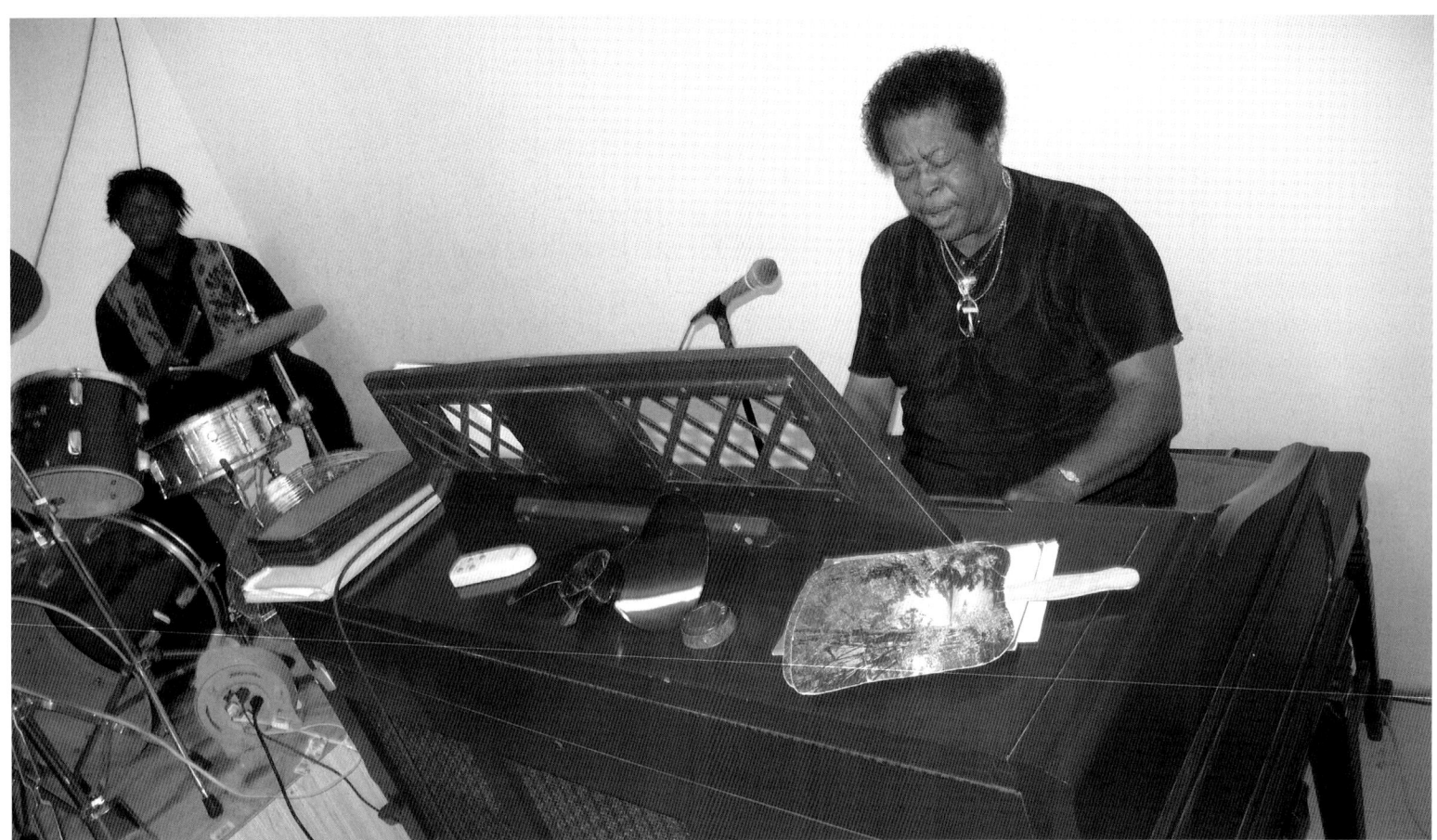

Mary Ann playing the organ and singing at her church, with her grandson Johnnie on drums, Fort Pierce, 2008.

foot-long photograph of a waterfall that is lighted from behind; when it is electronically engaged, the falls cascade. The Reverend Mary Ann Carroll, with her artistic talent, has created a divine setting here. Indeed, in this place worshipers can be transported from their daily grind and easily inspired to turn their thoughts to more godly things. The two metal roll-up garage doors in the back seem to vanish.

The church's setting has also improved. No longer is it a wasteland of cars needing paint and repairs. In fact, the vehicles have been removed; with the repair work accomplished, they have been returned to their owners or put away in the garages. The grass by the street has been mowed. The once undistinguished church in this unlikely location has become the site's focal point. A small hand-painted wooden sign reading FOUNDATION REVIVAL CENTER hangs above the air conditioner outside, between the two garage doors. The building is painted white above and gray beneath a one-foot-wide red stripe running across the church's exterior wall and continuing across the entire strip of car-repair bays, reminding all that this church is in a worldly place.

Mary Ann hopes one day to house the church in a standalone building, but money is tight. She supports the church through the sale of her paintings, and the improvements she has made have been costly. Attendees give as they can, but so far she is the main source of revenue. She takes no salary for her church work. "It's not about money," she says. The church attracts few people even during the winter season, maybe twenty-five on a good Sunday, and just one or two for midday prayer. "I don't give excuses for absentees," she says, adding that service is 24/7.

During services she leads prayer and song; she also reads and interprets scripture. Mary Ann wails, her voice dropping an octave or two as she belts out tunes like the best gospel preachers, inspiring those seated in the pews. As she lifts her voice and sings, "Give your heart to Jesus tonight," some rise and stretch their open palms upward, singing, "Thank you, Lord."

She preaches, in a raised voice, accentuating certain words: "Our trust is not in God. We are not really leaning on Him as our shepherd. We don't trust Him enough. We don't trust Him when we have some money in the bank. He loves us because we love Him. God opens the doors. I thank God for being God and I thank God for allowing me to be me."

On the west wall are the church's articles of incorporation as the Foundation Revival Center Church of Redemption, dated 1998. Next to this is an Appreciation, an homage that reads:

Founder and Overseer
Elder Mary A. Carroll
Pastor

Framed in gold above this plaque is a photograph of Mary Ann, a stunning young woman in her Sunday best. In the hand-tinted photograph, a common refinement of an image practiced before the advent of color negative film in the 1950s, she wears a dress her grandmother made for her. She believes that she was sixteen years old when the photograph was taken, but she looks older, more mature. "You must have confidence in yourself," she says. "Others can see more in you than you see in yourself."

In 1995 Mary Ann Carroll was ordained by the Genesis Ministries in Orlando "to retrain the minds of the lost" by accepting Christ. Her focus is on the Word, the teachings of Jesus Christ. "Something about God intrigued me. As a child I watched clouds shifting and drifting, and the sun making shadows dance. I liked to hear the wind blowing through the trees," she relates. It is clear that her reason for becoming

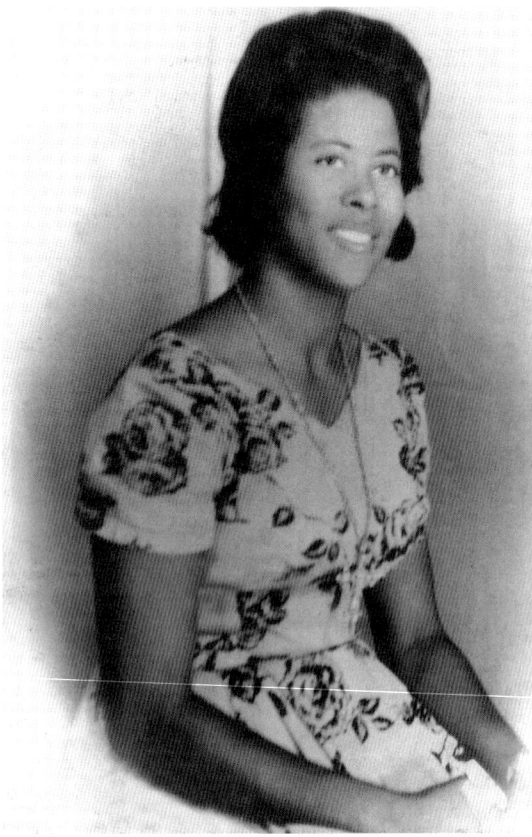

Mary Ann Sneed, c. 1957.

a pastor would also be the reason why she became a landscape painter. "Everything we can ever possess belongs to God," she explains, continuing, "The soul lives on." Mary Ann has performed many church roles throughout her life, including Sunday school teacher, choir member, and usher; she has functioned in "just about every capacity," she points out. For her, the church has always provided solace and instilled self-esteem. Consequently, her artwork expresses her love of God. To know God through the natural world was a popular and reassuring interpretation of the Highwaymen's art, as it had been for the tradition of American landscape painting a hundred years before, with its reverential tone.

Mary Ann has led an active yet solitary life. "I never had a change of pace," she says. Her life has been a cycle of family, art, and church, with little time for rest or leisure. Painting was the least consuming of her daily activities. "My grandmother didn't allow us to ask nothing from nobody. You earned it or you didn't get it," she reflects. Perhaps it was this early training that led to Mary Ann's sense of responsibility and her independent ways. These values have been her driving force. Given her sense of alienation from mainstream society and this moral conviction, it is little wonder that she founded her own ministry.

Mary Ann Sneed was born in Sandersville, Georgia, on November 30, 1940, the second child of B. W. and Leonora Jones Sneed. Her father—she isn't sure what he did for a living, maybe a railroad laborer or a sharecropper—and her mother, a nurse, separated before she was born. Mary Ann's early years were spent in nearby Wrightsville, Georgia. She first saw her father there when he was being transported in a prison work truck. The guards permitted him to get out of the vehicle as they approached the family house. Mary Ann recalls that "no one was on his back, no one had a shotgun [trained] on him." He came up to the porch and spoke with her older sister, Ruby. Mary Ann ran and hid in the house as he walked up to it. She kept an eye on him but didn't want to engage him. Mary Ann does not know exactly why he was imprisoned and says coyly, "I was afraid of convicts." She thinks he was incarcerated for having jumped a man on the courthouse steps. "Guess he was short-fused," she says. Mary Ann never saw him again.

Eventually Leonora married Delmar Pullen, a good man and a good provider, according to Mary Ann. Leonora would have five more children with Delmar. With their growing brood of offspring, the Pullens began to travel back and forth, following seasonal migrant work from Wrightsville to Fort Pierce, where Delmar had family. By the time Mary Ann was eight, the family had settled in Fort Pierce.

Because work in Florida's orange groves promised a source of steady income, the family's life there was somewhat better than it was in Georgia. While her parents worked, her grandmother, Mary Lee Brown-Jones, raised Mary Ann and Ruby. The children all grew up well under the guidance of their grandmother. Ruby entered the nursing field, while McArthur went into motel maintenance after returning from Vietnam. Marie and Chrissandra were housewives; Chrissandra also worked in restaurant management. Terry went from being an auto mechanic to drumming for a gospel choir. Mary Ann's youngest brother, Charles, worked at many trades: masonry, mechanics, electronics, carpentry, and landscaping. But as time passed, Mary Ann would be the sibling to have the most diverse and expansive work life. "I've been working ever since I was six years old, when I started babysitting McArthur," she says. During those early years Mary Ann's grandmother, who thought herself too young to be called by that title and went by Mama, instilled in Mary Ann a strong work ethic and a sense of right and wrong. These traits would continue to guide Mary Ann throughout her life.

Mary Ann attended the neighborhood school on Means Court between Avenues D and E. This frame schoolhouse had succeeded a shed on Brown's Court as a place of education for "coloreds" circa 1910. The

Means Court School opened as a junior high in 1923 and was named Lincoln Park Academy in 1924. A new building was dedicated on I Street in the heart of Blacktown in February of 1926 and accredited as a high school in 1928. The school would be strictly segregated for four decades until, in 1970, it became a middle school as the upper classes joined whites in a new high school facility south of Fort Pierce. Over the years of its existence as a Negro institution, Lincoln Park was a source of pride and an object of affection for black students and alumni. In spite of its humble beginnings and years of neglect by the white educational establishment, at LPA teachers and learning were respected and students were disciplined and nurtured. Ironically, the former "colored school" has become the county's premier school, so desirable that concerned parents register their newborns to attend.

Pre-integration education was a family affair at Lincoln Park, with church and school working together at the hub of the community. Parent-teacher conferences took place in church, and even at home. In fact, LPA teachers routinely went to the residences of their homeroom students to meet with the parents. Teachers were revered, remembers Rubin Johnson, a student in the Class of '64. "Lincoln Park Academy was run like an academy." Academic excellence was a priority. Teachers not only had responsibility, they had authority. There were no helicopter parents questioning teachers then. Teaching was a prestigious profession, on a plane with medicine. Lincoln Park residents thought of the teachers as wealthy because they had the nicest houses. Policemen, too, were part of the black community's striving for uplift, even though at one time a black policeman could only enforce the law with other blacks. "The policemen knew our parents. We weren't afraid of them," asserts Rubin Johnson. Later, however, mothers and grandmothers would threaten to call Officer Patrick Duval, the first African American sheriff's deputy in St. Lucie County, to deal with rebellious teenagers.

It was the parents and other good citizens on the Northwest Side who overcame official neglect to make possible the evolution from Means Court to the Lincoln Park Academy that was a model to the rest of Florida, an accredited black high school where Principal James Espy insisted on hiring only certified teachers. The black citizenry raised $2,600 toward the original accreditation demands, an amount the School Board could not supply in 1924. Later they raised money by selling ten-cent sandwiches to build a basketball court, which volunteers subsequently fenced in. The sale of tickets to home games contributed to the expansion program.

Despite the promises of the evolving education system, at least one student fell between the cracks. Mary Ann cites two reasons for her dropping out of Lincoln Park Academy at the end of the ninth grade; each is indicative of attitudes that would shape her adult journey.

Mary Ann was angry when she could not get her report card because her class dues were in arrears.

She simply did not have the five cents that she owed the school. She would not tell anyone, including her parents, nor would she ask them for the money. Additionally, her grandmother would not allow Mary Ann to wear shorts. Unable to don proper sports attire, she was not allowed to participate in gym, thus failing the class. Angry at these injustices, she dropped out of school in rebellion.

Her mother told her to get a job. "It was good advice," Mary Ann recalls, "but would have been better advice to go back to school." She managed her own life from that point on. As a little girl Mary Ann had worked in the gladiola fields, where she earned one cent for twelve flowers bound in a rubber band. Now she went to work there again, gathering the flowers after cutting them with her pocketknife. The brilliant full blooms dancing in gentle breezes resonated within the young woman. Mary Ann did some other field work, but she is quick to point out that she never picked oranges. "They are too thorny," she explains. Generally, no women of any race picked citrus, because it was considered too strenuous for them. Mary Ann also did some housecleaning when her mother was too sick to report for work. She was never afraid of heavy lifting and would later do "men's work" to support her family.

A brief review of the development of the coast north and south of Fort Pierce helps us to understand the role of African Americans in the region's variable economic makeup. With the coming of Henry Flagler's Florida East Coast Railway in 1895, Vero Beach, just north of Fort Pierce, benefited from his vision, as did many locales to the south including Palm Beach and Miami. With only a couple of station agents and redcaps, Vero's small depot facilitated the town's becoming a minor resort. Nearby Fort Pierce "became the division point of the FEC and was, in effect, for many years a 'railroad town' with a sizeable depot, yards and repair facilities, [with] a large number of men based there," writes historian Seth Bramson.

A cadre of African Americans came to live in Fort Pierce, to work as railroad firemen, porters, oilers, and machinists, and in the labor gangs. This workforce joined those engaged in the low-wage agrarian and cattle cultures in isolated Fort Pierce. The community of laborers included many seasonally employed migrants who lived inland near the fields or boarded the buses that would take them to pick fruit and vegetables. Their lives were far, literally and figuratively, from the ocean, where desirable homes and coastal tourism proliferated. Although Fort Pierce could boast about its deep-sea fishing, tourism was never its strong suit. This common source of revenue for almost all of coastal Florida, where fun-in-the-sun reigned, remained a world away from the homes of Fort Pierce's black residents.

Employment choices for Mary Ann were accordingly limited at this point in her life. Even while she was working in the flower fields, though, she was drawing and painting. These were activities she had enjoyed for as long as she could remember, recalling that she drew stagecoaches and horses while she was in school. She began painting in earnest in 1957, the year before giving birth to the first of her seven children.

Mary Ann had a romantic relationship with Jasper Reaves, and the couple had two children, Louise (1958–2002) and Ira Jay (b. 1960). Having children without being wed was her "biggest vice," says Mary Ann. "He was a grown man," she exclaims, adding, "I didn't know he was married! I was only sixteen, maybe seventeen." Jasper used to come to the Cozy Corner, a restaurant along Avenue D at 13th Street where Mary Ann worked. He was a farm contractor, hiring men for daily field work, picking them up in the bus he drove. Jasper died in 1961. During the latter part of 1962 or early in 1963, Mary Ann married James Brady Carroll, and the couple had five children—Marcus (b. 1962), Kandie (b. 1964), Rosa (b. 1966), Renee (b. 1969), and Tarsha (b. 1971). Mary Ann and James separated in 1976 and divorced within a year. "He left me and the kids," Mary Ann says without acrimony, adding that James did not want, nor could he handle, the responsibility of a large family.

Mary Ann was the breadwinner during her marriage. James worked for General Development Corporation and later for Club Med, both south of Fort Pierce in Port St. Lucie. He maintained golf courses for both companies. When he was laid off, he turned to the citrus groves, driving a van. He was not a field hand; he was not suited for picking oranges. As Mary Ann sees it, "He wasn't in love with a lot of work; they were all just jobs to him." Mary Ann didn't want to get married again. "I never thought about that life." She wanted her freedom; she wanted to live creatively. And by the time Mary Ann and James divorced, she was a well-established artist.

While she painted and raised children, Mary Ann worked in a number of labor-intensive jobs including stints as a delivery truck driver, restaurant server, and nurse's aide. Tireless and determined, she undertook a variety of home improvements—carpentry, painting, plumbing, wiring. She says, "I've been a worker all my life." She cut lawns, drove a limousine, and even sold bolita bets at one time. Bolita was an illegal but popular game of chance and superstition. Mary Ann was attracted to it when she overheard her mother mention "sixty-two" in a conversation and she bet the number to win, placing a dime and winning seven dollars.

Raised by her grandmother to be self-reliant, Mary Ann says, "I didn't see suffering as suffering." She was too proud for that. Pride gave her strength, and it elicited anger. She is quick to point out that she never lived in public housing—"I never had free rent"—or went on welfare. She did take government money once, for her children's medical bills, which she couldn't afford to pay herself. "I've been through the storm," she says in summation. She laments that her temper is her greatest failing and often gets the best of her. It may have given her a kind of arrogance, too; at times this attitude intensified into intolerance when she saw others falter. More than anything else, living righteously was and is Mary Ann Carroll's dominant life theme.

Salvation came through art, and God showed her the way there, Mary Ann would say. From a practical standpoint, painting would pay the family bills, and it would also lead her on an unimaginable trajectory. It began in front of the popular neighborhood juke joint, Eddie's Place on Avenue D, one day during the early 1960s, likely in '62 or '63, when Mary Ann, attracted by the flames that Harold Newton had painted along the sides of his Chevy coupe, approached him while he was talking to one of his friends. The two talked briefly, and that was that. Soon thereafter she observed Harold on Avenue Q and 17th Street painting a royal poinciana, the flaming tree igniting mundane surroundings. She meandered over to watch him paint.

As a teenager Mary Ann had copied pictures from calendars and church fans, painting with flat colors right out of the tubes. But this would change soon after she met Newton. They went to the Town and Country, a restaurant in the African American part of Fort Pierce that "was like the restaurants you'd find in the other part of town," Mary Ann says. It was the first date she'd ever been on. A platonic relationship ensued, Mary Ann was quick to point out, and it was all business after that evening out. "Harold was a real gentleman. He loved his women; he loved his children," remembers Mary Ann, adding, "He knew God."

Her art took root, as Harold showed her how to mix oil paints to achieve varied and nuanced colors. "The first three colors I learned to mix I learned from Harold," she recalls. "Pastel looking. Hint of blue and green," which she explains adds to the sense of receding space when properly applied. She trails off, saying, "Sky colors die in the evening." Mary Ann implies that her unique color sensibility was, in fact, the result of her inexpert blending of the pigments: "I paint the way I feel. Sometimes [the colors are] too bold. I leave them or tone them down."

Mary Ann was always drawn to Norman Rockwell's everyday scenes of a wholesome America. She found his illustrations "so distinctive and natural looking. It's what I wanted to do. I knew nothing about color then." Eventually she found her way into the American psyche through her own variants of the tropical landscape. The Highwaymen aesthetic required veracity, an authentic sense of the land. Pictorial realism was not their answer. Mary Ann's limitations became her strengths, and she codified the land according to her own perceptions and cultural influences.

Meanwhile Harold Newton, the iconic artist, was developing his own approach after abandoning the practice of painting religious scenes of Jesus walking on water or sitting at the Last Supper. The surrounding Florida landscape offered great opportunity to Harold and the fledgling artists. Many were then beginning to encircle Alfred Hair, who encouraged all to join him in his new enterprise. Mary Ann must have sensed this opportunity too. But she was more impressed by Newton's art, so she tried her hand at painting the land with increased care.

This effort must have come after her marriage. An early crude painting of Mary Ann's was discovered in 1997 in a shop in Titusville with the signature M.A.S. Carroll—the S being for Sneed, her maiden name. Although it held sure signs of what was to come, this painting, along with her other early creations, is not quite a Highwaymen interpretation of the land. No paintings are known to exist with the signature Mary Ann Sneed—or "Snead," as her maiden name was often misspelled, even appearing as such on one of her children's birth certificates. Mary Ann does not recall how long she signed with the S before dropping it, only that she included the S intermittently until it vanished. By then she was well on her way. In fact, another painting signed M.A.S. Carroll was auctioned in Vero Beach in 2012, and it was a refined example of her work.

Early Highwaymen paintings were loose and gestural, palette knife passes so exuberant that paint was pulled off the board. The resulting pieces were raw, yet formally resolved, demanding in their own spirited and carefree way, and certainly unmatched by other artists.

In the early 1960s, Fort Pierce was ground zero for the proliferation of Highwaymen paintings, and Mary Ann Carroll became one of the nuclear members of the group of artists. Alfred Hair, Harold Newton, Livingston Roberts, James Gibson, Roy McLendon, along with Willie Daniels, Al Black, and Mary Ann, originated and defined the group's shared characteristics and the aesthetic parameters of its art. Luckily or unluckily for Mary Ann, Fort Pierce was her home; given her family responsibilities, she could not easily move from its stifling Jim Crow environment. Assailed daily by the subtleties and suspicions of segregation's unwritten laws, her point of view would only harden with time.

"Nobody else was worthy of raising my kids. It was my responsibility from day one," Mary Ann says. She was well prepared. "I raised my mom's kids, then I raised mine—then I raised my daughter's [after Louise died]. I went through some struggles," she asserts. Her religious beliefs as well as her youthful experiences, and perhaps something in her genes, equipped her to surmount difficulties. "Faith is the only thing that works," she tells others. "You can't have doubts."

God, she says, gave her power and wisdom. She nurtured her strength from the start. "I chose to be able to defend myself. I could throw a guy. I could box. I could run real fast." In fact, it would have been difficult to intimidate Mary Ann. Her pride and the reality of her surroundings dictated that she be strong. "You don't take nothing from me. If I give it to you, that's different," she explains. She always carried a knife, and later a gun.

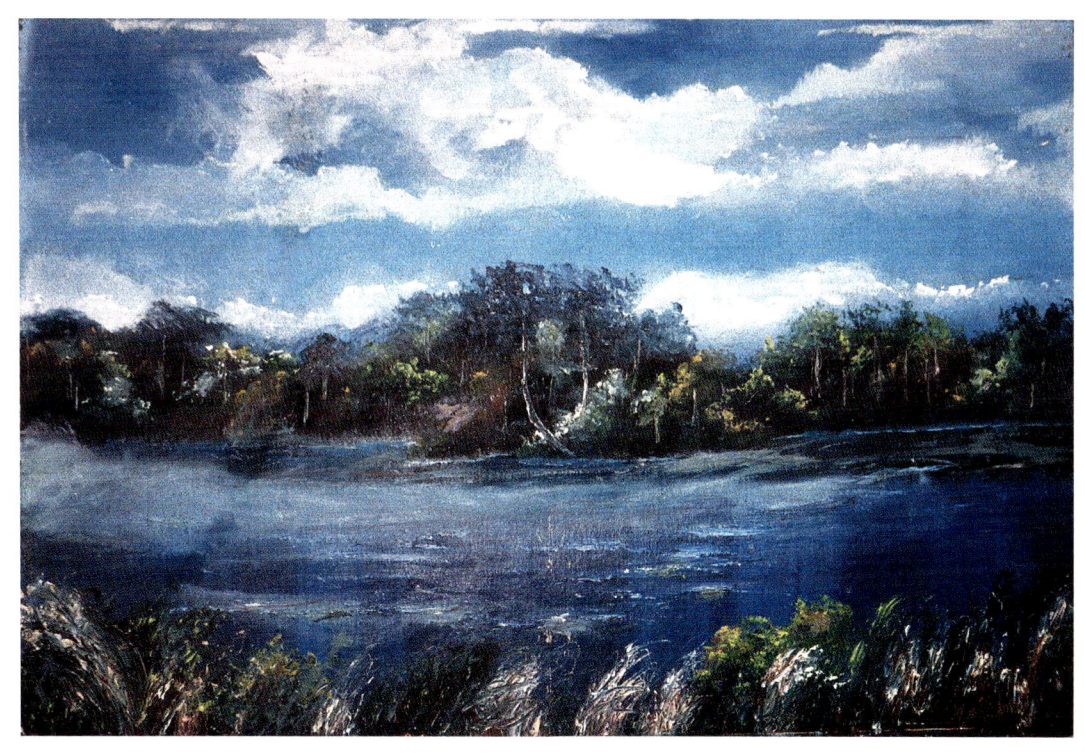

Paintings signed M.A.S. Carroll.

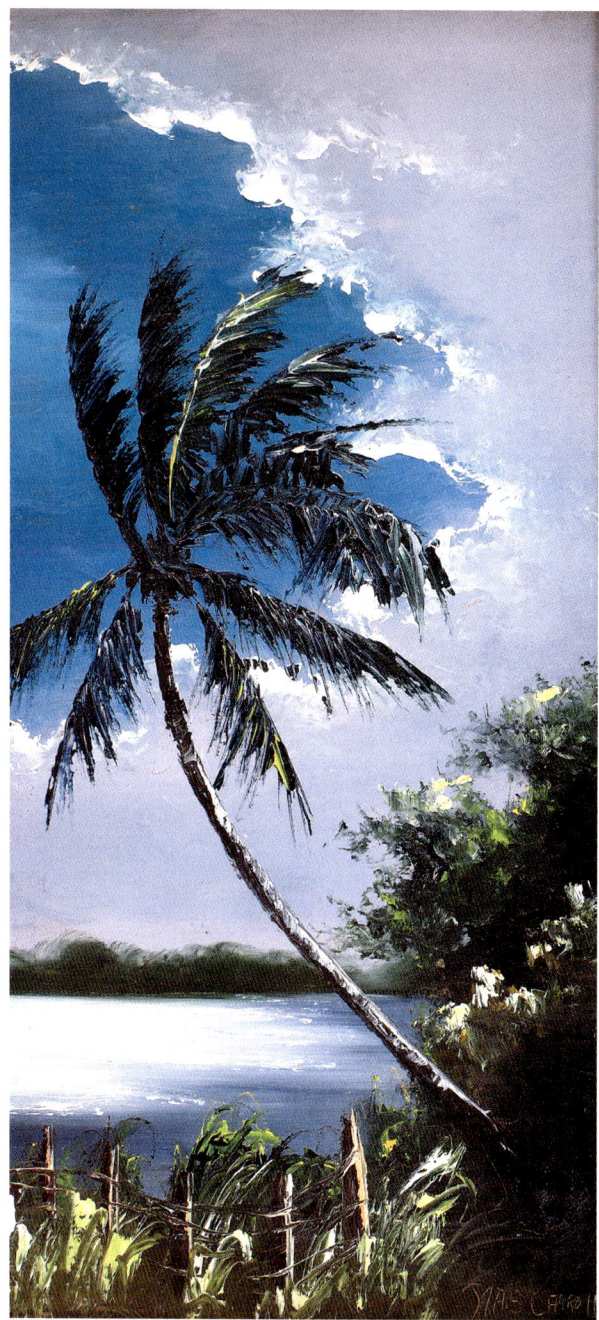

Recalling an altercation with a fellow Highwayman, she says, "I had to whip Lem Newton. He tried to keep my painting. I had to body slam him to get it back. I was tough. I could whip a monkey in a minute if he made me . . . [but] I always liked peace." These abilities underpinned her self-confidence when she began driving the roads to sell her paintings. She used her God-given wisdom, though, instead of her physical abilities when threatening events occurred. Although she kept her gun nearby, her manner or her artwork defused any tensions with customers or with others she encountered along the way. The Highwaymen were consummate salespeople—deferential, polite, and respectful.

Before Mary Ann became involved with the visual arts, she played music. "It's always been a love of mine," she says, going back to her early childhood in Georgia. Although she was attracted to her uncle Isadore "Buddy" Jones's guitar playing, he would not let her touch his guitar; he wouldn't even teach her a note. When he returned the instrument to its case after strumming and singing, he would tell Mary Ann that "snakes are in there" as he slid it beneath his bed. But when he and the other adults in the family went to work in the fields, Mary Ann would pull the case out from under the bed and attempt to play the guitar. Eventually her grandmother taught her the basic chords C, F, and G, which were considered "hillbilly chords." Music became an integral part of her life.

Mary Ann would lead church choirs, singing hymns and songs of praise, as she played guitar and piano. In the early 1980s, as her children were growing up and the Highwaymen's painting enterprise was dwindling, Mary Ann formed her own gospel group, Wings of Faith. Of the seven members, two were her children: Louise sang and Ira played drums. The group traveled around Florida, Georgia, Alabama, Mississippi, and Tennessee. Along the way, when Mary Ann heard street people with good voices, she would invite them to join the band, just as Alfred Hair had welcomed anyone with the inclination to paint for a living. This openheartedness was consistent with both the Highwaymen ethic and her religious convictions.

↓ ↓ ↓

Mary Ann's painting venture took hold in the mid-1960s when she could bring home hundreds of dollars after just a couple of hours' work. "My favorite places to sell was where they bought more than one or two paintings," she says with a smile, adding, "Do you know how much twenty-five dollars was in the sixties? You could buy the family groceries and put gas in your car." She remembers one day when Livingston Roberts and two of the group's salesmen asked her to drive them on a sales outing. She agreed as long as they would help her sell her paintings; she was shy back then. They hit the road together in her Buick, and she was initiated. "I was so happy. I think my husband got angry because I made more money than him. I always did. I was cutting yards, six people's yards a month in between painting. My kids had to eat, wear clean clothes, and have shelter," she explains. She did what needed to be done.

As the money from the sales of her paintings began pouring in, she painted even more to keep up with demand and with the other artists. Isaac Knight smiles, saying, "It was not difficult or awkward having her around. Mary Ann probably can beat [up] half of us. She'd love to put you to work . . . move her stuff for her. It was fun. She was always a sweetheart. There wasn't anyone [among us] selfish." A family of sorts developed quickly. They learned from one another. Mary Ann explains, "Each goes to see if the grass is the same green. Saw things through our own eyes of what the others did. We influenced each other. Seeing what the others were doing, seeing if you can do it better. Each artist had a touch on another."

Yet, as the sole young woman in the group, she stood apart. "I didn't participate in partying. Never. The guys, McLendon, Castro, and some of the others, were all drinking together. I've always been around church. I always loved the Lord. I lived on the rim, not sanctified or holier than thou. I didn't drink, didn't smoke, and didn't shoot pool. I was a young lady in the midst of all these guys. They respected me when I said 'no.' They were gentlemen. There was no dogs among them," she contends. "Most all of them made a pass at me. But they respected my 'no' for an answer. I was pretty but never thought of myself like that. They were all gentlemen. Everybody was friendly, never bothered me. All of them already had women," she adds.

As to how the artists were treated by their fellow African Americans, Willie Daniels offers this: "The women liked us and the guys hated us. Highwaymen were drinking beer all day, and they'd be picking oranges." Mary Ann quickly adds, "Women and men hated me." Men seemed to be intimidated by her ability to make money, although she believes women did not like her because they were jealous. Mary Ann explains, "I was a woman and I been around the guys." Other women saw her as a rival for male attention, while she was, so to speak, one of the guys. "I never put on eyeliner and high heels and skimpy clothes. That wasn't an intent of mine," she says.

"I had different dreams from most of the women I knew. My thoughts in life were different than other people's." Never flashy, she wore and still wears pants all the time and has avoided "lipstick, powder, and paint." She has never worn bright colors or delicate prints, never liked those "girlie things." She says that after her artistic success, "I would not allow my neck to stick up. I felt the same as I felt before. I just had some more money." Racing cars and CB radios were among her interests; she saved the aesthetics for her artwork. Life was clear-cut for Mary Ann Carroll: "All I know is that you're going to be right or wrong."

Righteousness led to a fascination with and, ultimately, a study of law enforcement. Mary Ann once took a private investigation correspondence course from New York City, in which she learned the basics of fingerprinting, surveillance, and more. "Eighteen courses in all," she says, "the whole nine yards." Mary Ann got to use these skills when she witnessed an accident one night and helped the Fort Pierce police track down the offender. She still has her Code of Ethics certificate.

These interests go right back to childhood. Mary Ann not only had roles in school plays and was elected to the student council, where she served as secretary, she also served as lieutenant of the Safety Patrol and joined Junior Crime Fighters because it challenged children to do better. Always in control of her life, she says, "I could have been just as much trouble as anyone else, but I chose not to. I've never been an average person. I was a challenger, daring."

Fort Pierce's Lincoln Park neighborhood, anchored by Avenue D, was a good place for African Americans to live during the era of segregation. Surrounded and shaped by institutional racism, with a strong sense of collective identity, the community thrived. Cafes, juke joints, bars, liquor stores, pool halls, dime stores, drugstores, clothing stores, furniture stores, meat markets, icehouses, shoe stores, hat stores, barbershops and beauty parlors, restaurants and bakeries, boardinghouses and hotels, laundries, insurance agencies, professional offices, and even a movie theater were among the businesses that lined Avenue D. "You didn't have to go to the white side of town. Anything you wanted you could get on Avenue D," remembers Deputy Duval.

"We had more than one of everything," Mary Ann recalls. "Avenue D was the big spot then, on Saturday nights. That's where we were," remembers Mary Ann's schoolmate Janice McGriff, who became a teacher and taught for thirty-five years in Fort Pierce and who still recalls "hearing my feet up and down the hallways" in the old Means Court School. Back then Avenue D was paved only from US 1 to 13th Street, less than half of its length, but it was a center of African American culture. This was the place to buy whatever was needed or wanted and the place for socializing. D Street, as it was also called, attracted African Americans from around the nation.

The Chitlin' Circuit was the name given to the string of clubs and halls throughout the segregated South where black entertainers performed to enthusiastic black audiences. Jacksonville, near the Georgia border, had been a center for black film production and was a major stop on the circuit. Gainesville, with its famed Cotton Club, and Eatonville near Orlando, one of the nation's first all-black incorporated towns, also hosted these traveling performers, as did Overtown's Lyric Theater on the edge of downtown Miami along with small venues throughout Florida.

The acts came to Fort Pierce to play on and around Avenue D. In those days Baker's Flamingo Bar and Grill was center stage; motel rooms behind the lounge welcomed performers and visitors from across the

United States. Baker's hosted professional boxing matches when the likes of James Brown, B. B. King, and Sam Cooke weren't on stage.

The residents of Fort Pierce's African American community didn't feel deprived, nor did they want to cross Moore's Creek, the racial demarcation line. In fact, Levie "LB" Baker would even take the black acts across town, where they performed for white audiences at the National Guard Armory. In their own cordoned-off community, blacks found a sufficient and satisfying mix of business and pleasure.

"We all grew up in a community together," Janice McGriff says. "Parents were working hard. People were more concerned about each other and their children." Mary Ann points out, "We stayed on the north side of Orange Avenue," a few blocks south of the canal. The area's black citizens didn't venture out too far beyond that, especially at night. Even though it was "whites on one side and blacks on the other side," McGriff says theirs was a self-contained neighborhood. "We had everything we needed." Blacks could go elsewhere, of course, if they did not mind feeling unwelcome.

Isaac Knight came to a relatively tranquil Fort Pierce in 1959. "Black people embraced each other," he says, recalling the spirit of the community at that time. Relationships with whites were on an even keel, but with Martin Luther King's assassination in 1968, "blacks and whites absolutely didn't trust one another." Young African Americans began "burning up Avenue D, setting up fires," says Mary Ann. The police barricaded 7th Street to keep rioters from entering downtown. "It was chaos—burning stores, breaking out windows," remembers Willie Turner, a retired African American officer with the Sheriff's Department. Unleashed anger was the rule of the day. Elder Ernest Walters, who occasionally preaches at Mary Ann's church, offers, "When Martin Luther King got killed, blacks went haywire. There was no business, and blacks couldn't afford to rebuild."

Along Avenue D, whites were major landlords with black partners who operated businesses alongside black-owned establishments like Stone Brothers Funeral Home and Baker's Flamingo Bar. There were black-white partnerships like that of Dr. Clem Benton, the black community's beloved physician, and Harry Center, the white pharmacist and proprietor of the white community's oldest drug store, who were co-owners of the Lincoln Theater. After King's death, white investment in the area dropped off and conditions worsened. Whites didn't rebuild partially because they could no longer get insurance.

A lot of people gave up and left the area. Following the flight of stable community assets, transients and migrants dominated the visible landscape of Avenue D. Integration meant that blacks could finally live, work, and shop where they pleased; they could venture outside their neighborhoods, and they did. "Then we didn't have to come to Avenue D to buy groceries, to buy clothes," explains Havert "Coach"

Fenn. Besides, many things were less expensive in the white community because of greater sales volume. Avenue D and the surrounding neighborhoods were sinking as their residents located elsewhere. Drugs and prostitution would become the norm in this once vital neighborhood.

According to Officer Turner, Fort Pierce was a hard place to be an African American; it was "low minded. Second class citizens, that's what you were . . . felt like fifth or sixth class." Coach Fenn thought that all places were alike until he moved to Fort Pierce from the depressed town of Palmetto on Florida's Gulf Coast. He soon heard "weird stories about when the sun goes down." He explains that in Palmetto, African Americans could go wherever they wanted. "Here it was 'don't get caught' . . . I had never really experienced anything like this; here I was told where I could, couldn't, and shouldn't be after sundown. Fort Pierce was different than anyplace else I've lived. We knew in other places to get on the back of the bus. It didn't bother me, but it bothered me in Fort Pierce. I saw so many things that should not have been."

Fort Pierce had its share of Ku Klux Klan activity. Kirby Loop was said to be one of its strongholds. Living on a few streets flanking the town dump, some two miles from the black neighborhood, Kirby Loopers were a tribe of poor whites who, in the 1940s and 1950s, were especially threatening to the blacks. "Blacks traveled in pairs on Kirby Loop. But I went there alone. I paid my dues. I went by myself in the redneck country," Mary Ann affirms.

Lincoln Park's downward spiral worsened without bank loans, investments, and cash flow. Meanwhile, in this town especially, neither Supreme Court rulings nor an awakening national conscience supporting integration managed to end segregation. "It was racial as hell," Elder Walters says; segregation was intact into the early 1970s. Crosses were still being burned in Fort Pierce and throughout Florida then. Twenty were reported in Dade County, in Miami and Homestead: six-foot-tall fuel-drenched wooden crosses set aflame over a few months in 1972.

A year before that, in Fort Pierce and greater St. Lucie County, four crosses were burned including one on the lawn of Fort Pierce Central High School. Racial strife and altercations between blacks and whites at the newly integrated high school reached a boiling point. Pent-up hostilities were unleashed; reconciliation faltered in spite of the efforts of several interracial committees. The official story of the school troubles of 1971 is an ambiguous one. According to at least one witness, black youths set the crosses on fire. "That's something they would have said then," counters area historian Jean Ellen Wilson, a white native of Fort Pierce. Her colleague Joyce Jackson, a black woman who lived in Fort Pierce during desegregation, doesn't believe that African American youths lit the crosses either. "The black kids wouldn't have the nerve to do something like that," she asserts, adding that "the Klan lived in White City," the adjacent town.

Earl Little, born in 1926, graduated from Lincoln Park Academy and later taught music there. He was teaching when the schools were integrated and says that the main problem with integration came from the senior class. When the new central high was built, whites were forced to abandon Dan McCarty High and blacks were forced to leave Lincoln Park Academy to attend a new school as seniors, leaving behind their respective schools' cultures and traditions. The outstanding football team, with great athletes from both schools, had a triumphant season and united all the students in the excitement. But there was a letdown after that. Seniors were upset that they could not graduate from their respective schools. That, Mr. Little points out, is what led to the discontent in February of 1971.

The reporting of the *Fort Pierce News Tribune* is sketchy about the discord. Vero Beach Public Library's research librarian and genealogist Pam Cooper offers that "as usual, from that time period, I find the newspapers are very selective about what they published." Fort Pierce seemed to hold firm to its reluctance to change and held on to the past with a vengeance; it seemed more determined than other communities to keep out of step with social progress. Librarian Cooper adds, "Dealing with some of our local historians—I believe they only want to know and print the fictionalized version."

Doctors in Fort Pierce continued to have two waiting rooms. Separate service windows and counters for blacks remained the norm. Second water fountains and separate restrooms vanished slowly, "until they got it right," says Elder Walters's wife, Gloria. Journalist Anthony Westbury, with the Treasure Coast Newspapers, quotes Samuel Gaines, a Fort Pierce civic leader and director of the African American community's Stone Brothers Funeral Home: "It was just the way it was. Yes, I can remember when there were two windows at the courthouse, one for blacks, one for whites, but, no, that didn't bother me. That was the mindset at the time."

At another time, Sam Gaines put it somewhat differently. "We didn't know we were segregated. It didn't matter; it was a very close-knit community." He remembers that along 8th Street off Avenue D, the hub of commerce, were more successful black-owned businesses—shoe stores, banks, doctors' and dentists' offices. As a child Gaines watched the Ku Klux Klan march along 7th Street from the second-floor porch of the funeral parlor, which was also the family home. "We had no sense of fear, because we were sheltered," he explains.

By "sheltered" Gaines means two things: before integration, young blacks were part of a community that valued education, and these youths were not exposed to antisocial behaviors. Pride was reflected in the Lincoln Park Academy motto, "We do right because it is right to do right." Accomplishment and self-worth were instilled then—qualities the students were not allowed to tarnish. As Rubin Johnson explains, "It was ingrained in you after twelve years." School fostered a sense of community in myriad ways. Mentoring was common. Older boys would choose a younger one to practice sports with; this bonding led to socialization and bred confidence.

Graduates were prepared to enter the workforce or any other aspect of the real world. In those days, social standards were set in school, too. Students were expected to speak well, tuck in their shirttails, wear belts, doff their sunglasses indoors, remove caps before entering classrooms, keep their hair trimmed, and, of course, not talk back to those in authority. Johnson explains sheltering as "shielding us to not get in trouble." Serious trouble could get one sent to the reform school in Okeechobee or to the military. At the very least, it would get a student a meeting with Robert Jefferson, Dean of Boys and Physical Education, who was in charge of discipline at Lincoln Park Academy. Rubin got paddled more at school than he did at home.

Jefferson, professionally and affectionately addressed as Coach Jefferson, was a no-nonsense man and a fierce disciplinarian. He came from the same sort of background as the students he served, and he pulled himself up by his own bootstraps. He brought the discipline he learned in the military to Lincoln Park Academy. The students, he believed, needed it, and he dished it out evenly and fairly. Coach Jefferson would also give students the shirt off his back or, more accurately, shoes and overcoats when, for example, they were leaving for college up North and needed warm clothing.

Chores and after-school jobs were the norm. Parents often took their children to work with them, and children often had responsible positions at work. Rubin Johnson worked at Duval's Grocery, where he was trusted with the cash box. "We didn't see pimps and prostitutes. We didn't know what drugs were. We picked up on those we admired," and Johnson admired "nice trucks with chrome wheels, like Ernest Holmes and 'Tater Boy' owned." These men worked their way up to own fruit harvesting companies and "owned eleven trucks between them."

A work ethic and entrepreneurialism were instilled in these children. If someone skipped school, it was generally to work. They could go to the loading ground on Avenue D by the Lincoln Theater, board a bus to the fields, and join a harvesting crew. Working from Friday through the weekend in the fields would provide well-deserved earnings. But come Sunday night, these students "would be glad to see school start on Monday." They could really relax once they got past Coach Jefferson. This was no easy feat, since Jefferson knew every student by name. And when he called their names, they'd freeze in their tracks.

Jean Ellen Wilson, through oral histories she's collected, learned that most people didn't realize they faced discrimination at every turn, having experienced it consistently during their entire lives. "We knew who we were. You knew what you could do and you knew what you couldn't," says Joyce Jackson. "That was the status quo. It was natural then," she adds. "It was accepted," historian Wilson clarifies. Whites set the rules including where blacks were allowed to be, and when.

Outside their neighborhood, blacks faced being detained and interrogated by white police officers and even being beaten by them. Fear-inducing patrolling was treated as a sport. A devoted collector of Highwaymen paintings, whose name is withheld at his request, had a PhD-holding cousin there who used to ride along with a policeman at night just to harass young black men. They liked to "thump them" every once in a while. One white policeman told historian Jean Ellen Wilson he arrested black men for "reckless eyeballing," the supposed sexually aggressive or otherwise inappropriate glance at a white woman.

Up until integration, their neighborhood had clearly been a good place to live and a safe place to be. But with the neighborhood's core waning, the social fabric was deteriorating from within and being ignored from without. An environment previously enriched by caring people became a place where people were poorly connected. It happened in other places as well, of course, with the advent of forced integration.

Joyce Jackson points out, "It was a great village; without benefit of telephones, people knew what was going on with each other." Jean Ellen Wilson says, "People watched out for each other's children." This cut down on truancy. Jackson relates that "by the time a child got home from cutting school, word of mouth would have tipped off the student's mother, who would be sitting on the front porch, waiting. She'd ask: 'Don't you have any sense?' You'd still get whacked." Education was taken seriously then. One simply didn't split an infinitive in Mrs. Pierce's class, for example. "You did not under any circumstances misuse the English language," says Jackson.

Deputy Duval relates that "back in the day" Lincoln Park Academy's competitive football team was given one football helmet for the entire team by its counterpart white school. This wasn't sportsmanship and this wasn't a prank. It was the way it was. The battered, outdated textbooks in African American classrooms also came from the white schools. In them were the names of white students who had attended the schools from which they were handed down. Earl Little recalls that the books "might have been a bit tattered, and sometimes pages were missing, but if you are determined to learn a formula, it's just as good in a used book as it is in a new one. Also, we often had to buy our own books, and we'd look for used books to buy, so if you got a free used book you felt like you had gotten something. One thing was, the books from the white schools might have the answers written in, and that seemed like a good thing, but then we found out the answers might be right but they might be wrong. But you see, our parents wanted so bad for us to get an education—to them and to us, an education was such a prize."

Little did not feel the sting of segregation until he went into the service in World War II. In his youth, like so many other blacks, he thought the dual system was natural; used books seemed like part of an unquestionable order. All the elements were natural to him. He said, "Nothing surprised me. I would have been surprised if anyone had gone against it." He does not recall an instance where he, individually, experienced discrimination. He just says, "Nothing happened to me that didn't happen to everyone." During segregation, public areas, even the St. Lucie County courthouse, had two water fountains, one marked "Colored" and the other marked "White Only." There were no restrooms in downtown Fort Pierce where "coloreds" were allowed. Like other overt markers of our racist past, these would, with time, fade away. However, as Mary Ann observes, "Fort Pierce was one of the last on the market list to come out of segregation."

Many African Americans enjoyed attending movies in downtown Fort Pierce at the plush Sunrise Theater, once the largest one on Florida's east coast. However, they weren't allowed to enter through the elegant front doors. They had to use the back door, which gave them entry to the balcony, where they were segregated from other moviegoers. "We had to go upstairs and sit in a box," Gloria Walters explains. "We had to climb a flight of stairs on the outside of the building, and go in the box—a small room. If you weren't there in time to get a seat, you couldn't go up, and you certainly couldn't sit downstairs. There was even a ticket window, upstairs, for black people."

In Fort Pierce the Burger King fast-food restaurant accepted blacks' money at the front counter, but these customers then had to go around to the back of the building to pick up their food. Reporter Anthony Westbury points out that this Burger King was built on Orange Avenue, at the edge of the African American community, in the 1960s. This was the time of school integration dramas and mounting racial tension, and being rejected by a national restaurant reinforced blacks' growing consciousness of their own oppression.

Avenue D with its many juke joints and good times had long attracted African Americans from around the country, and northern blacks visiting or living in Fort Pierce, as well as in other parts of the South, saw things differently from those who were raised there. On the cusp of national social upheaval, attitudes were still entrenched in this community. Gloria Walters recalls having to stand in the rain to get her food at Burger King: "A white lady invited me to come in out of the rain, and then another white lady walked out. The two white ladies working there told me to wait outside. I asked for my money back;

they wouldn't give it to me. One lady said, 'You'll just have to wait for your food, because you're not getting your money back.'"

Janice McGriff, the first African American cashier at JCPenney in white Fort Pierce in 1966, remembers only one incident of relatively mild, yet stinging, discrimination. A white woman to whom she had offered assistance told her, "I don't want you to wait on me." When her manager offered solace, she simply replied that she understood, saying, "My parents raised me to be kind to people." Or as Joyce Jackson puts it: "I'm not going to hate a race of people because of the stupidity of one person."

But it was more than one person.

↓ ↓ ↓

This was the racial backdrop for the Highwaymen. It was important that they avoid drama on what had been, and could again become, hazardous streets. They were able to negotiate this uncertain and potentially dangerous context with their good manners and their desirable paintings. "There was no racial tension," Mary Ann contends, as she and her cadre displayed their artwork. She points out that the artists had what people, who were overwhelmingly white, wanted—pleasingly framed oil paintings at reasonable prices. It was a win-win scenario. Furniture store owners would buy paintings to warm up their showroom displays. In addition to hanging them on their offices' walls to serve as incentives to closing sales, realtors would give paintings as housewarming gifts to new homeowners.

The artists became, in effect, goodwill ambassadors between black and white communities. Their glowing paintings warmed people's eyes, hearts, and minds, as well as their homes and businesses. They appeased the white clientele while bridging troubled waters. The artists were welcomed in spite of "No Nigger No Mexican" signs posted at certain businesses in the state's interior. Isaac Knight remembers, "I never been treated bad on the road, not even in Okeechobee." During the messy aftermath of Martin Luther King's death, he adds, "I still didn't have any problems." Business relationships had the chance of taking hold when people met as individuals, away from the masses. The Highwaymen were seen as nonthreatening; they came bearing a desirable cultural currency.

The Highwaymen had reached full stride when the Civil Rights Bill was enacted in 1964, while "separate but equal" restrictions lingered for another decade. Even after the rioting in response to Martin Luther King's assassination, the artists sold their paintings at breakneck speed throughout the region. Perhaps dealing one-on-one with white customers assuaged guilt, or perhaps customers found the artists to be like anyone else who was young, eager, and polite, with something to sell at a good price.

Their grit and tenacity, key tenets of the American spirit of independence, brought them respect while they were selling their creations, and the paintings themselves helped squelch racial discrimination. "The paintings sold themselves," says Willie Daniels. "If it had the colors they needed, they'd buy it." He adds, "Some people would buy to help you out." There were stumbling blocks, to be sure. Beyond the Cinderella story of the Highwaymen's success—making terrific paintings that were marketed with aplomb and relative ease—at times "selling was rough," says Daniels. Not every white customer was smitten with the black artists and their artwork.

Willie Turner offers, "There was some deep-seated resentment toward black people, but for the Highwaymen there was a lack of hostility. They were there legally, selling paintings. They posed no threat, and people wanted their paintings." Mary Ann goes further: "In white homes you were offered drinks, something to eat. Made welcome. Not have to sit in a raggedy chair. Even during racial tension we were treated . . . like people. Yeah, like people. We had what they wanted, and they got more than what they paid for," she declares.

"Some whites knew what it was to suffer," Mary Ann concedes. She adds that these people paid full price, $25 or $35, depending on the painting's size. Others, though, in Mary Ann's term, were just snotty. Still, "for every snotty person someone was more kinder. The compassion was so great. But sometimes people probably bought something so we wouldn't steal."

Of course, bargaining was a common practice. Mary Ann would accept less for her paintings before the rest of the Highwaymen would yield to offers below their asking prices. If a painting was offered at $35, she was quicker than her male counterparts to accept $25 for it; she simply could not afford to lose a sale. "I had to feed my family. I needed money for food, not for liquor or beer." She hadn't the time or inclination for haggling.

The artists became common fixtures as they traveled regularly, mostly working the east coast from Fort Lauderdale to Flagler Beach. At certain area businesses, "No Solicitation" signs popped up in the 1970s. Willie Daniels says ruefully, "By the time you got to your car, the cops would be there." But when the law enforcement officers noted the wet paintings, they concluded that the artwork had not been stolen and that the person in possession of the pieces had painted them.

"Some let you go, some checked you out. And some issued a citation [for solicitation]," Daniels says. His use of "you" is rhetorical; few others had legal difficulties worth noting. The artists, however, didn't routinely have permits, although one was needed for each town in which they intended to sell paintings.

Mary Ann, like some of the others, did eventually buy one. She also got a sales tax number. Al Black bought a permit only when he got caught without one. Mary Ann got hers preemptively. Without permits, the artists could have been detained and possibly arrested. In either event they would not have been selling paintings, and to the Highwaymen a painting wasn't completed until it was sold.

Mary Ann believes that "the scene, the color, and compassion," usually sold these paintings. People bought for themselves when something struck a nerve. Many women purchased paintings before redecorating their homes, saying that they "changed the color of their walls to match them." There is a quality of remembrance in Highwaymen paintings, a connectedness to Florida's past and its natural beauty. The landscape is continually being altered. Mary Ann cites this as the reason for the current resurgent interest in the Highwaymen and their paintings. "Now they are buying them because everything is fading away."

However, in some ways Highwaymen art does alter nature, as these artists were not concerned with factual representation. For them, veracity was realized in the gestalt; the feel of reality was achieved through gesture and color. "Nature's never wrong," says Mary Ann. "If I add a tree that's not there now, doesn't mean it's never been there." Color functioned metaphorically as well. Perception was experience, and experience was knowing. Highwaymen patrons did more than know what they liked—they liked what they knew, and what they knew resonated within. These images evoked empathy. More, they compelled the viewers to place themselves in that Promised Land.

People didn't care about photographic realism. If they did, admits Mary Ann, "they wouldn't have bought my paintings. It's what a person sees that makes the difference." That was, and is, the allure of a Highwaymen painting—each scene's depiction seems customized. Maybe it is the brushstrokes, as bold as they are carefree, or the idea that little matters in paradise, as their painterly manner suggests.

For the male Highwaymen, selling began with scouting and a knock on a door. Mary Ann, though, was more deliberate in her preparations. She began by checking to be certain that she had enough gas to get there and back: "I would not like running out of gas in my car. I had to turn around and get back to pick up my kids. I wanted to make sure they were properly supervised."

Most often the artists and salesmen looked for businesses "where there was more than one employee working," Mary Ann explains. She would generally bring ten paintings on her sales trips, safely nesting one in the other on the backseat. The large trunks of the luxury cars the Highwaymen favored held their largest paintings, typically 24" × 48". Mary Ann, unlike her flashy car, was anything but ostentatious.

The artists knew the importance of first impressions and proper attire. Dressed in her usual uniform of pants, blouse, and polished shoes, she would knock on the door and ask permission to show her paintings. She might state factually, "I have some paintings. Would you like to buy some?" Mary Ann is quick to point out that she "never took it [acceptance] for granted." She was polite, even deferential, in this still-segregated region where the threat of conflict lay just beneath the surface of a racist attitude.

"I could take five [paintings] in each hand," recalls Mary Ann. She would not say much as she leaned her landscapes along a wall. She didn't have to talk; indeed, it was better that she didn't explain her artwork. She would answer questions, however, such as "Where is this?" She would never say, "It's wherever you want it to be," although that would have been truthful. The Highwaymen's images may have been based on actual places or hybrid perceptions of various places and experiences, or they may have been borrowed from Backus. But the artists' renditions were their own, and through their process they stripped the landscape to its barest, leaving it less observed than imagined, and open for interpretation. This engaged viewers, and their excitement was contagious. "Sometimes," Mary Ann says, "they wanted the same thing." She realized, as did the other artists, that archetypal images were best aligned with the understandings and tastes of potential patrons. Success in sales sprang from a visceral reaction.

Throughout her children's youth, sales of Mary Ann's paintings would be the family's primary source of income. Painting required time, and it was demanding. Sometimes she painted through the night; she more often painted while her children were in school. She generally produced in quantity. She wanted to have more than enough paintings when she was working areas far from home; indeed, the more she had, the more incentive she'd have to continue selling. Occasionally Mary Ann would need a supply of paintings for the Hungry Artists Gallery in West Palm Beach, which bought and resold her paintings. "I was full of energy," she recalls of driving regularly to "West Palm Beach, Miami, Daytona, and Jupiter." Her paintings were at times used to barter for services or goods. She paid a dentist for a gold crown with one of her creations, and she similarly traded one for a set of tires for one of her cars.

Feeding her family was the prime motivator, and the spirited competition between the artists upped the entrepreneurial ante. She was determined, dogged even, about keeping up with and surpassing her male counterparts. Of course, no one could top Al Black's sales ability, not even Mary Ann. Nor did Mary Ann have Alfred Hair's drive to keep a constant inventory. "I was not a Speedy Gonzalez. I did four at a time but wasn't rushed. I left stuff out when I rushed," she explains. There are paintings in which, for example, tree limbs don't reflect in a pond below. But these flaws are dismissible, if even noticeable, because in the scheme of things they do not matter; they do not drive the content of her creations, or of any other Highwaymen paintings for that matter.

Mary Ann learned her strengths and her weaknesses. "I don't draw cows, because my cows look like pigs," she admits. This worked to her advantage, because barnyard animals and other accoutrements would only detract from nature, from the sense of wilderness which enticed buyers. She, like the others, learned what sold. "People always liked royal poincianas," she observed. Mary Ann favored ocean scenes and painted many backwoods and glades as well. She gravitated toward tranquility.

↓ ↓ ↓

In this media-drenched world where readers devour salacious gossip and accept each piece of insidious innuendo as fact, Mary Ann Carroll is angrily dismissive of rumors about an affair she allegedly had with Harold Newton decades ago. The claim is an undercurrent that has become part and parcel of her narrative now that she's achieved celebrity status, and it even made its way, subtly and possibly with guile, into a Highwaymen biography.

She forcefully addresses the suggestion about herself and Harold Newton: "That's a lie! I don't like lies. I'm not going to live one." Then Mary Ann, in an offhanded way, recalls that "there was as many white people as blacks making passes at me." In her acerbic comment is a lot more of bitterness than the juicy stuff of rumor. It embodies the racism and shifting tides of the Jim Crow double standard of the 1950s and 1960s.

As for the book that claimed she had an affair with Harold Newton, Mary Ann did not attempt to correct the misstatements of the author; instead she crossed out the reference with a black Sharpie when asked to autograph the book. This action is vintage Mary Ann Carroll. She is angered easily by a thoughtless, often unfair, world. She subsequently charged five dollars to autograph that book.

The money, she explained, would benefit her church. Whether or not these payments, which irritated many of her fans and drove some away, made it directly to the church coffers is irrelevant, because much of her income supports her church. She reckons, too, that many of these autograph seekers are making an investment. Her signature makes their books more valuable, as the Highwaymen phenomenon has been, to Florida's east coast, the equivalent of the Old West gold rush. Further, none of the Highwaymen has benefited from the escalated resale value of their paintings. This reality, although standard practice in the visual arts, raises the ire of some of the Highwaymen including Mary Ann, because it reminds them of the injustices of the not too distant past.

She never accepted things like the "Colored waiting rooms in doctors' offices, the wooden chairs, no padding, that was unlike the wooden chairs in the white reception areas, which were padded." She noticed and was angered by all the symptoms and symbols of segregation; even today she seems to still live with them.

Mary Ann knew she was separate but unequal, and it was always gnawing at her. Her angst was hard to contain. The everyday attempts to humiliate her angered her, then as now, while other African Americans seemed to take them in stride. And that angers her too. "I'm not the most liked person in Fort Pierce by some of my own people," she acknowledges. "Nothing was too much for me to challenge." She is well liked and respected, though she has offended certain people, whether it is by charging them to autograph their books or by speaking her mind. She's a vocal critic, albeit a somewhat passive-aggressive one. Her feelings otherwise might be rooted more in self-image than reality, though she's not one to compromise. Besides, she was and is today a salesperson, and in this capacity she has to please others and keep any anger concealed.

Sam Gaines looks back at the 1950s and remembers seeing the coming changes. He also recalls hearing from his grandfather about "the pole," which once stood on a now asphalt-covered 8th Street and Avenue C by the Masonic Hall. Here black men were brought, tied, and beaten, the message of "know your place and stay there" sent right from the heart of the black community. From having seen the Klan march in his youth, from remembering how blacks had to get off the sidewalk for approaching whites, and later, from participating in the early days of the civil rights era, the old ways were no longer acceptable to him, and they were especially not acceptable to those African Americans who were coming home from colleges. They had a new sense of self; they saw themselves as equals. "We saw things differently than what we grew up knowing," Gaines says. He, like other African American parents of that day, sent their children to black colleges with the idea that their offspring would know who they are and where they came from. "Young men," he says, "were no longer quiet."

Black children were instructed by their parents to be prepared for unfair treatment. Gaines points out certain rules: "Be careful. Remember your color. You won't be treated properly. Don't get aggressive with an officer. Be permissive." Something else was behind the passivity. He told his own children: "I need you to know who you are. If you get kicked in your ass, you need to have something inside of you to pull yourself up and keep going." Rubin Johnson's list was similar: "Stay out of certain situations. Be aware of where you are and what you are doing. Don't draw attention to yourself." His number one rule was "Don't break the law; you'll be treated differently." Lives were lived in the shadows. But things were about to change; it was the eve of integration.

Youngsters in Fort Pierce's Blacktown were well prepared to enter the world with the abandon of aspiring young men and women who would find their places and make their marks. Of course they were also shackled by the color of their skin. It was a tall order. "When we left Lincoln Park Academy, we didn't know what we knew," Sam Gaines says. "We could stand alongside anyone."

They were prepared, but perhaps not for the onslaught of forced integration. Their close-knit community began unraveling from inside and from outside. Gaines unabashedly sums up the problem: "Black children were exposed to what white kids got away with." The ideals that the Lincoln Park community had propagated so well were being dismantled. Low-mindedness was increasingly muscling aside the high-mindedness of integration. Court rulings, for example on bringing a certain number of black teachers to white schools, seemed gratuitous and caused animosity.

Being sheltered meant being alienated, but it was in part separation by choice. It required strength and knowing. Sam Gaines describes an "intuition" that is shared by black people who have been subjected to prejudice: "We can tell when we're being tolerated but not wanted." It's a deep-rooted distrust of intentions, a suspicion of the motives of white people. "It's in us, to always be looking or listening for what's not being said. That's something that is inbred in us that you can't take from us. It's a feeling within . . . that we can look, and just see, and get the sense of whether or not you're sincere. Now, my kids don't have it, because they came up in altogether different times."

Zora Neale Hurston once said, "The Indian resists curiosity by a stony silence. The Negro offers a featherbed resistance. That is, we let the probe enter, but it never comes out. It gets smothered under a lot of laughter and pleasantries." This adage rings loud and clear for Mary Ann Carroll. She apparently possesses this survival skill whereby a black woman can guardedly disclose information sufficient to satisfy white curiosity without revealing too much of herself, her world, or her truths.

Mary Ann is bothered a lot by what she feels are dishonest or disrespectful attempts at relationships. Hers is a constant struggle in which her Bible is her only source for determining right and wrong. Further, her moral interpretations are unyielding, making conflict unavoidable. Living in her hometown brings back all the memories of the inequities and blanket judgments that white society has cast on black people. In spite of great accomplishments, the reminders of erasure, as a vestige of social racism, continue into the twenty-first century, especially, for Mary Ann, in Fort Pierce. This is a burden she carries.

The creation of public art commemorating the Highwaymen—an obelisk in November 2009 and a mural in August 2011, along Avenue D—are signs of positive change there. But recognition came too little and too late to appease some of the artists, Mary Ann Carroll foremost among them. The selection of artists and artworks and installation requirements for Public Art, paid for by tax dollars entrusted to local city, county, and state government entities, is subject to rules and regulations. The process requires a publicly announced Request for Artists; the application makes the selection competitive. Of course, materials used must be suitable for these site-specific artworks, and only artisans capable of creating in such ways would be considered for these commissions.

In spite of a legally advertised submissions call, the Highwaymen knew nothing about the obelisk until its construction was under way. Mary Ann was dismayed. When she learned that a Miami-based white female artist from New York received $90,000 to create the sculpture, she was disillusioned. At first she could not understand why one of the Highwaymen wasn't selected, then why the project wasn't made a collaborative effort involving the local artists. She found it even harder to understand why the Highwaymen weren't at least consulted as to what they might like to see representing themselves. She was in disbelief when she realized the commissioned artist didn't even bother to share her plans with any of the Highwaymen and, further, that none of the city commissioners or their administrators urged her to consult with the artists. Mary Ann would have "liked to have been consulted." She adds that she may well be capable in the use of the required materials, but this is beside the point. She didn't express her feelings about being excluded. She harbored them instead, allowing animus to form. There was no civil discourse, no conversation at all.

Mary Ann says that many of the Highwaymen were irritated when they learned that another non-Highwayman was commissioned to create a mosaic mural of a Highwaymen painting at a new bus station on Avenue D. Holding no malice toward the regionally respected artist who was chosen, Mary Ann let her ire turn to apathy. For her, this response was safer than disgust.

Then again, maybe Mary Ann felt helpless and believed that the world is unjust. Her behavior might at times look like arrogance. But her attitude stems more from elusiveness, a learned way to survive in a world in which she was racially a second-class citizen as well as a woman in a man's world. Mary Ann's truculence, in part a way of coping, may not be the best or most productive way. Underlying her anger is her feeling of exclusion, her feeling that she was driven away from something to which she has ownership rights. Mary Ann believes she should have been afforded a discussion with the powers that be and that she should have been included in the public art tributes to her and other Highwaymen.

Decades ago she had no choice. Indeed, institutionalized racism bothers Mary Ann more than interpersonal experiences of bigotry or discrimination. She recalls lots of little slights, and she says, "I can see things most of the others didn't pay attention to." She adds, "It's been totally unfair. It didn't make me happy."

↓ ↓ ↓

The Highwaymen's audience is not now, nor has it ever been, at home in Fort Pierce. Indeed, it was from the start a flight of fancy, not about getting away from home and family, but about eluding the inevitable future that loomed ahead of young black people in St. Lucie County in that day—labor in the grove and field, labor lifting and loading, labor menial and repetitive. It was about finding or creating alternatives. Harold Newton was a wanderer, fishing when he wasn't painting, and painting generally to pay bills. He traveled northward, appreciating the St. Johns River. Its laid-back environs were more to his liking than the urban south of Florida, with bustling cities whose pace was suited to Alfred Hair's temperament and ambitions. Both men, as well as those they inspired to paint and those they employed to sell their paintings, found and built clienteles throughout the seaboard's towns and cities. They aspired to saturate the state with their paintings, and they soared above and beyond their hometowns. The artists and their paintings were everywhere.

Of course, most of the twenty-six Highwaymen were not itinerants out to sell limitless numbers of paintings; most were living satisfied lives at home, enjoying the benefits of full-time employment, even. But the core group, some eight artists, knew nothing else. They were artists living artists' lives. Harold was relaxed; his skill alone determined his success. Alfred's cadre was driven to create a market as well as artwork to satisfy it, yet their lifestyle was fancy-free. Mary Ann could not afford to be relaxed, nor could she live loose and carefree, not with seven children to raise alone in Fort Pierce.

The lack of recognition at home bothers Mary Ann today; the feeling of not being included and, worse, of being exploited and ignored, gnaws at her. But she aches not just for herself; she carries the weight of a traumatic history, an African American's burden. Those old shackles are hard for her to break. She cannot find satisfaction or take pride in a place that cannot take pride in her. Recognition at home came too late to be meaningful to her. She finds fault in a well-intentioned obelisk, a mosaic mural, and local festivals because they reek to her and others of exploitation and racial inequity that is supposed to be over. She doesn't feel that we, as a society, have moved on, at least not in her hometown.

The intuition Sam Gaines says black people have developed that, like radar, questions white people's intentions is ripe in Mary Ann. It tells her that the recognition being accorded at home is disingenuous. Not all the artists agree or care; they are appreciative of any accolades, whether at home or from far away. Their attitude is good business. In fact, some of the once loose-knit band of artists, more like-minded than unified, have come together to form their own 501c3 nonprofit organization. They are a business now, protecting and promoting themselves. In 2012 they launched this new campaign with a successful fund-raising luncheon in Fort Pierce to an enthusiastic crowd of corporate sponsors, friends, and politicians. Most of the Highwaymen are celebrities nowadays, honored at festivals and featured guests at a variety of places. Branded and packaged, they take advantage of their newfound popularity as an opportunity to sell paintings. Mary Ann, critical and often poignant, questions the self-congratulatory group's motives. She pays a price for her moralistic and, at times, self-defeating, attitudes.

Dedication day for the obelisk came on the kind of morning that gives Florida its "sunny Florida" tag. It was a brief but sweet enough small-town ceremony that also served to kick off a Highwaymen festival. Sponsored by the Lincoln Park Main Street Association, it would have recognized the Highwaymen on their home turf and brought attention to the African American community, which was undergoing municipal redevelopment. But it was poorly organized and poorly publicized, so it failed to attract visitors. It was promised to become the central Highwaymen event—and, as the only such festival endorsed by the artists themselves, with many dozens of such festivals throughout the state annually, it could have been—but instead it was a significant loss to the community and a personal blow to the artists. To a critical and dispirited Mary Ann, it was a travesty, not a learning experience that would lead to a grander celebration of the Highwaymen at home.

Sam Gaines argues that Mary Ann's angst is not just a case of sour grapes. Now that the Highwaymen are so widely recognized and, indeed, famous, the city of Fort Pierce wants "ownership," Gaines says. "When they were struggling, no one paid attention to them."

A decade after the country woke up to the article in the *New York Times*, National Public Radio produced an extended Highwaymen series. It was no accident that it aired on Independence Day. The Highwaymen's history is established: Their story is inspiring, their paintings are symbolic of an era in our country's history, their meanings are enduring everywhere but not, it seems, at home. Veteran NPR correspondent Jacki Lyden, who spent a week in Fort Pierce conducting nearly thirty interviews, zeroed in on the story but found it a struggle to tell. She did an excellent job with the unusual three-part coverage, but she felt compelled to go beyond the Highwaymen's quasi-transcendental journey that empowered a virtual art-and-society movement.

What Jacki Lyden found bothered her, and she toiled over it. She heard "inflammatory words that hint at a broader divide in Fort Pierce. Not just an art spat, but perhaps vestigial racial tension from Jim Crow to the present. Fort Pierce recognizes the Highwaymen, but it doesn't seem to know how to include them." She goes on to ask, "So where is the spirit of tolerance and inclusivity that everyone remembers from Beanie Backus's home studio?"

Mary Ann Carroll likes the succinct reminder that "we had a struggle," but beyond that sound bite she does not care to argue what she sees as obvious. Instead she references her Bible—"A prophet is not without honor except in his own hometown." Perhaps these artists have no hometown. Being black in the America of their youth while witnessing their parents' and grandparents' lives was like being there but not fully; it was as if they were possessed, like farm equipment. Their elders' lives belonged to others. Nor were the lives of the young people who would become known as the Highwaymen fully their own.

Maybe the Highwaymen's name is more fitting for its allusion to how they lived than to how they sold paintings. In fact they drove away from Fort Pierce in search of riches, or, at least, of better lives. They came home at day's end to a warm and wonderful place because the Fort Pierce of their youth was just that. But that was then. As Thomas Wolfe wrote, "You can't go home again": you will be disappointed if you try, because home is no longer the same place. Indeed, it may no longer even be recognizable.

Jacki Lyden's prose becomes poetry; perhaps this is essential to the word-picture nature of radio storytelling when practiced as well as this veteran reporter does. Perhaps, too, the Highwaymen succeeded in creating visual images that worked more in the mind than to the mere delight of the eye. And like radio that creates visual allusions, the paintings created narrative allusions, and the purchasers told the stories. They imagined their own destinies with these glowing landscapes as backdrops. In this spirit Jacki Lyden concludes, "And that transformation is the story of art—and of young black Florida painters, now elderly, who once drove up and down US 1 selling wet-to-the-touch landscapes out of the trunks of their cars . . . shining like the American dream."

Stylistically, we know that the Highwaymen settled rapidly upon their primary scenes. They borrowed from Backus's oeuvre, but their images were truly unique to them. They may have started with his classical model, but they reinvented it, transformed it to leave fresh and original artwork. Mary Ann Carroll acknowledges that the paintings rendered by members of her circle "are not markedly different" from one another, but she points to distinctions that identify each painter's touch. "I might have turned my [tree] trunks to the right; they might have turned theirs to the left," she observes. It is a minor distinction in light of how remarkably varied each artist's output actually was. All, though, painted in the moment, unconcerned with traditional European rules of representation to establish their shared aesthetic, an aesthetic that upholds the tradition and meaning of landscape paintings, and that is the very definition of art.

"Everyone started laughing at my wild colors," Mary Ann remembers. She even thought, at times, that her hues were too vivid. "Sometimes I get into a trend and can't get out of it—too dark, too light. Sometimes perfect." She adds, "I always liked perfection. I didn't always do it, because I'd never get anything done!" For sure, it is a good thing that she did not focus on perfection; doing so would have made the paintings too defined and too predictable. And it would likely have hindered, tamed even, her expressive use of color.

Unlike the objectification of the landscape by high-minded artists with something to say, the Highwaymen's paintings are less like objects than experiences. A viewer can relate because they are accessible, and even flawed. These unusual paintings capture, with minimal effort, the sense of Florida in its rawest,

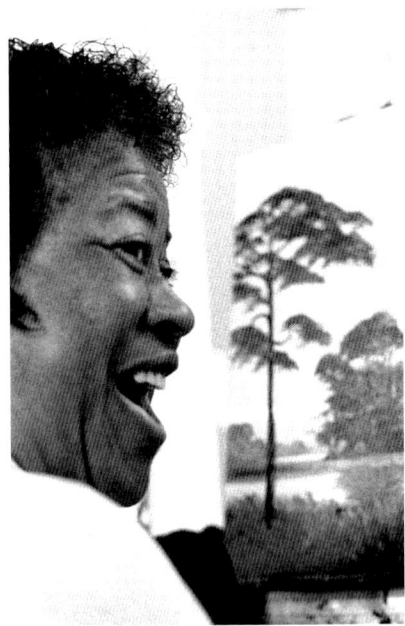

Mary Ann Carroll, Fort Pierce, 2000.

if not most sensual, form. "I guess I've always been a person who likes nature not domesticated," Mary Ann says.

The core group of Highwaymen established the aesthetic range of their genre and set the pace of their business enterprise in a social climate that was unwelcoming and at times hostile to African Americans. Through their energy and vision we see an idealized version of the Florida that well suited those looking for paradise in the 1960s and 1970s. At the intersection of their Floridian-pastoral creations and their entrepreneurial spirit, these young African Americans overcame Jim Crow obstacles and exemplified the American dream—success through hard work and creativity. None of the other artists, though, had quite the same obstacles as Mary Ann. The twenty-five male painters had a latitude that she did not. They were, for the most part, carefree. "The difference from the guys and me is that they didn't have to baby-sit and I did," she points out.

Willie Daniels adds, "Mary Ann, she hung around with the painters. [But] she never came to Eddie's; that's where we lived. We got through selling paintings, that's where we'd go drink beer. The painters set up the tables." Mary Ann did not partake. For her, the Highwaymen enterprise was all work. "I had bills to pay. I had seven kids to feed," she asserts. The only table she was setting was the one in her kitchen.

By the early 1980s, the artists had run out of steam and their enterprise came to a near halt. Sales became a shadow of what they had once been for those continuing to earn their living as painters, as Mary Ann did; the market for their images vanished as the culture shifted. People looked elsewhere for ways to decorate their homes and offices. The artists could travel freely and safely by then, but they had fewer reasons to "run the road." Some of the painters, including the remaining core members whose work set the Highwaymen's aesthetic standard—Harold Newton, Livingston Roberts, James Gibson, Roy McLendon, and Mary Ann Carroll—had eked out a living with brushes and palette knives since then, but most of the others drifted away from their craft. Art had been a ticket to fly away from their drab realities, and the times had changed. They returned home to a new drab reality.

Eventually, beginning in the mid-1990s, they were rediscovered and soon revered as artists and un-intentional pioneers. When they first began painting, it was hardly imaginable that young black people would lift themselves in a storybook manner from the shackles of segregation, realize the American dream, and leave a visual legacy of modern Florida. That's what happened, though, and it was even more unimaginable for a young woman to do this, as Mary Ann did.

In 2004, forty years after their major successes, the Highwaymen were inducted into the Florida Artists Hall of Fame by the State of Florida. They are alongside such notables as writers Ernest Hemingway, Tennessee Williams, and Zora Neale Hurston, musicians Jimmy Buffett and Ray Charles, and the visual artists Martin Johnson Heade, James Rosenquist, Robert Rauschenberg, and the man they admired, Beanie Backus.

Mary Ann Carroll continues to reap rewards as singular as her own biography. On May 18, 2011, she was honored by Michelle Obama at the First Lady's Luncheon at the Congressional Club in Washington, D.C. There she was the guest of honor, recognized for her achievements, achievements made in spite of discrimination. On the other hand, perhaps her achievements were accomplished because of the discrimination she has suffered and her contrary nature; she fought back, nonviolently of course, with fierce determination and countless tubes of oil paints.

Mary Ann stood tall, drove down the roads and walked along the streets, as she "looked beyond what was there." She saw beyond enduring discrimination and refused to accept being cast in a lower station than other citizens. Her art and its social marketing helped change that reality. Mary Ann, like the others of the coterie, broke barriers. She knew she had arrived when she presented one of her paintings, a flaming royal poinciana tree, to Mrs. Obama, knowing it would hang in the White House. "I felt like a champ," she exclaimed.

On the surface, Mary Ann Carroll's story stands apart from all the rest of the Highwaymen because of her gender. It would be simplistic, though, to define her merely as a woman who painted with a group of men. Mary Ann Carroll is a resilient survivor of some of the harshest times in American society, as well as a painter, preacher, and mother. In the true sense of the word, she is a victor, not only over the times in which she has lived but also in her chosen fields of work and in her luminous life.

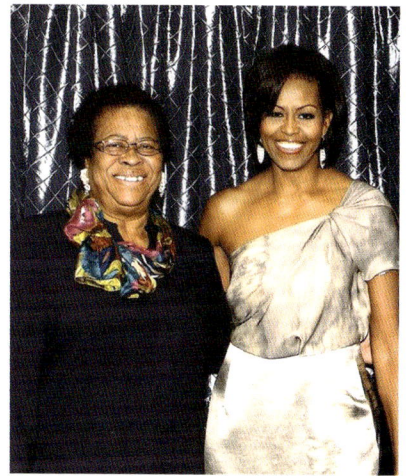

Mary Ann Carroll and First Lady Michelle Obama, Washington, D.C., 2011.

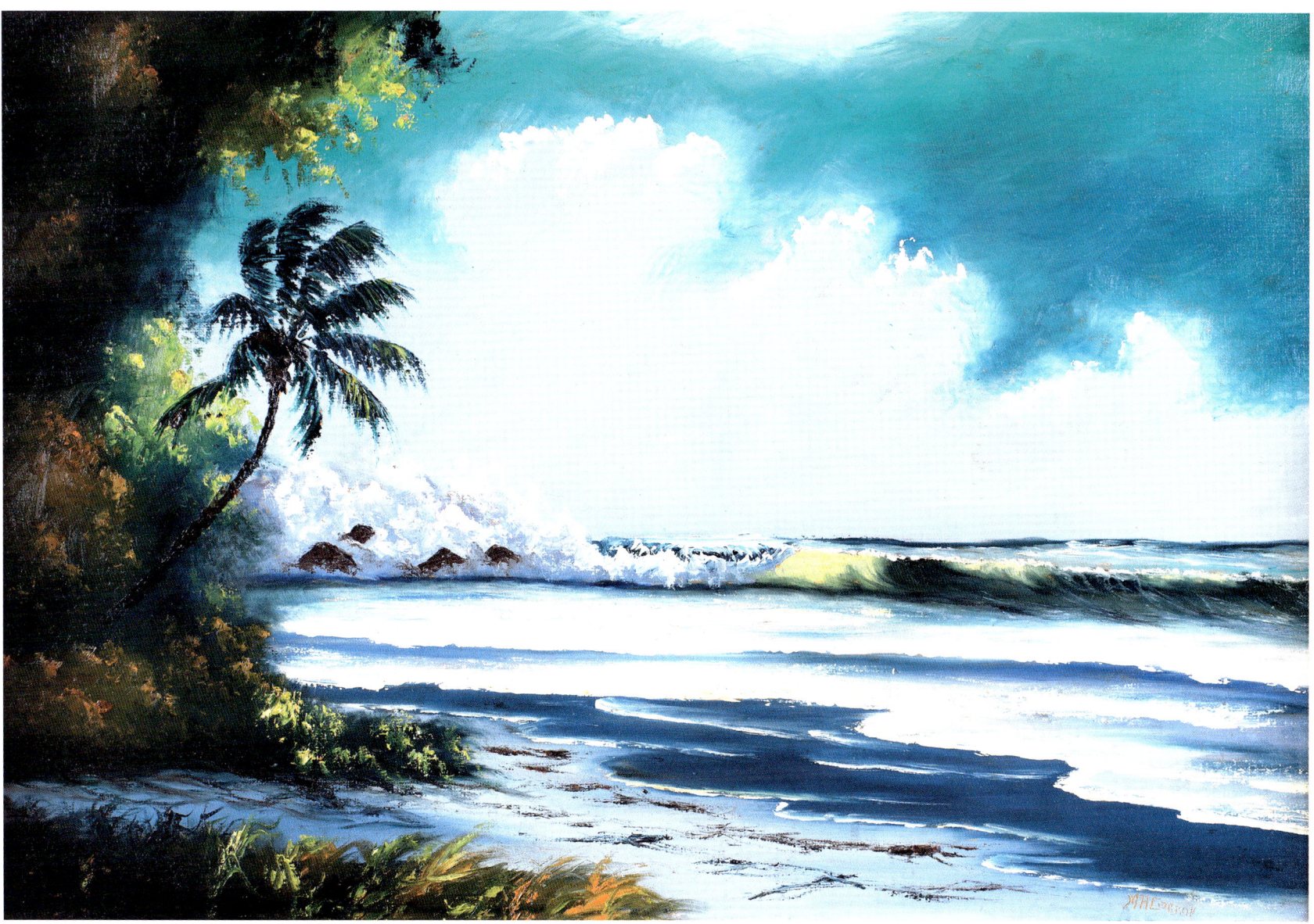

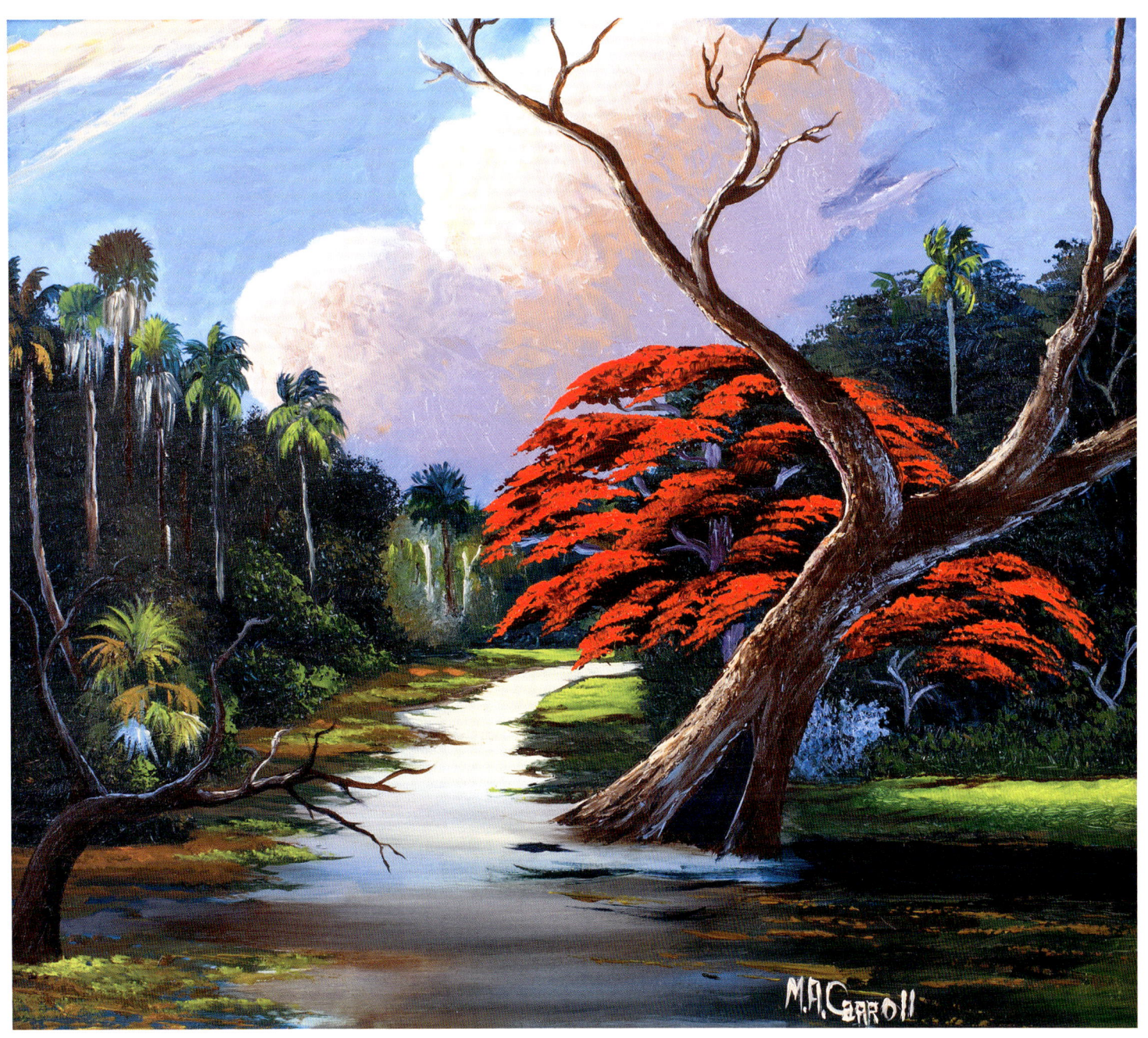

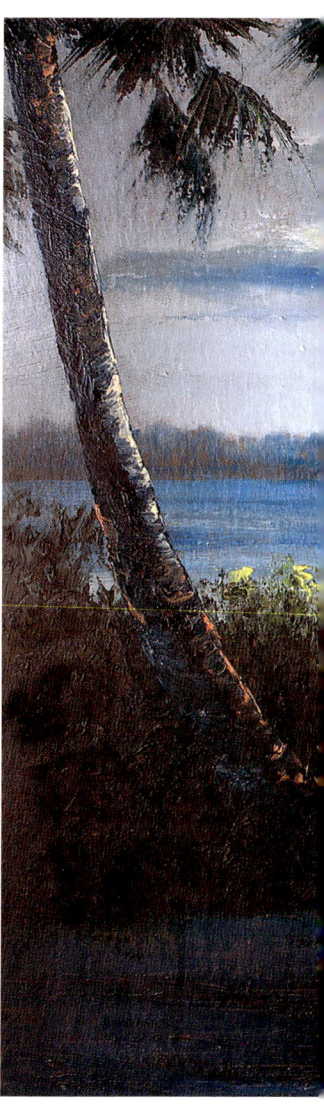

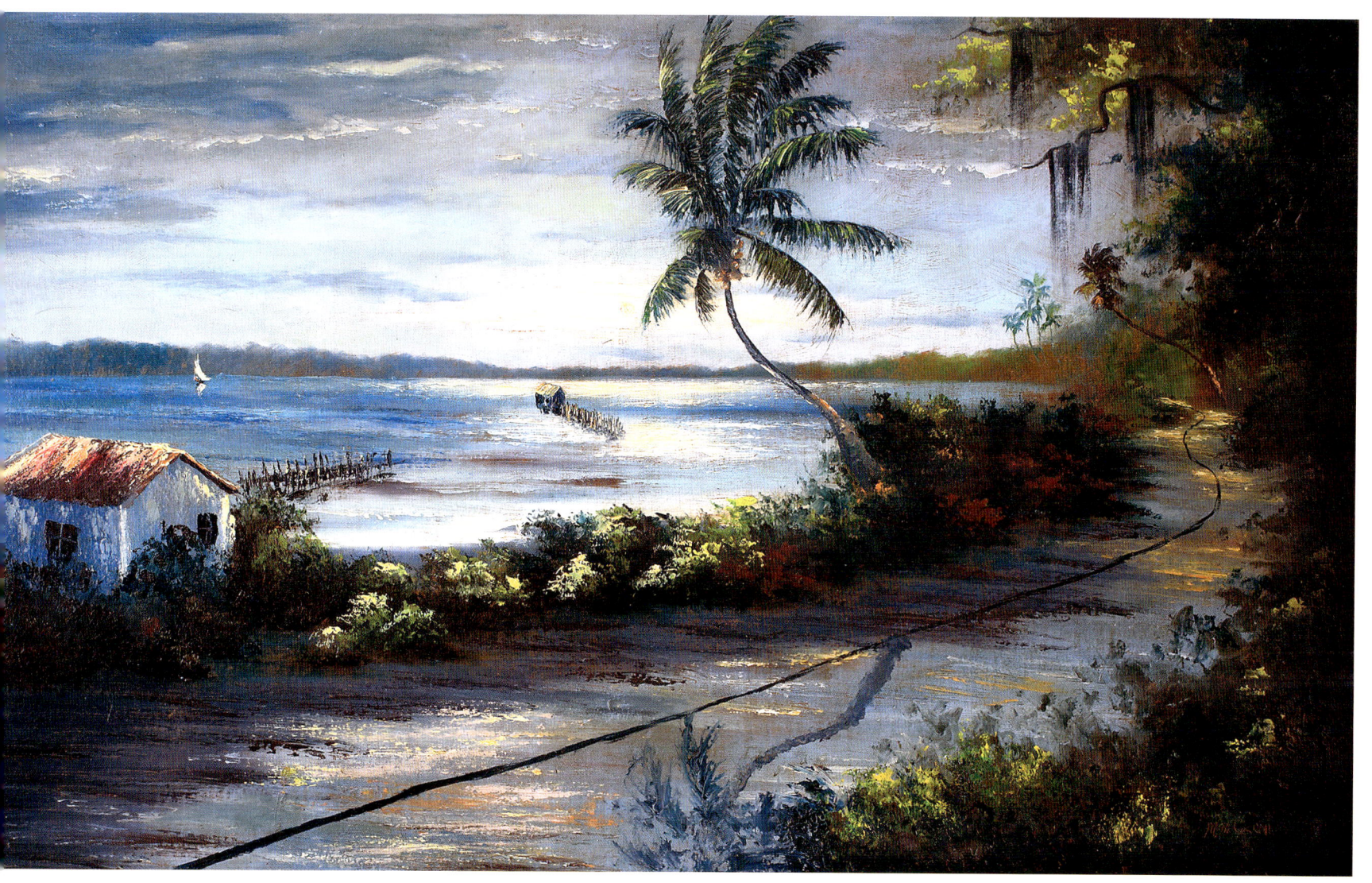

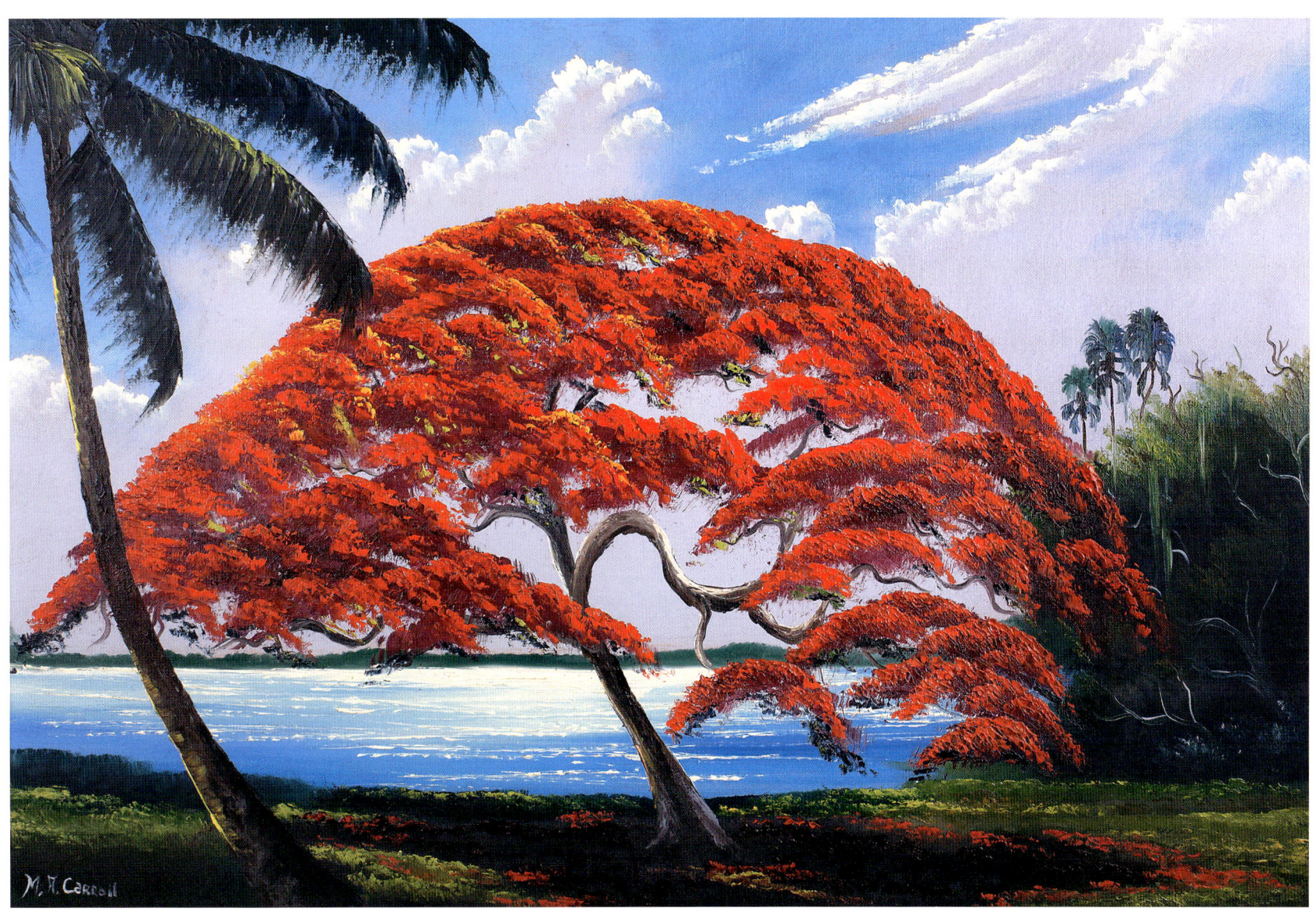

M. A. Carroll

48

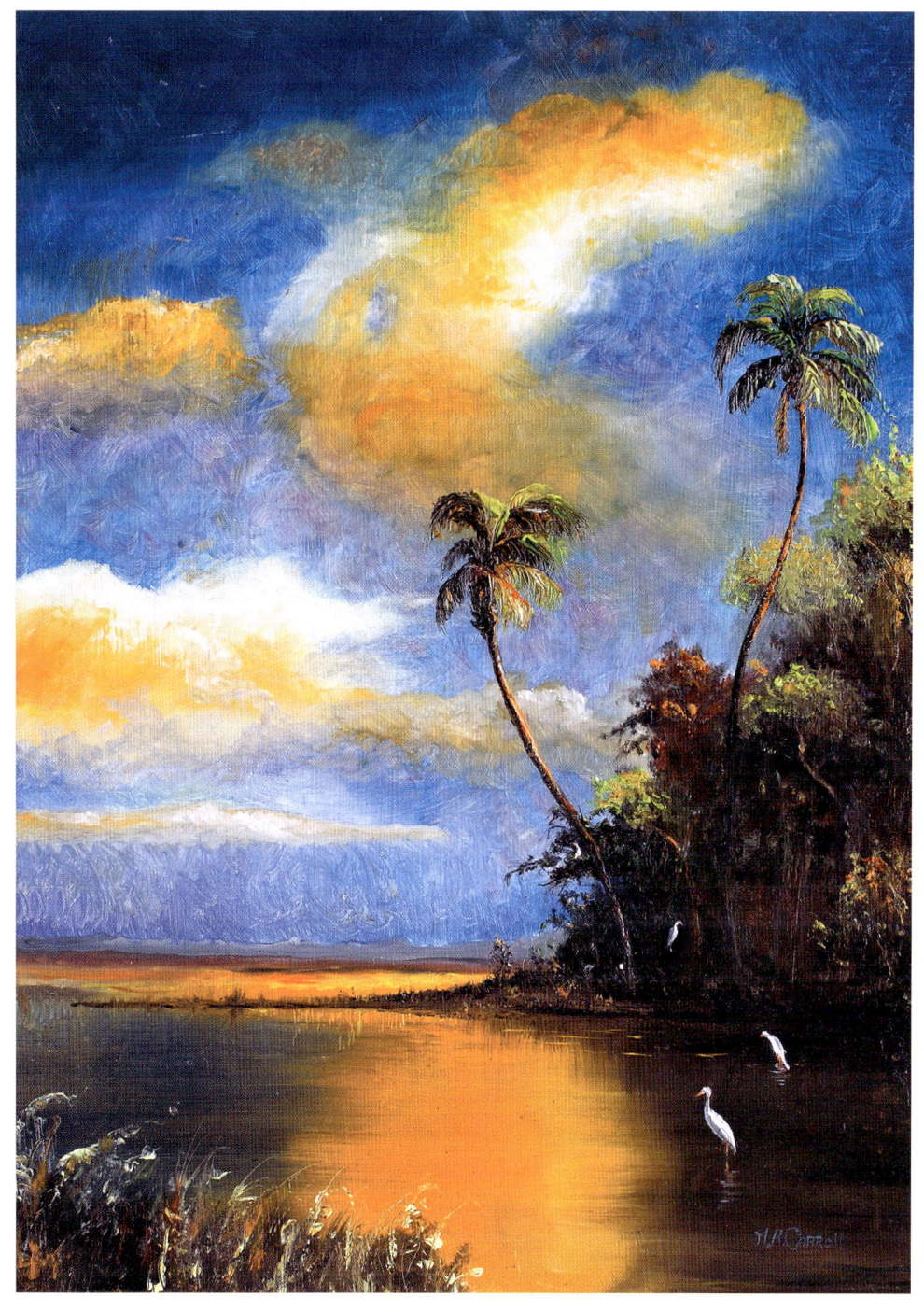

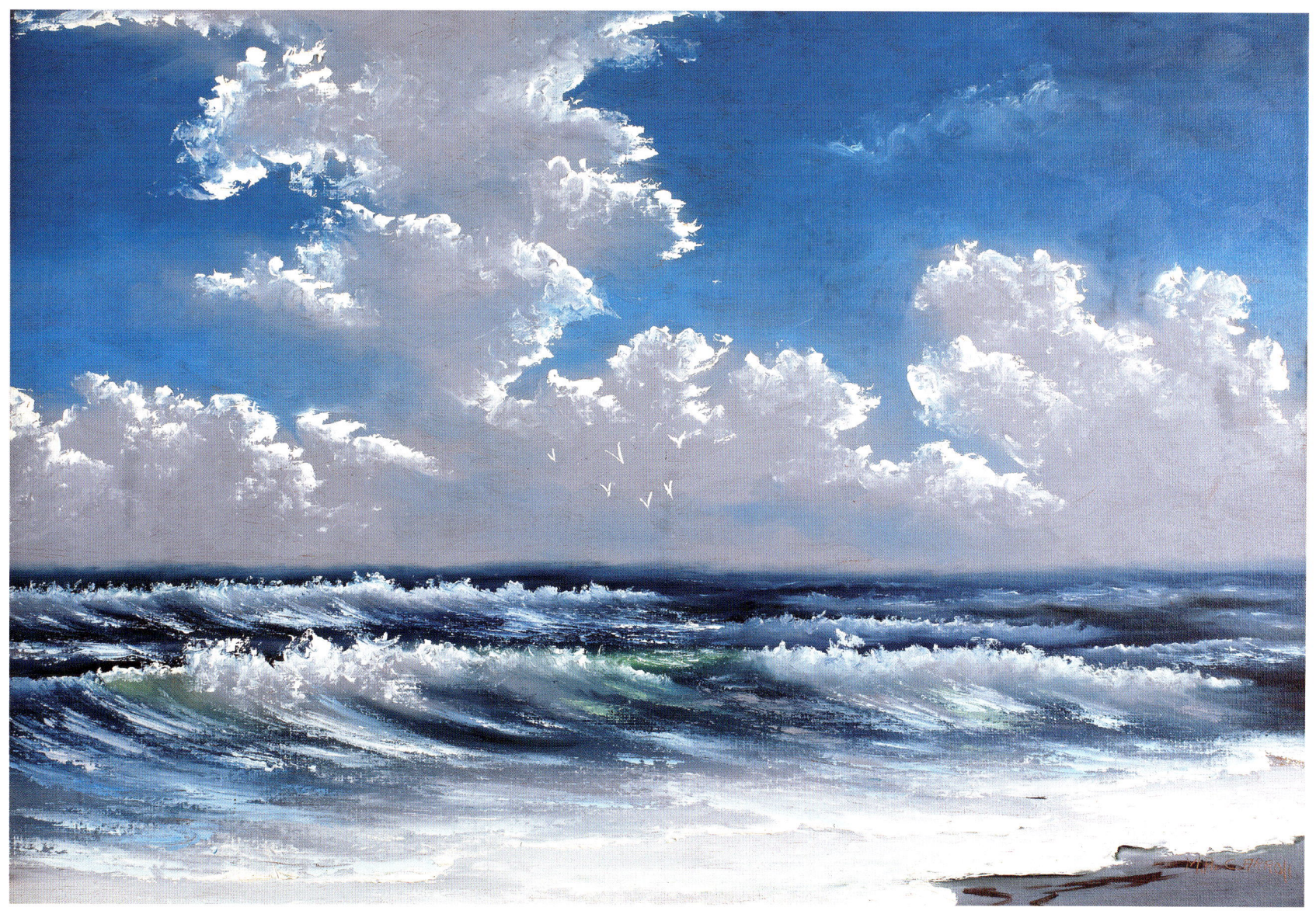

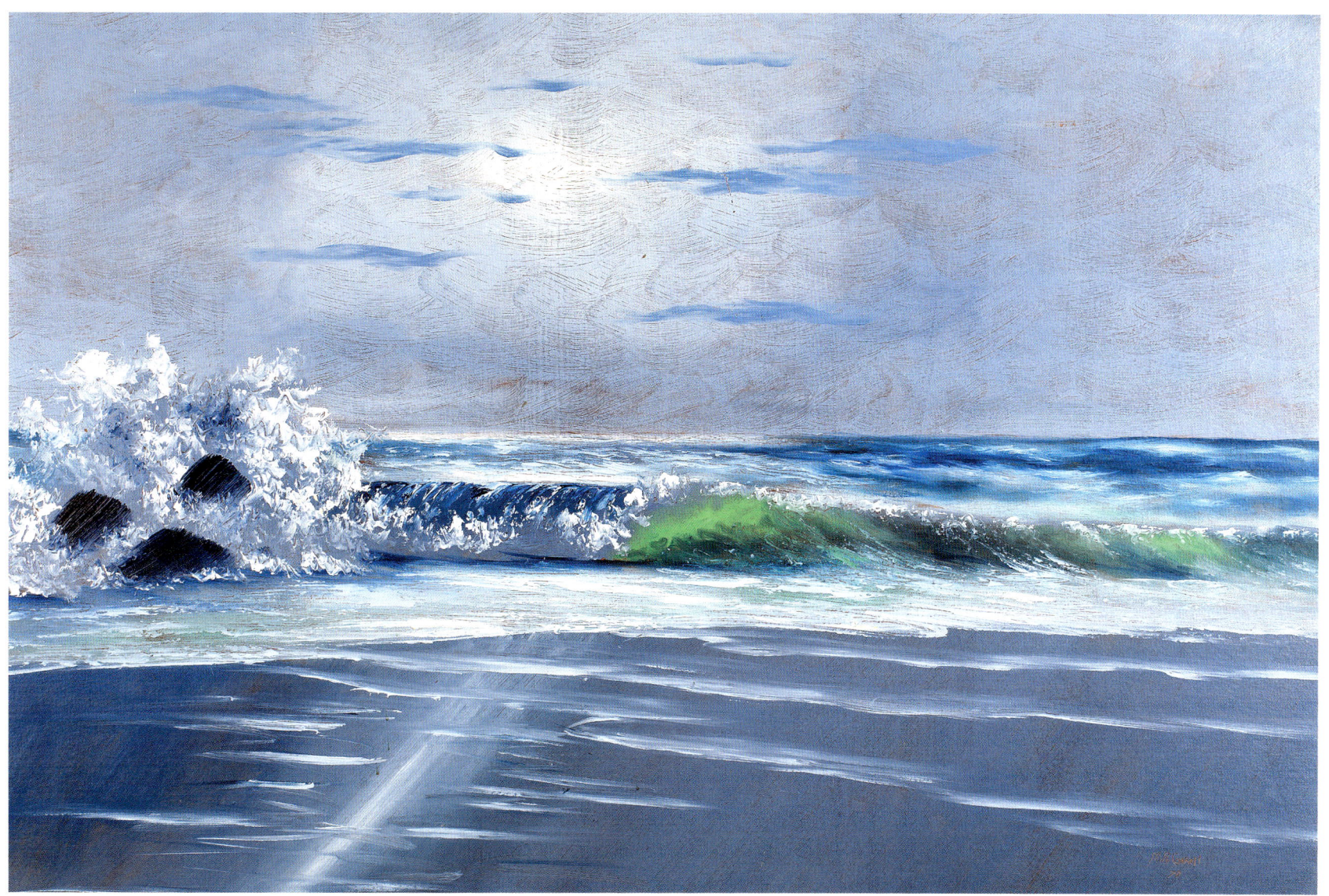

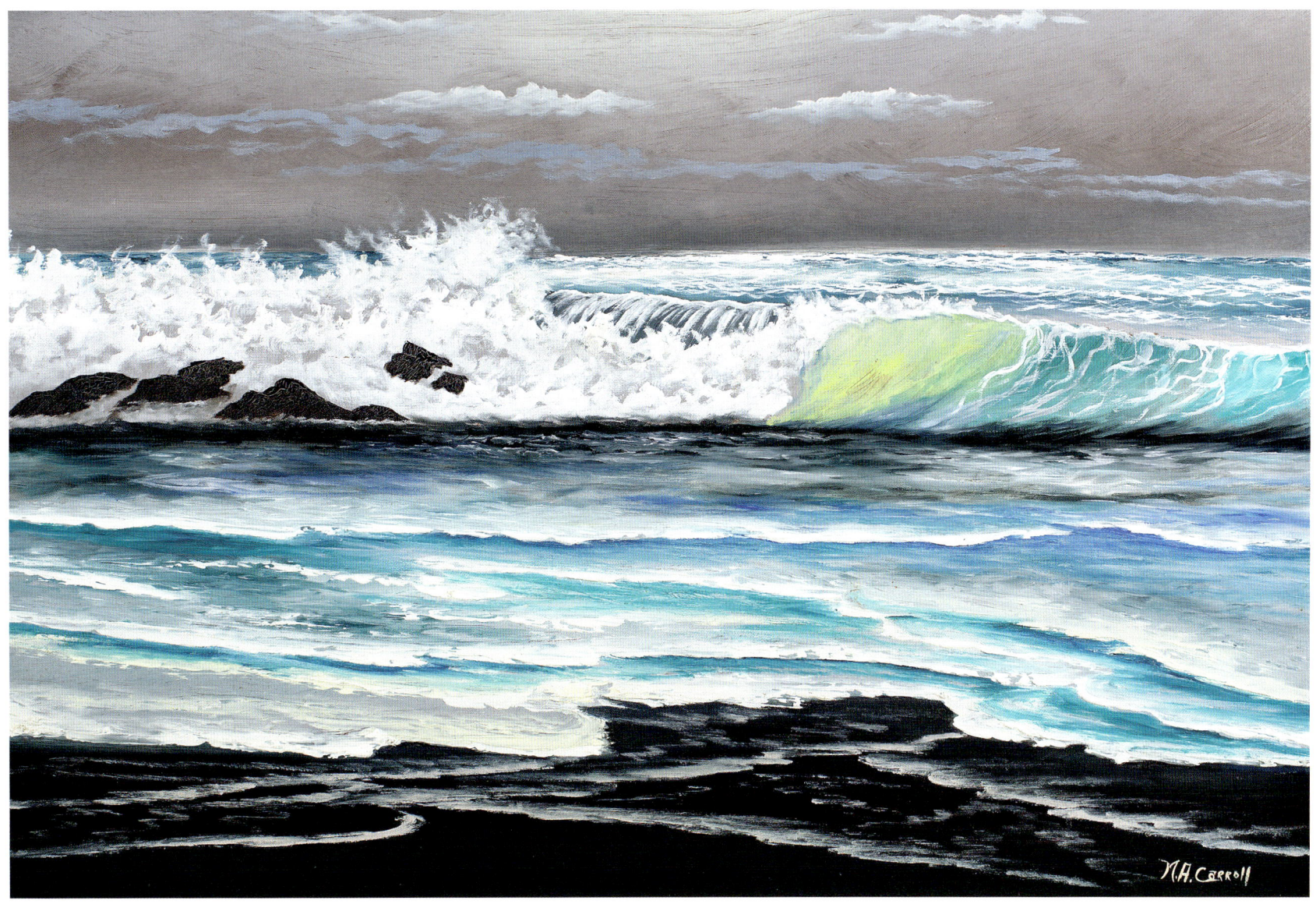

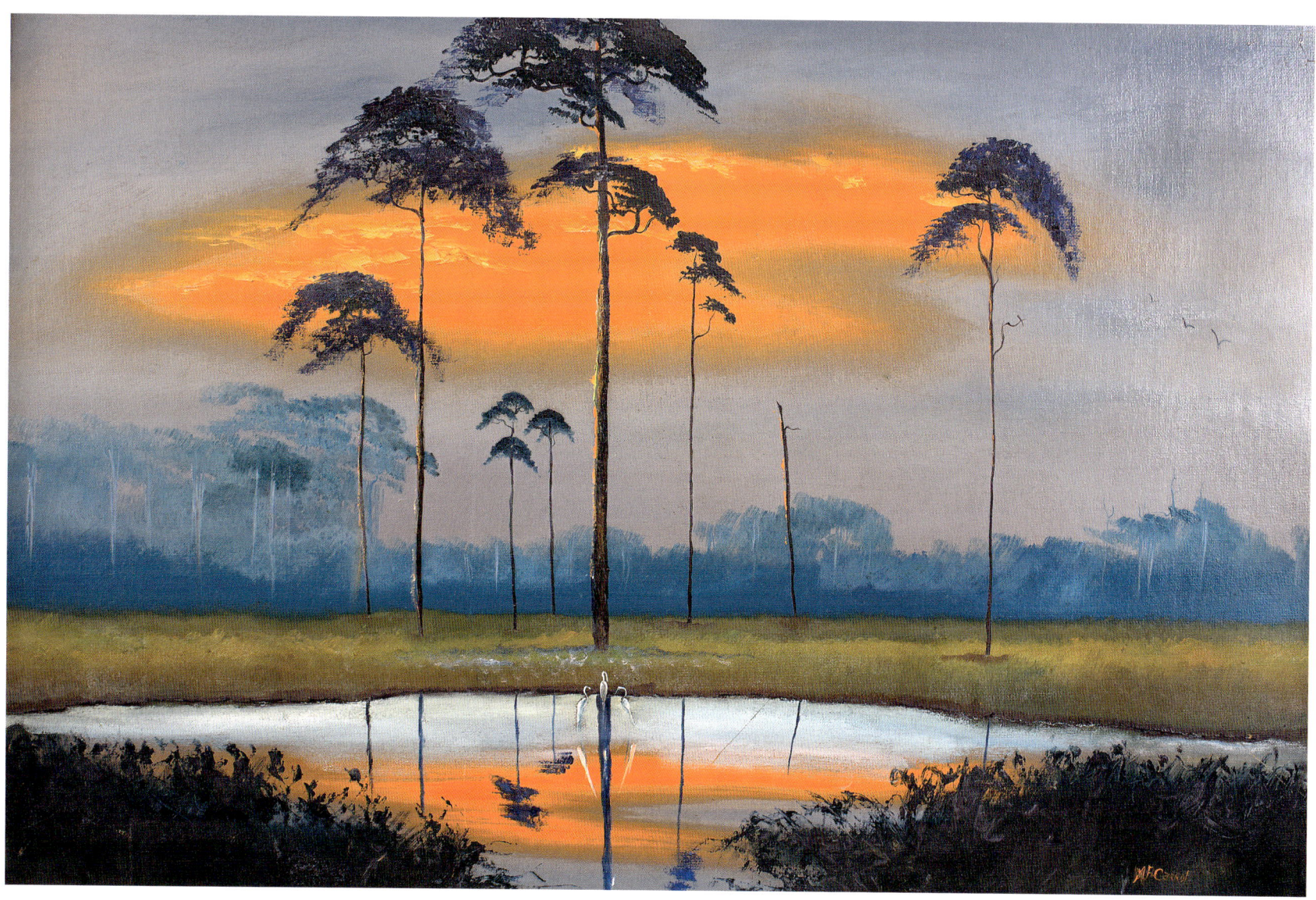

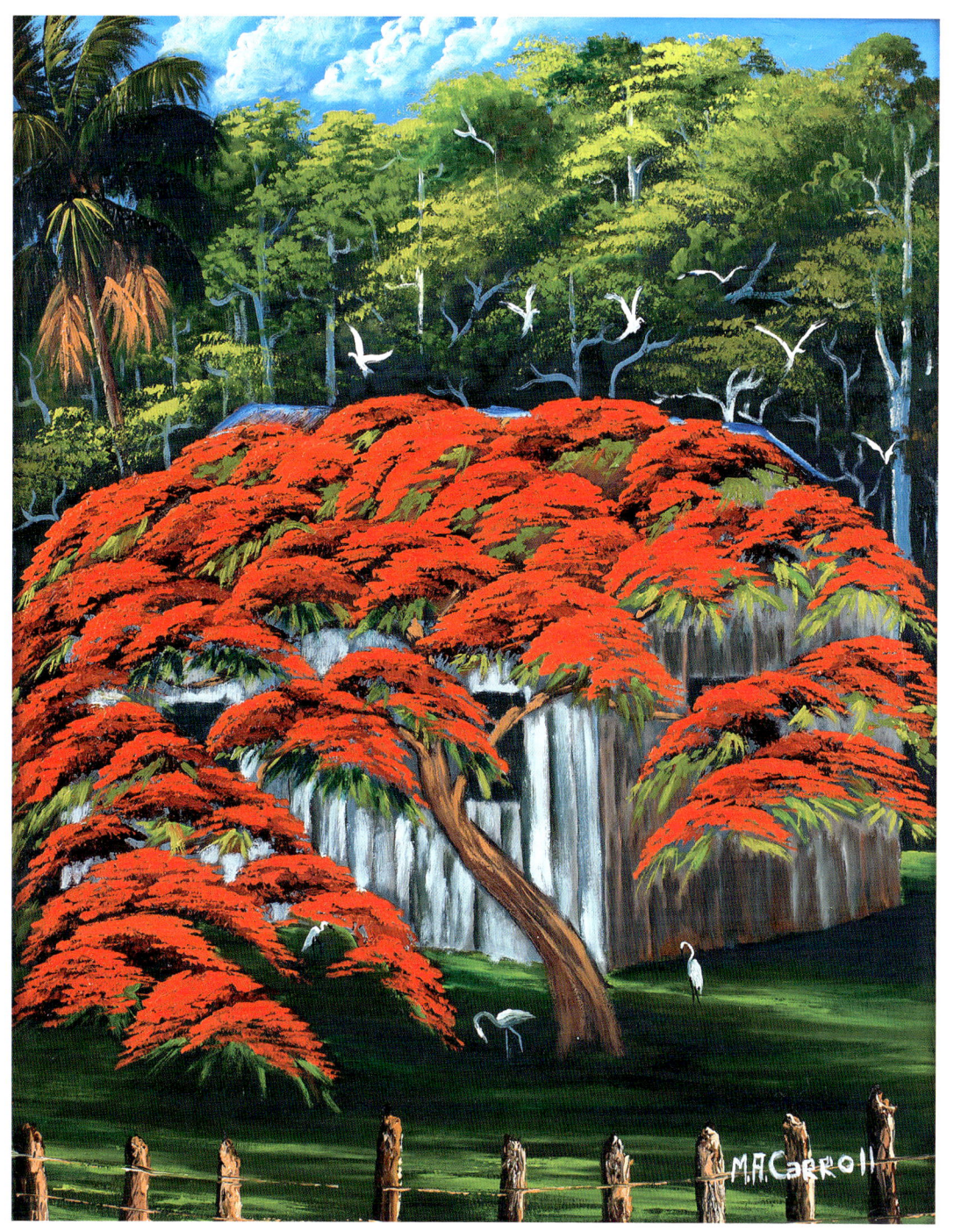

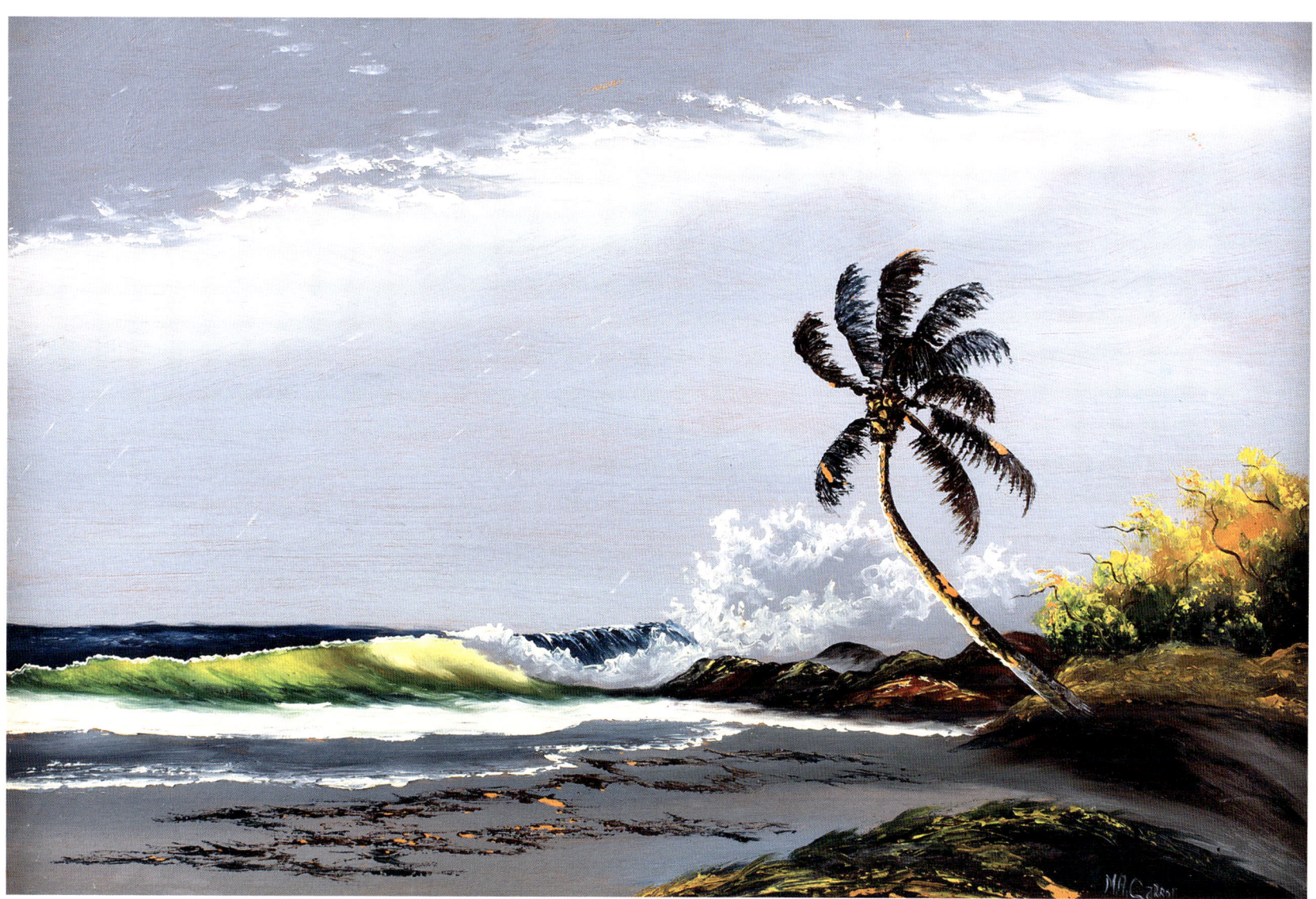

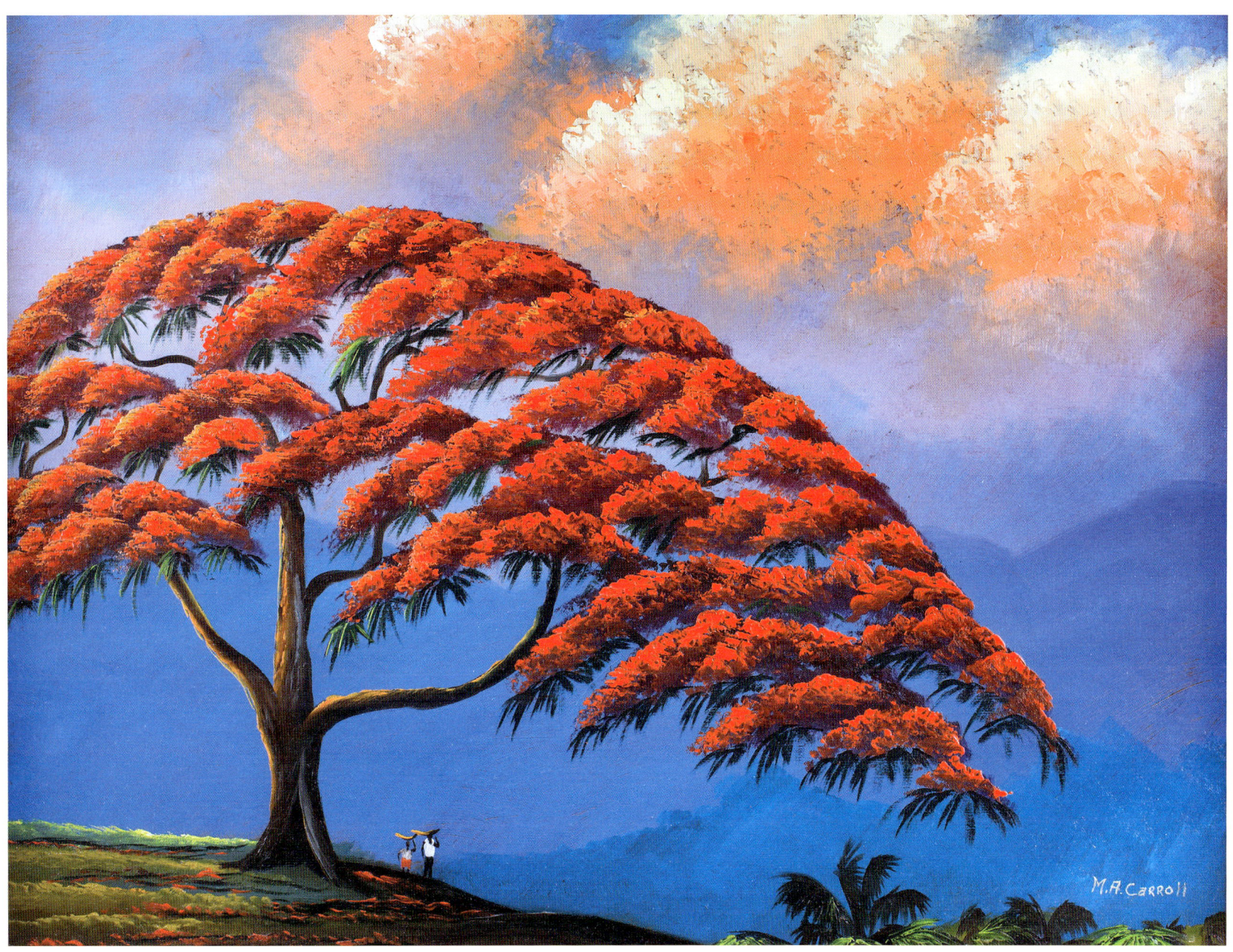

64

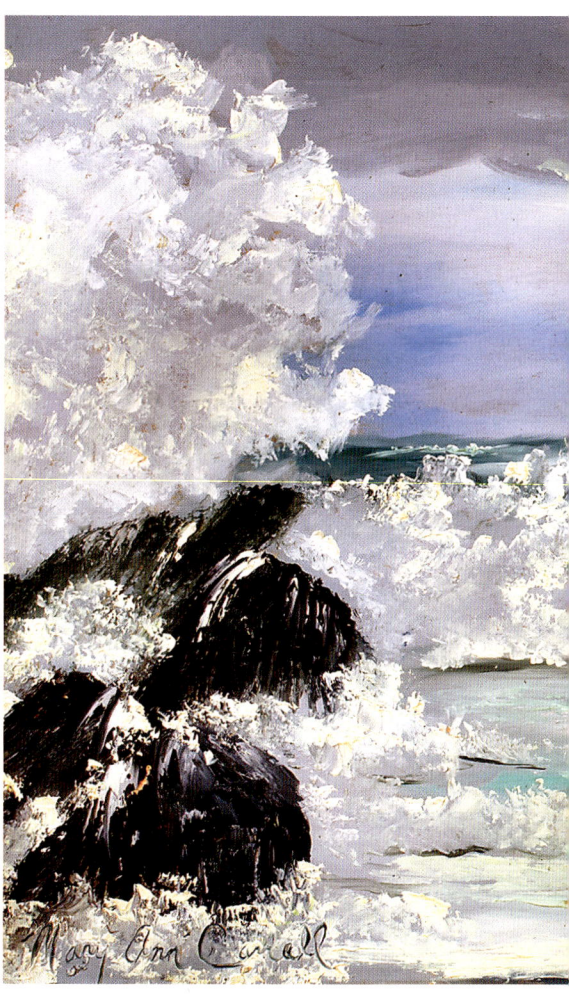

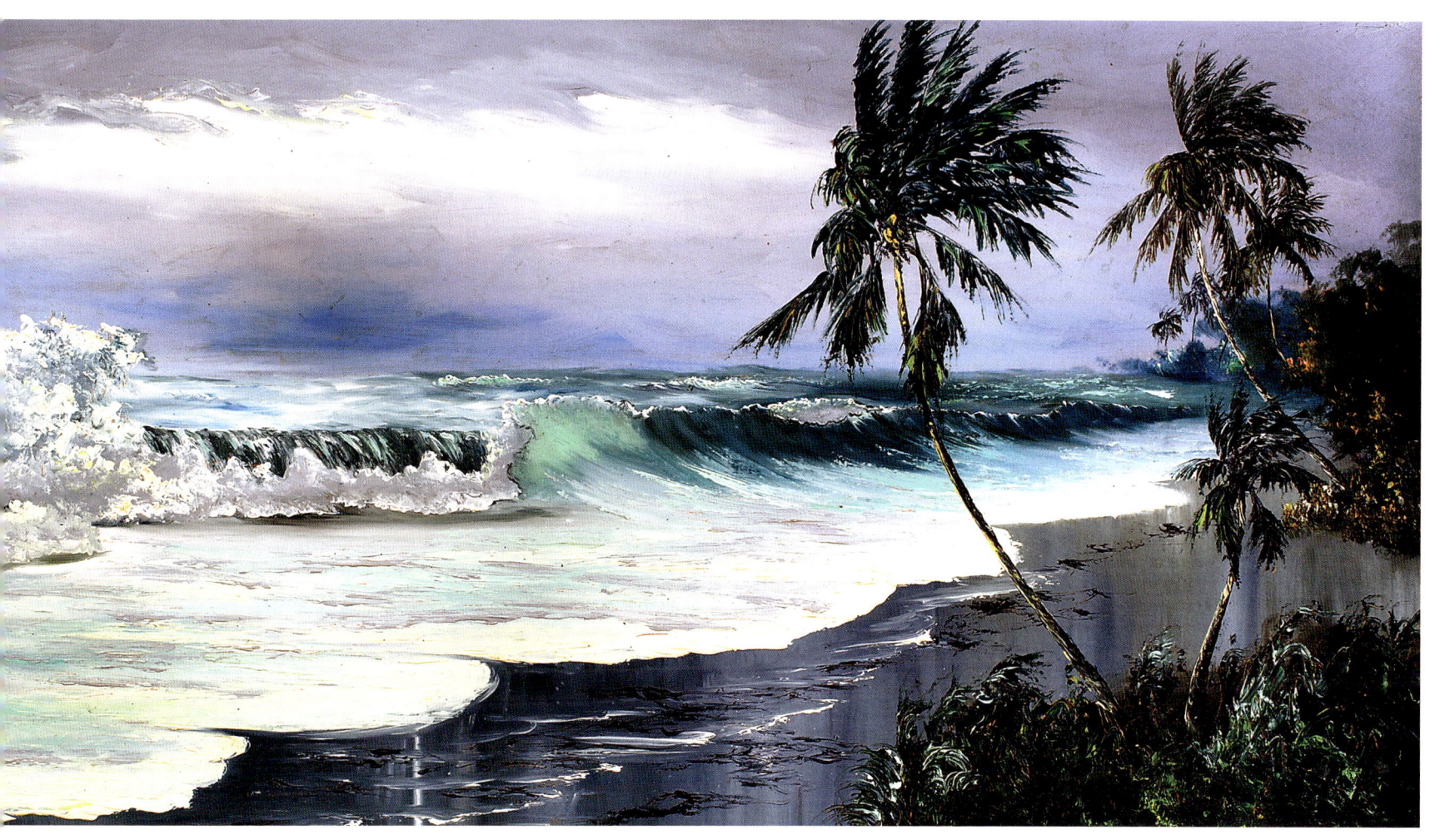

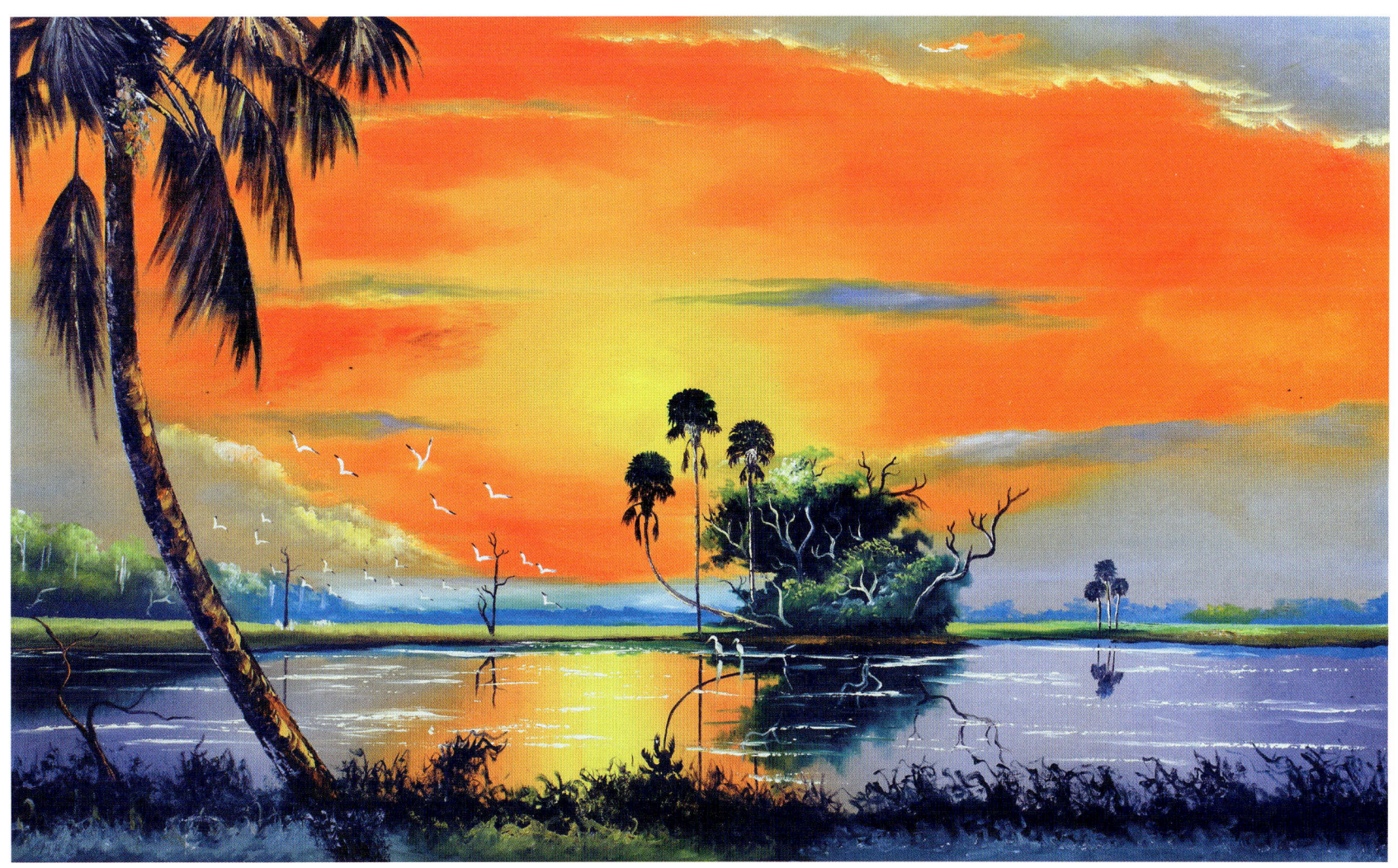

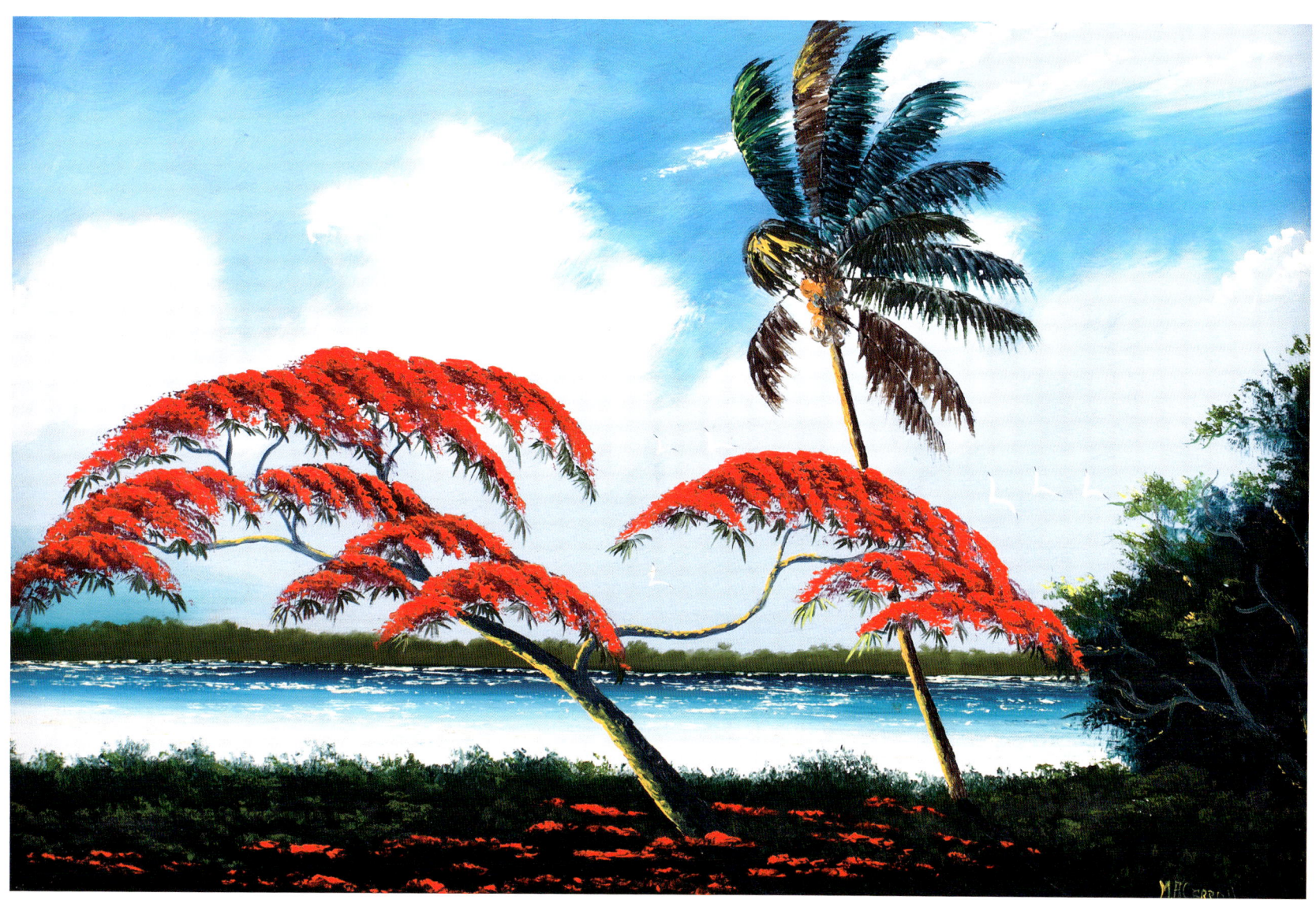

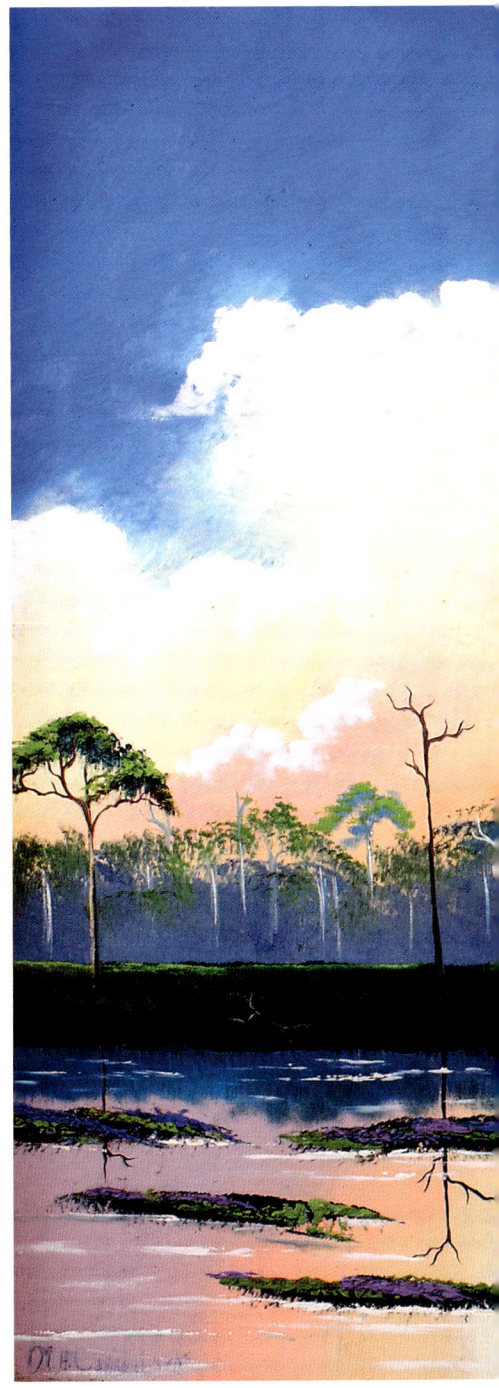

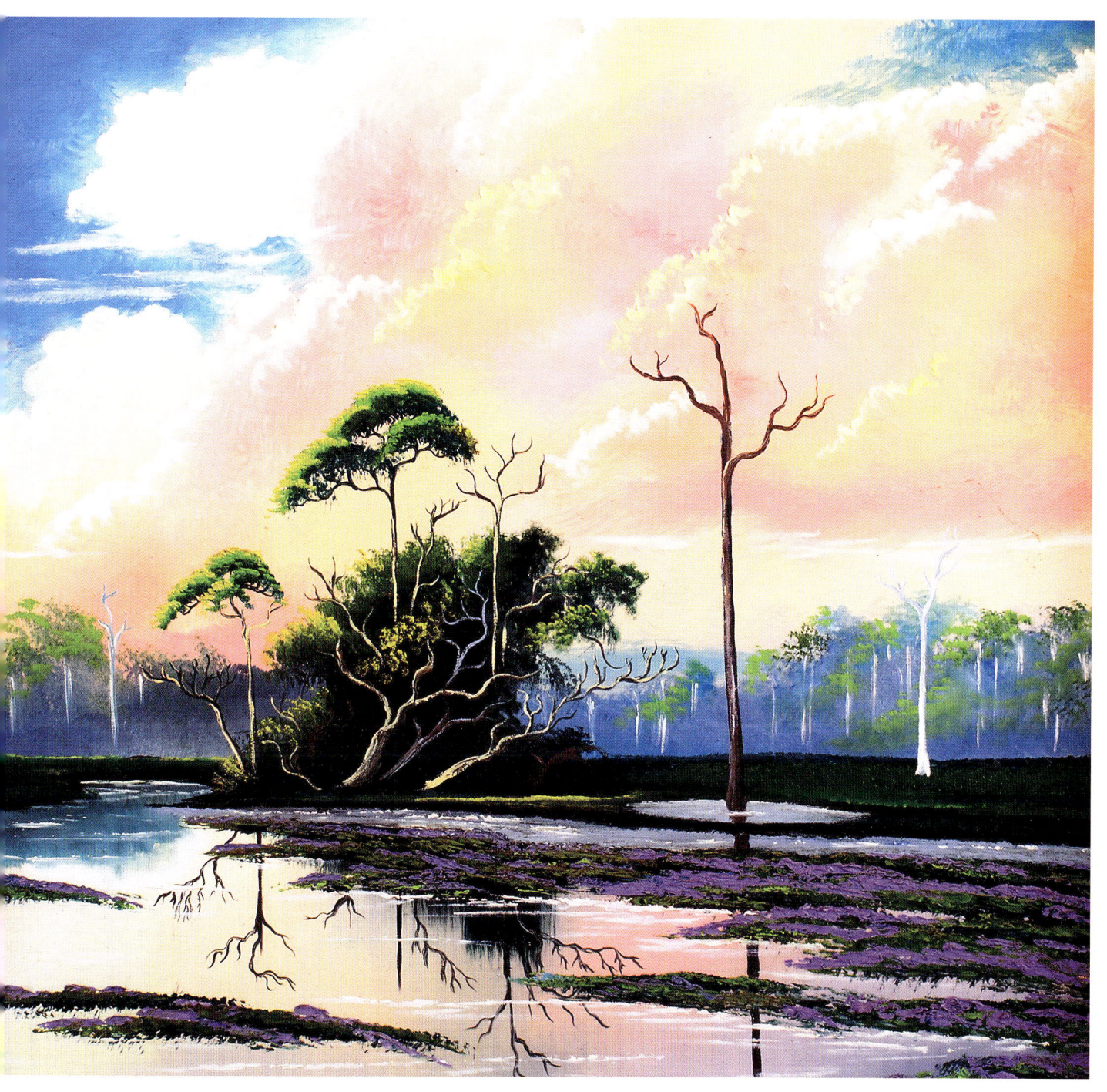

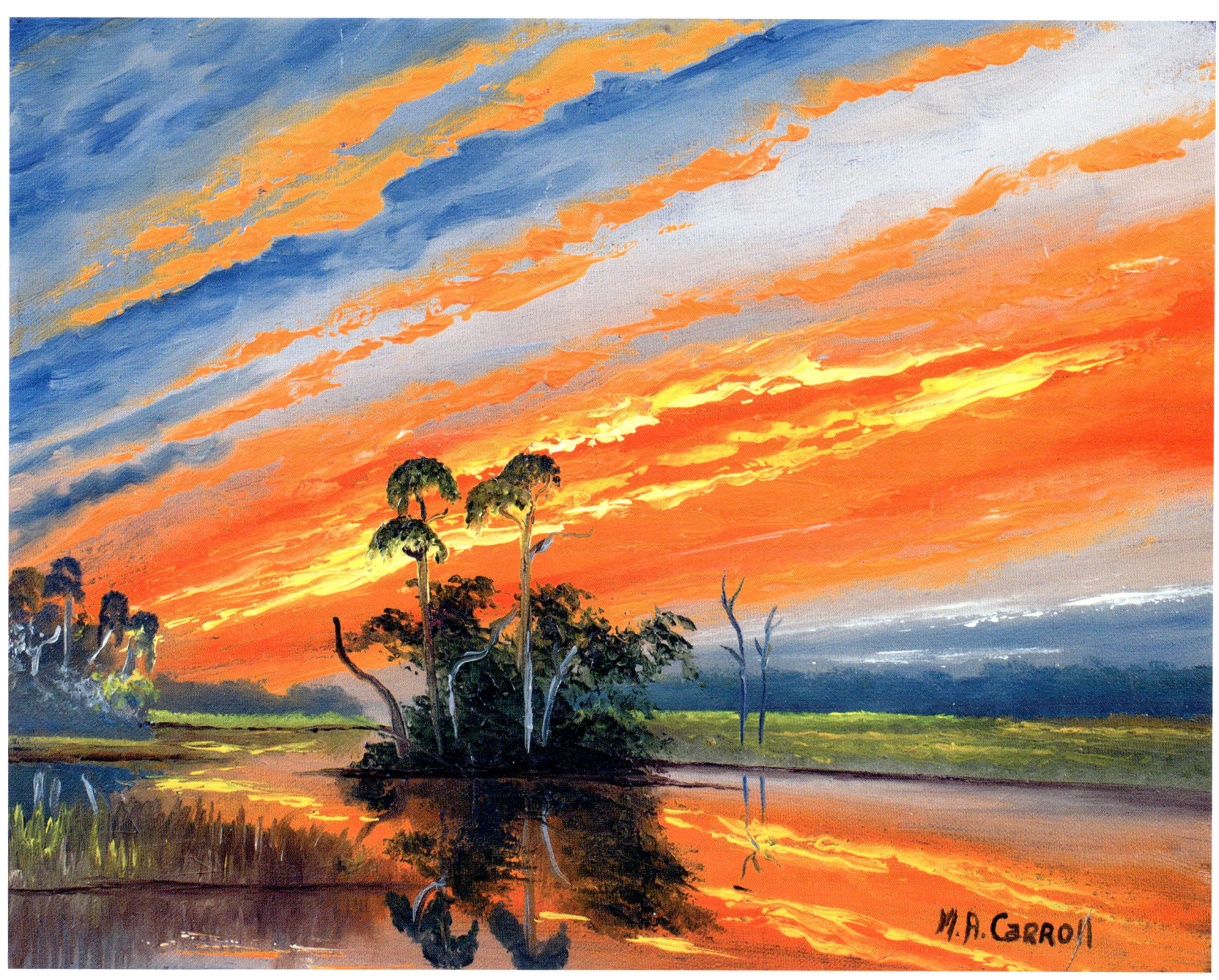

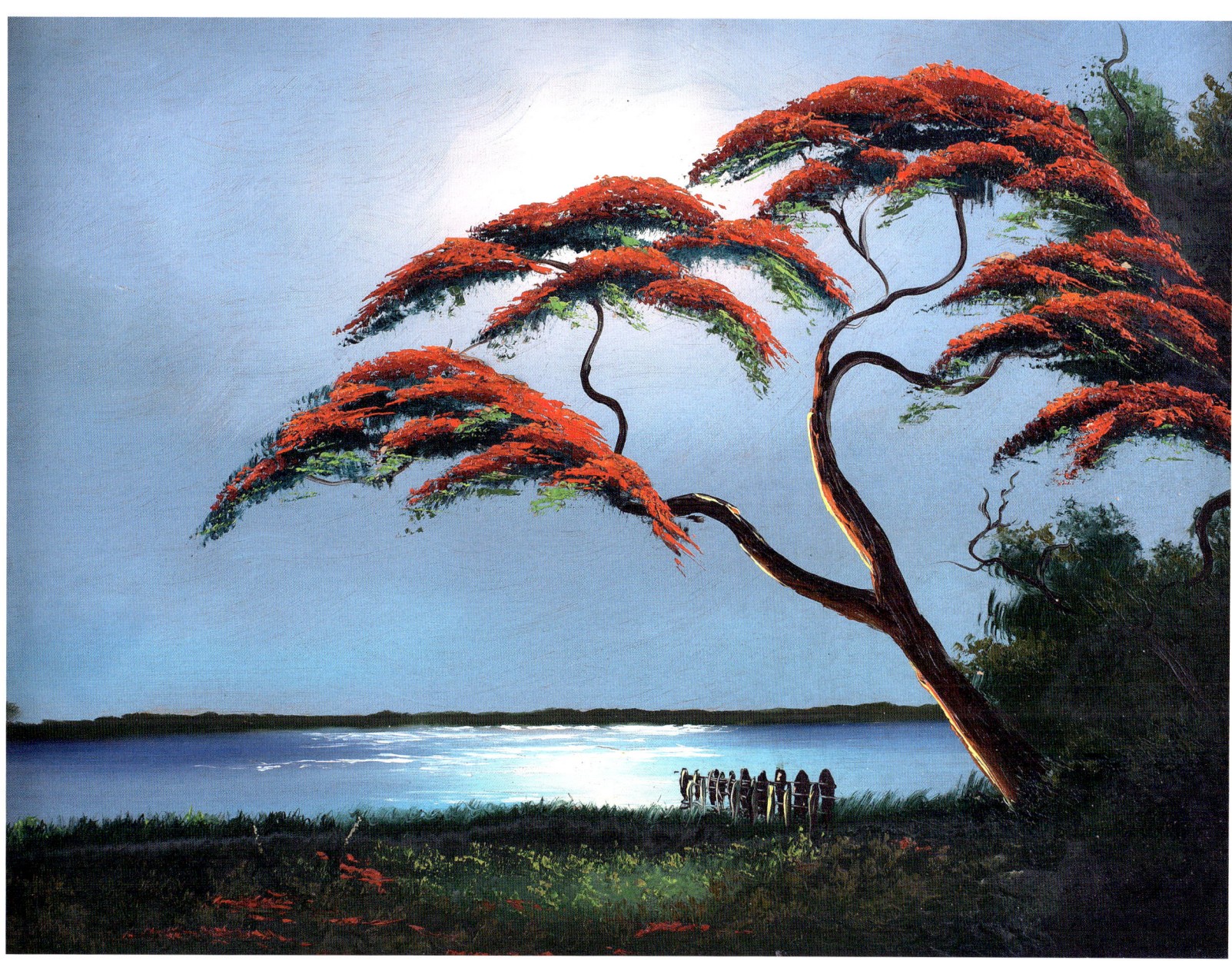

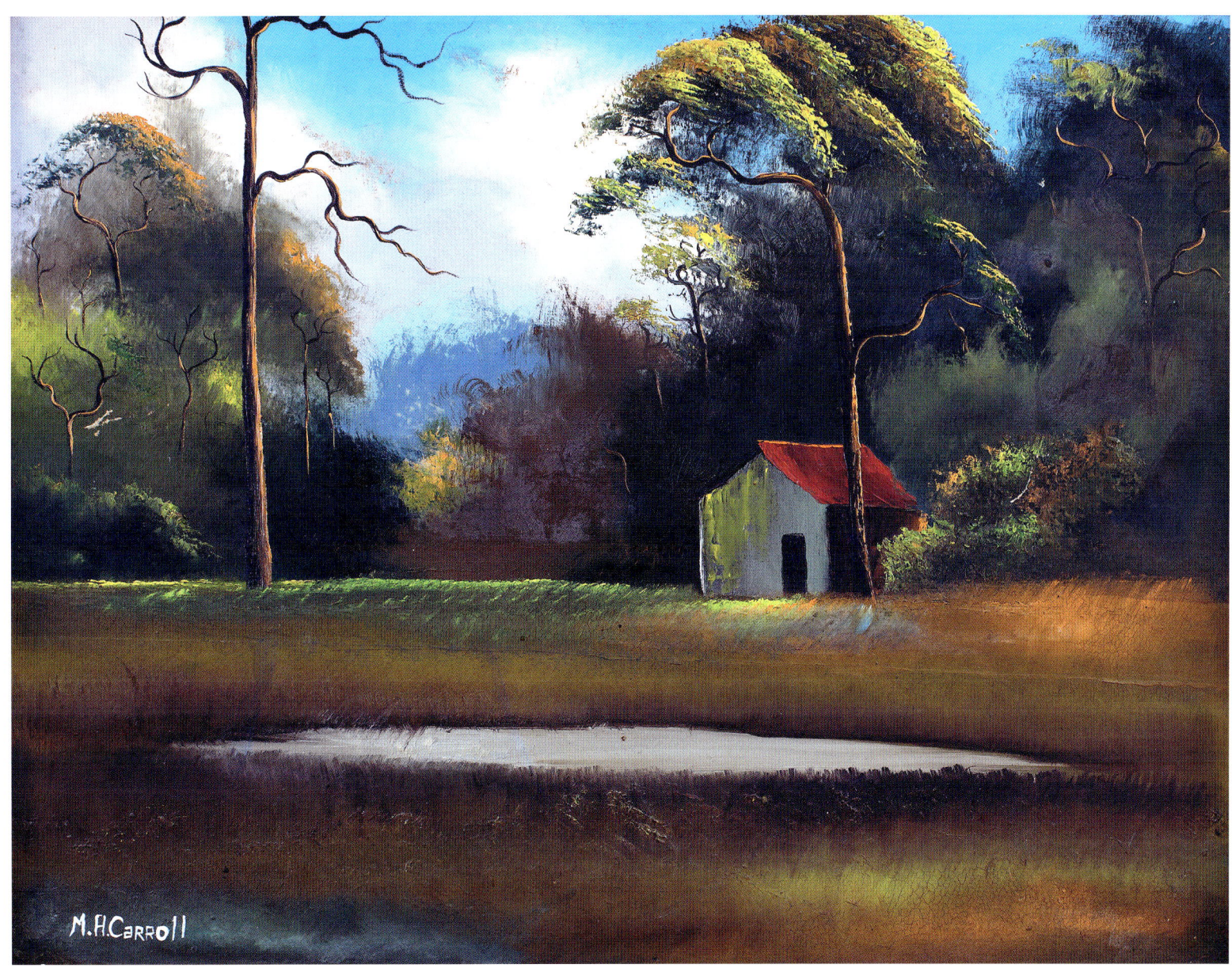
M.H.Carroll

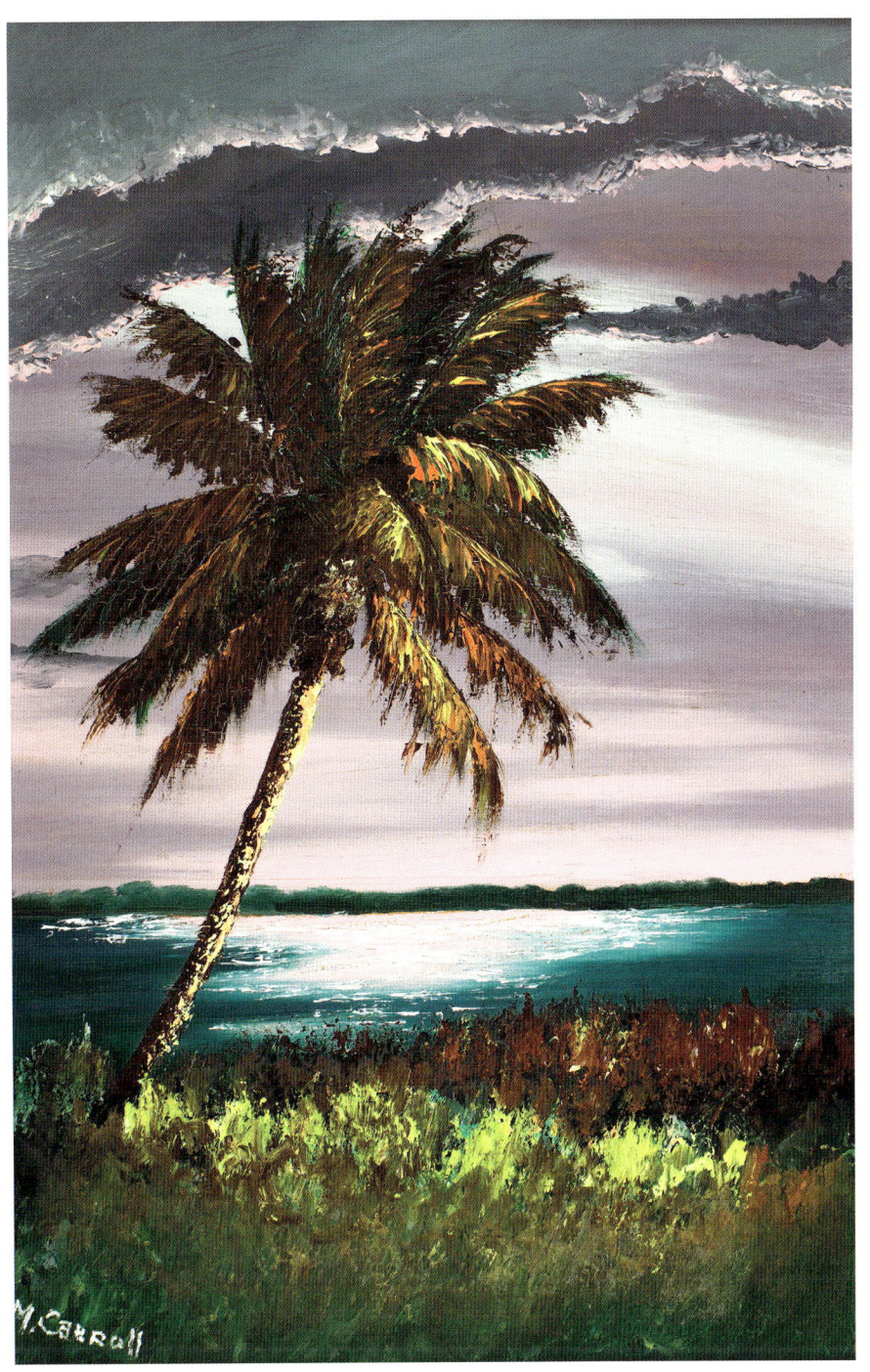

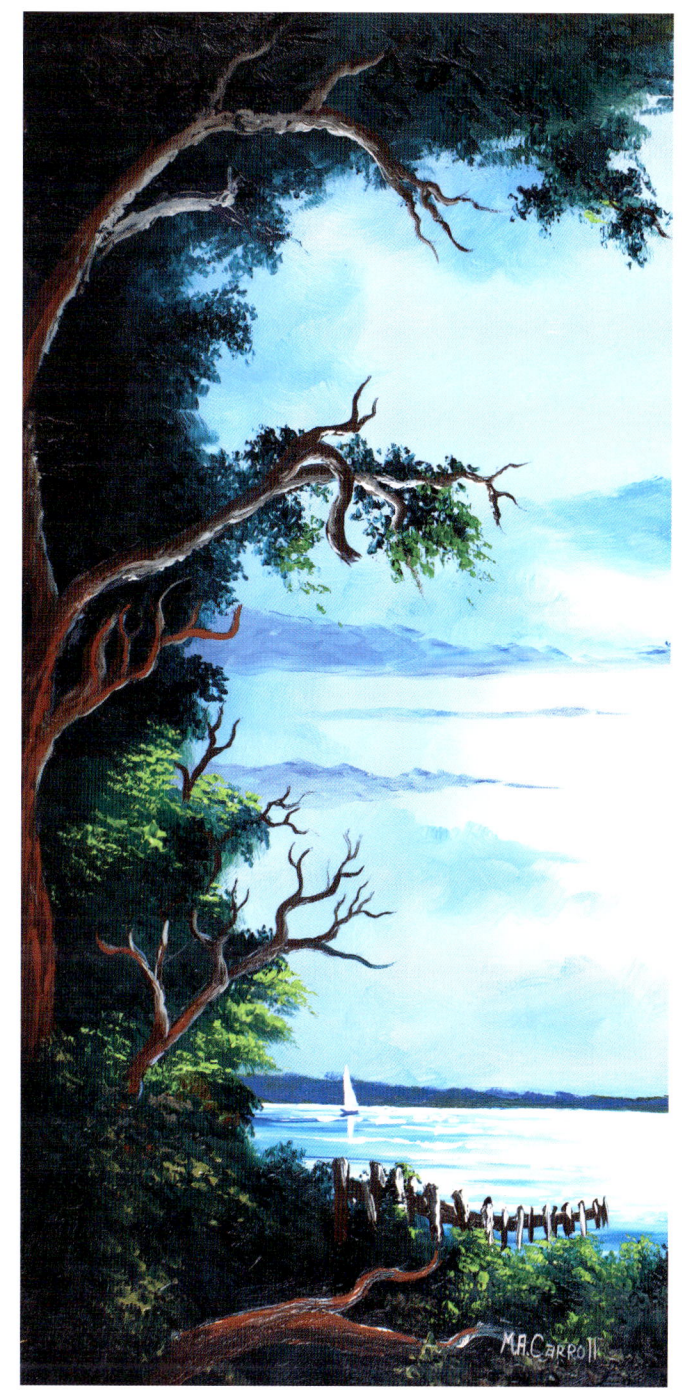

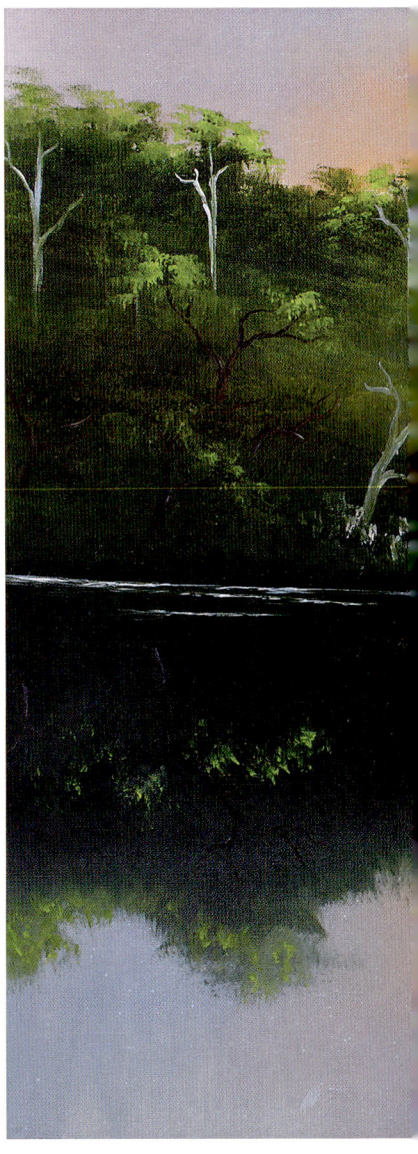

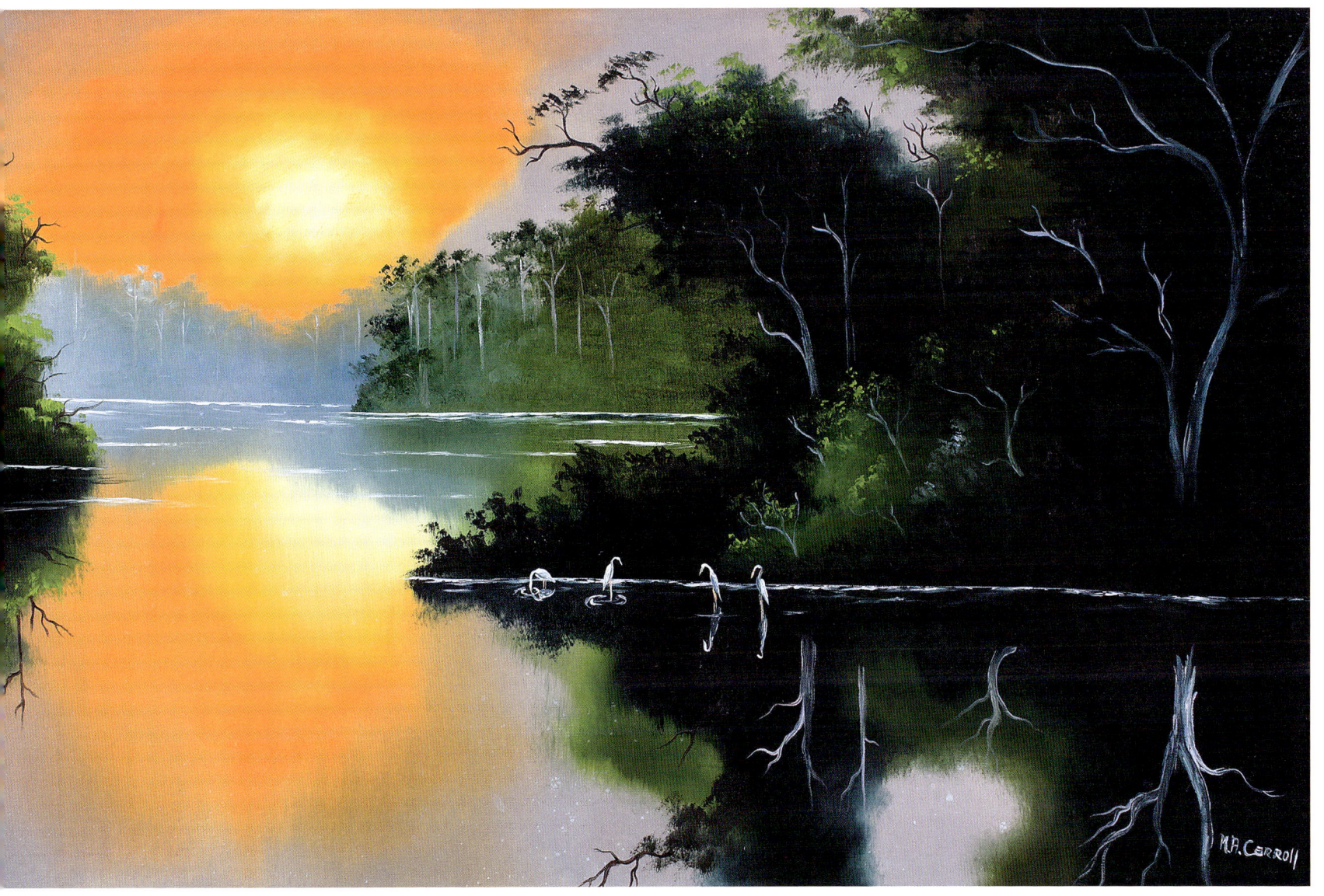

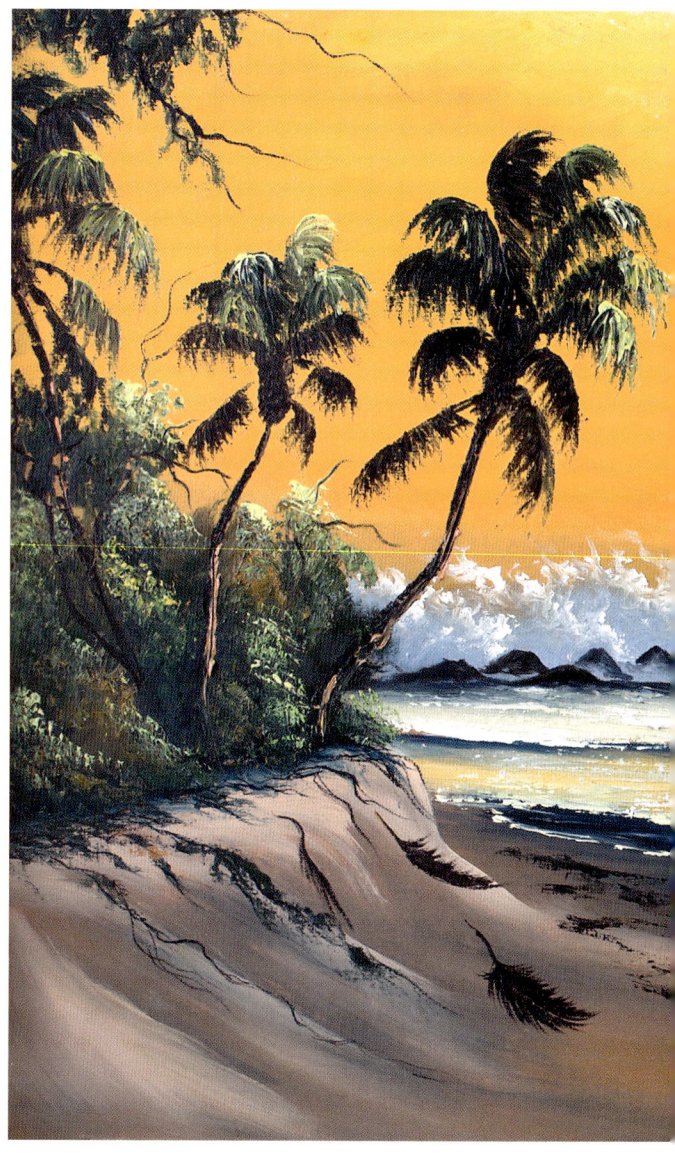

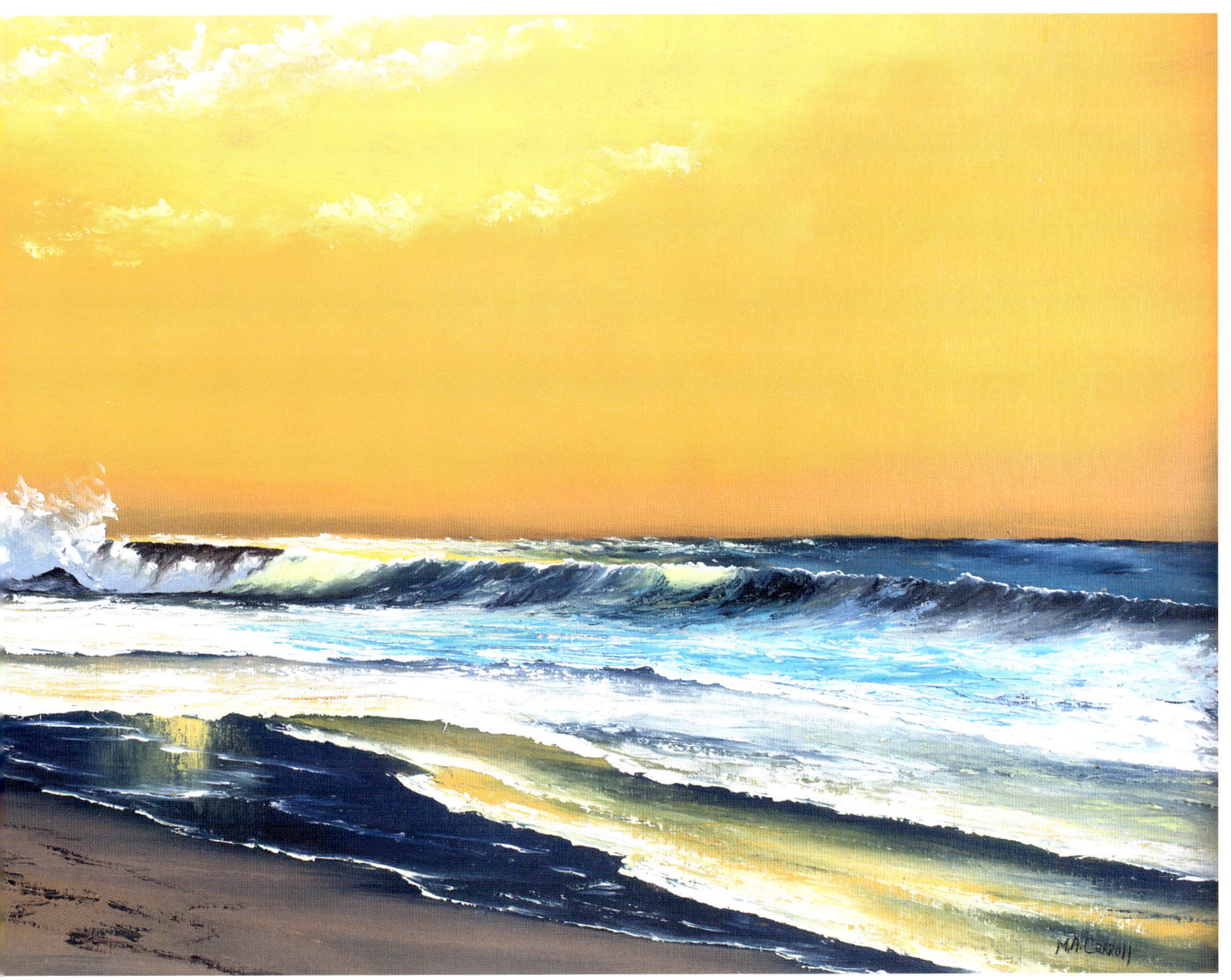

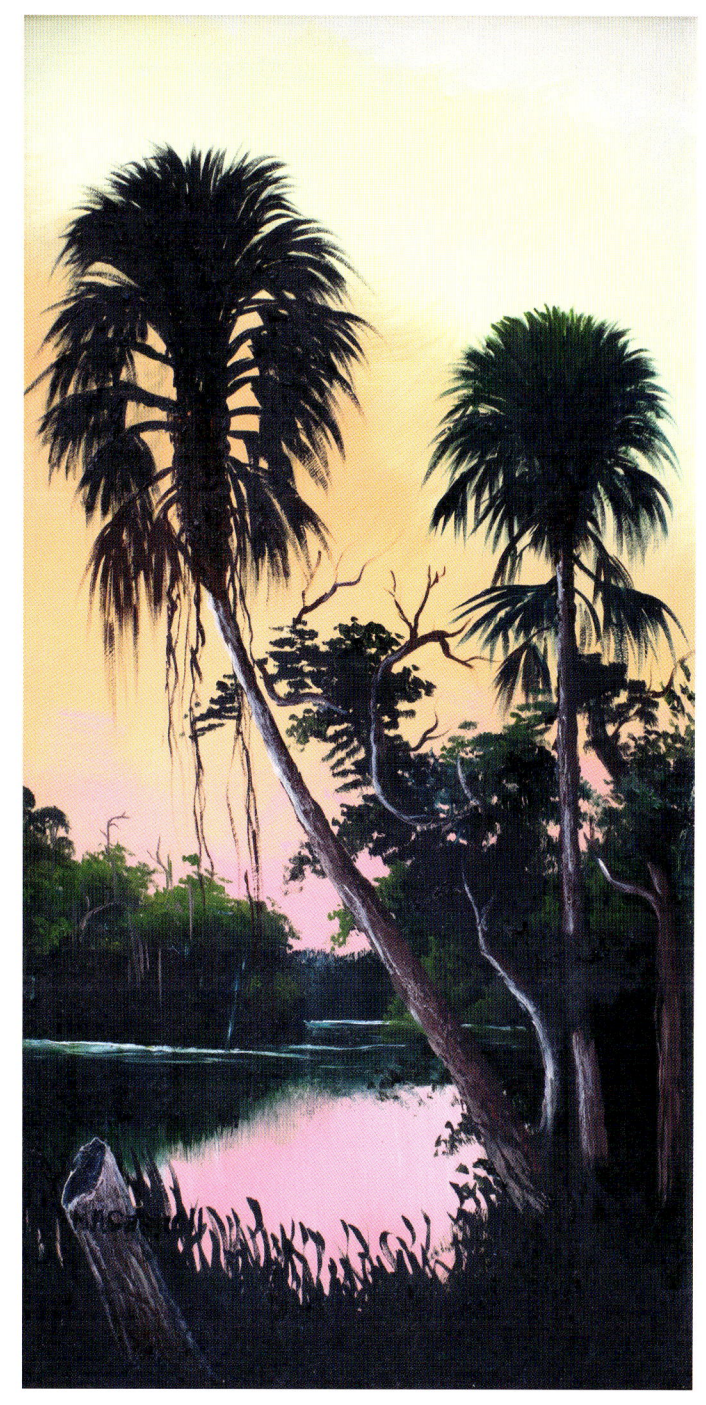

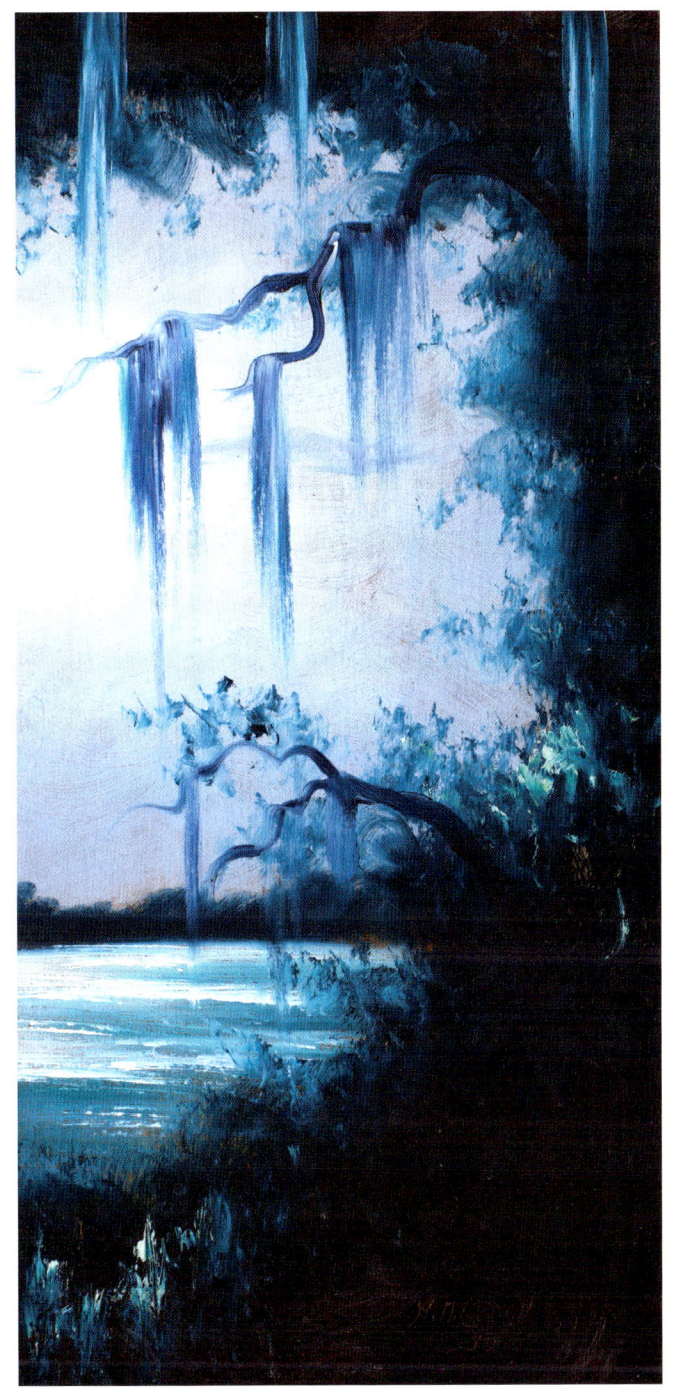
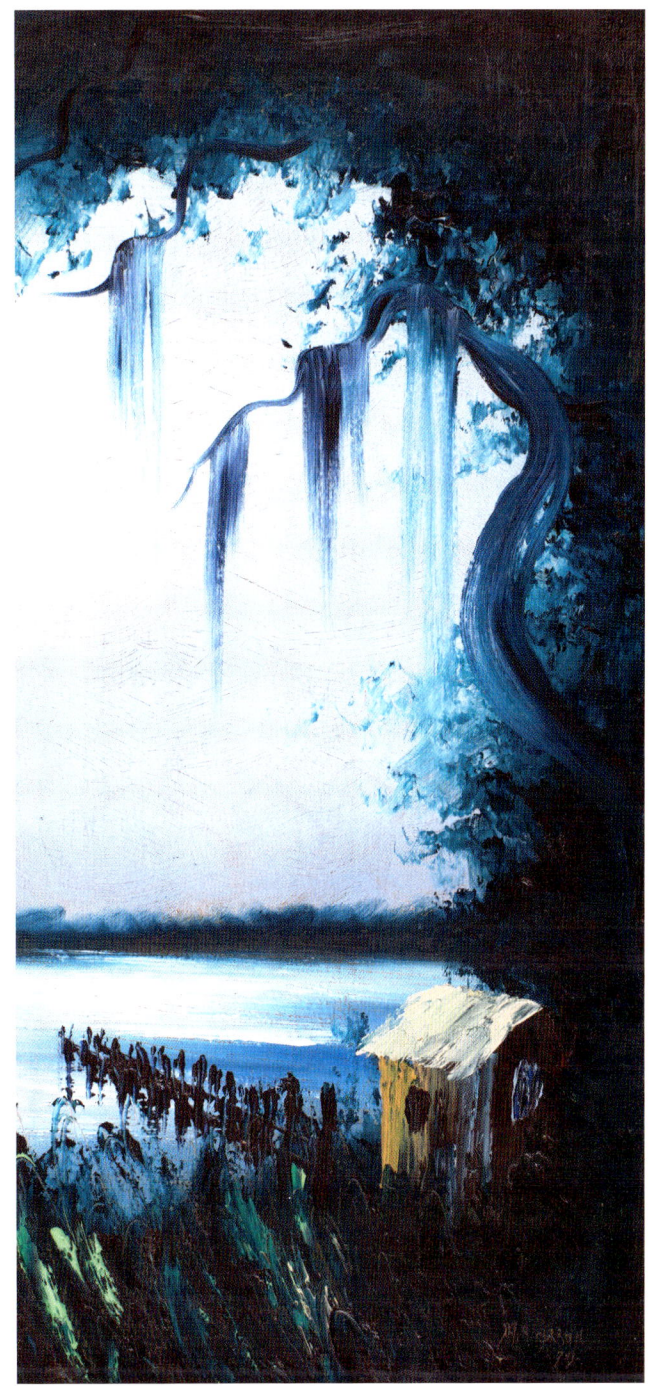

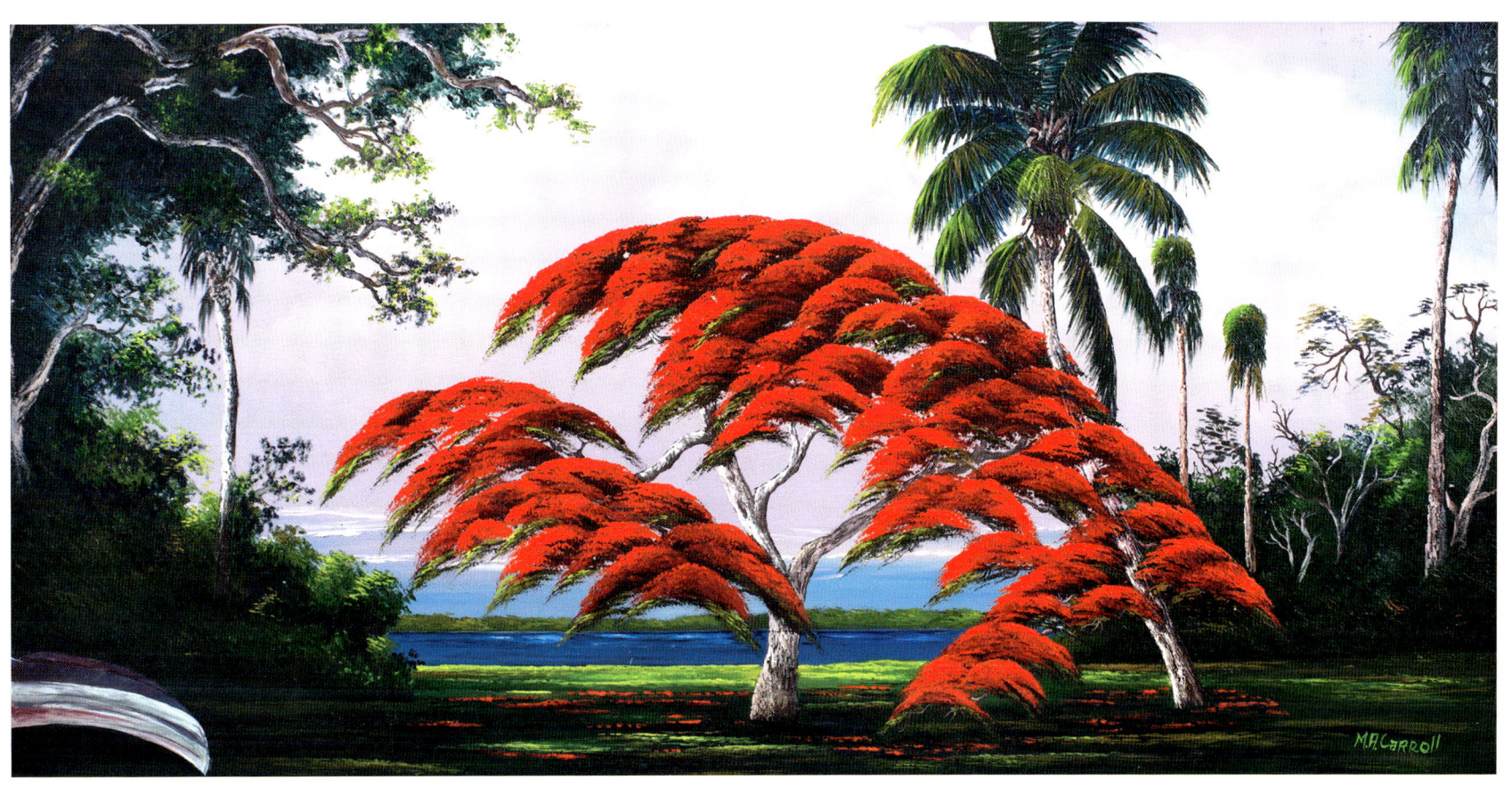

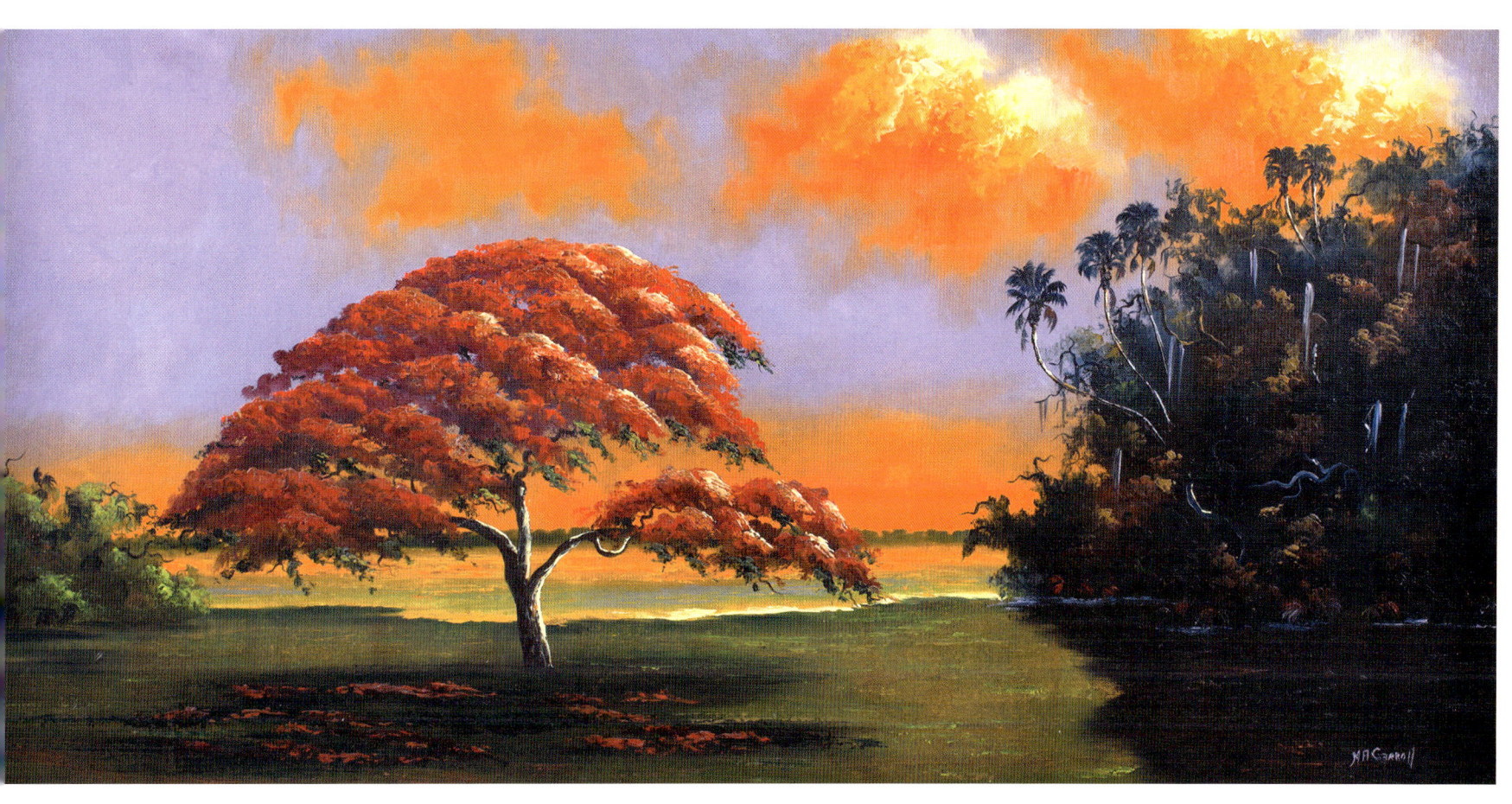

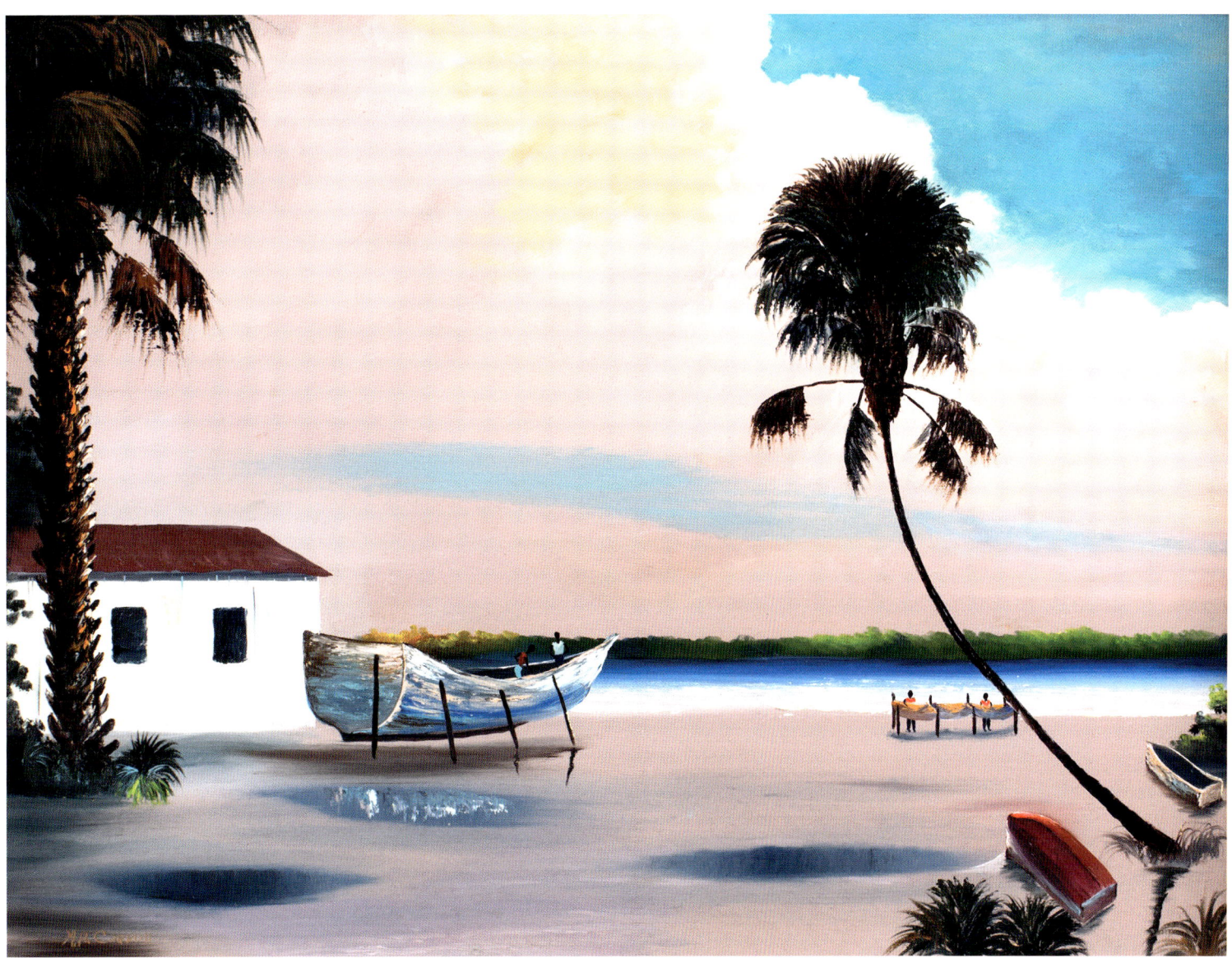

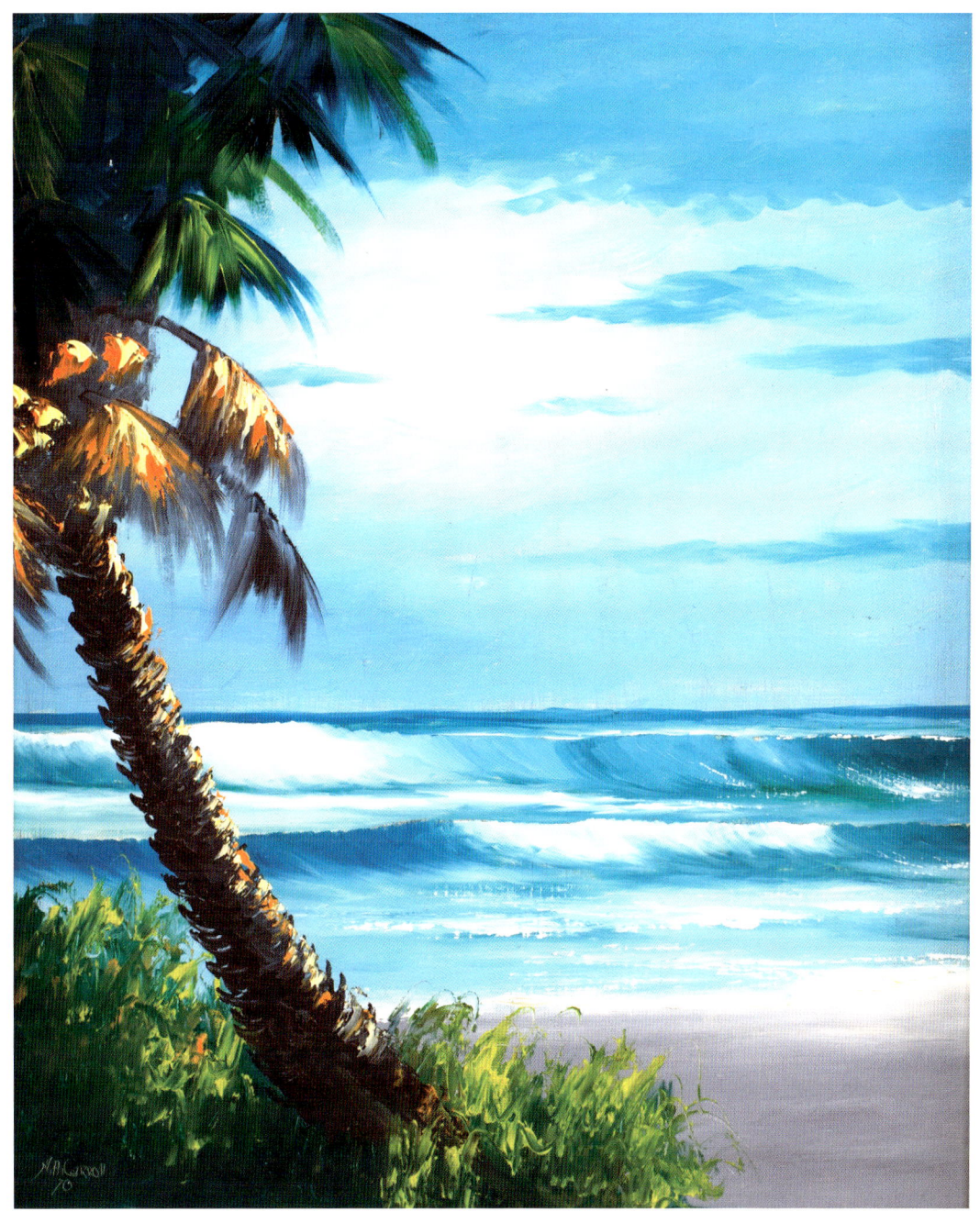

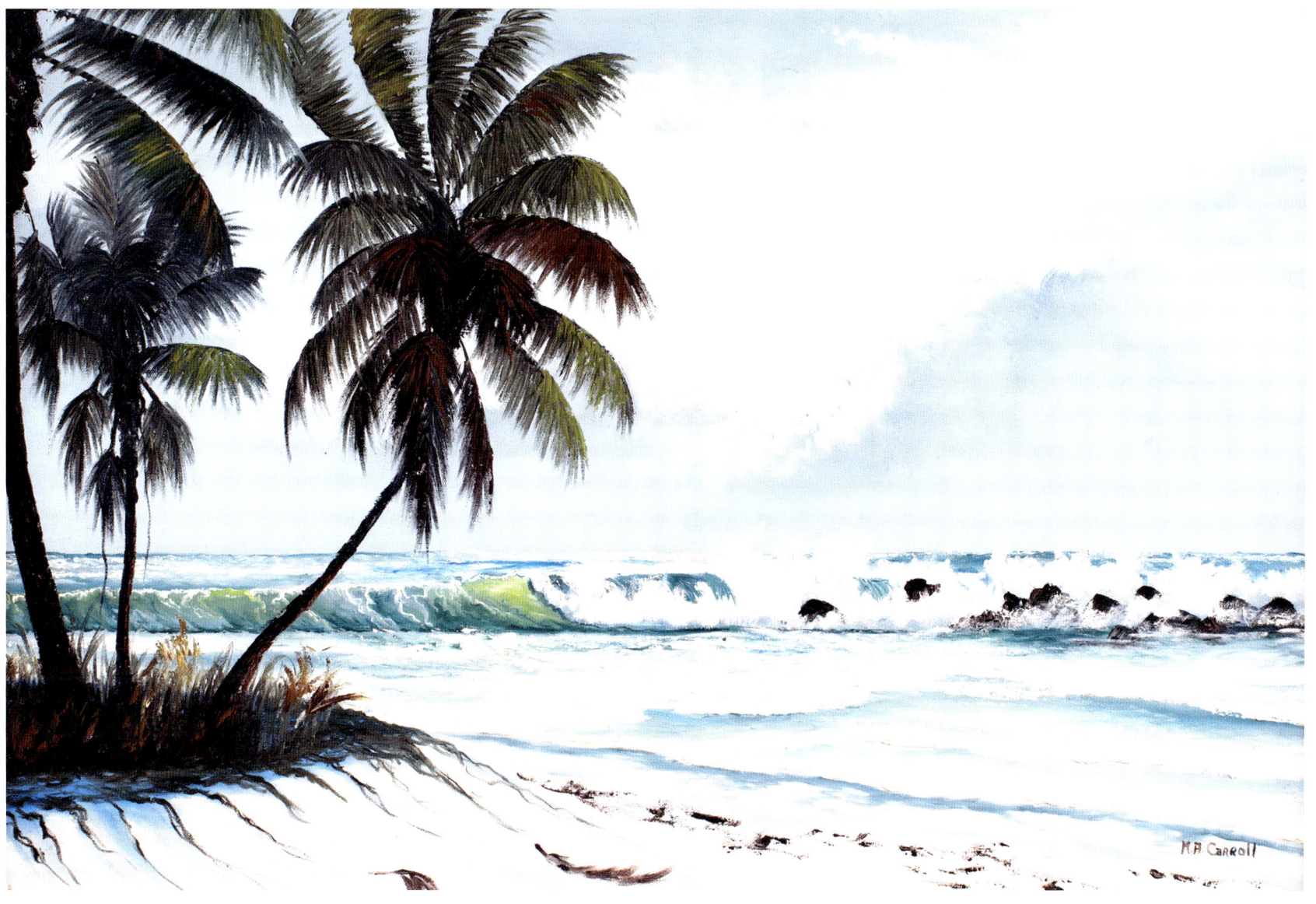

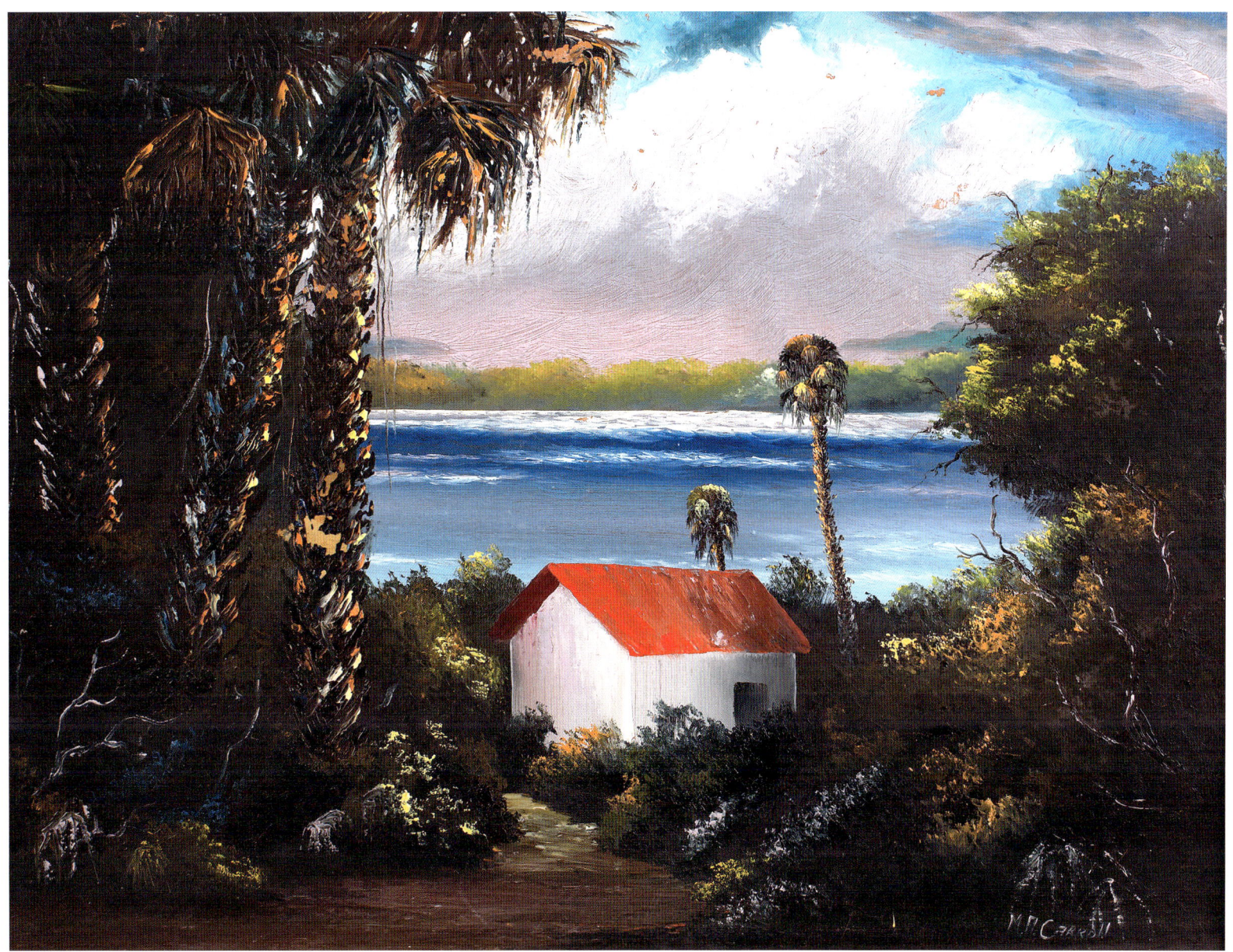

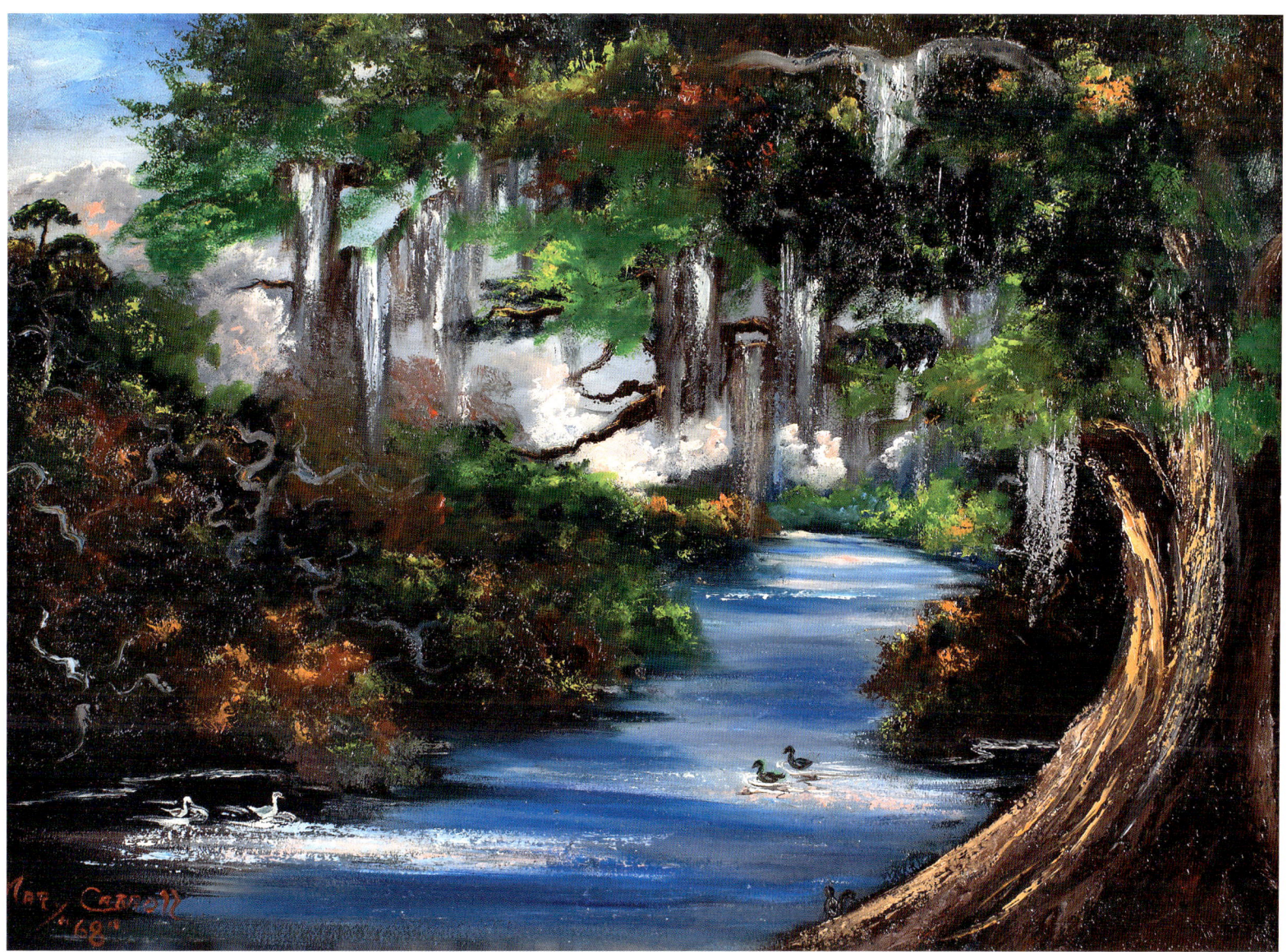

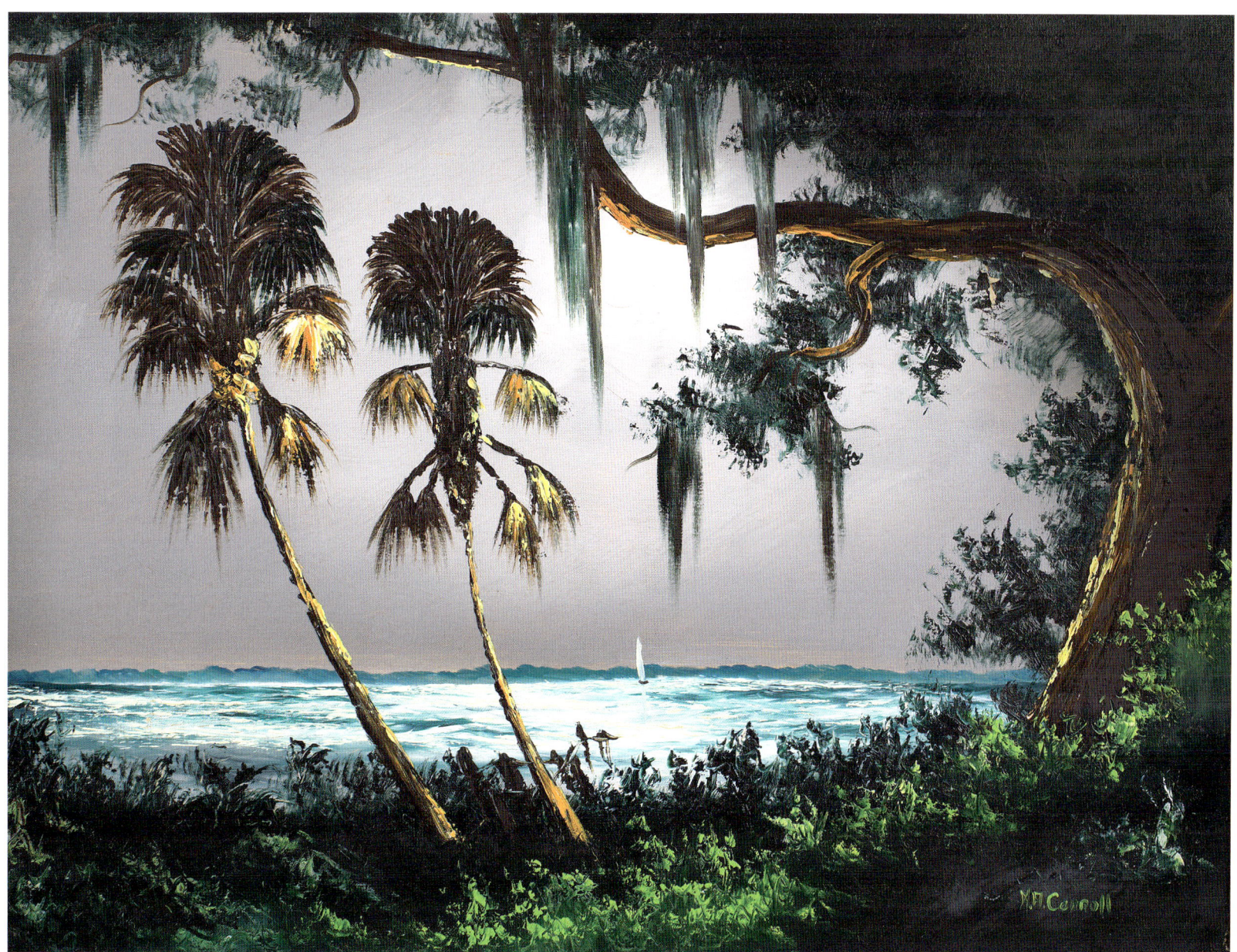

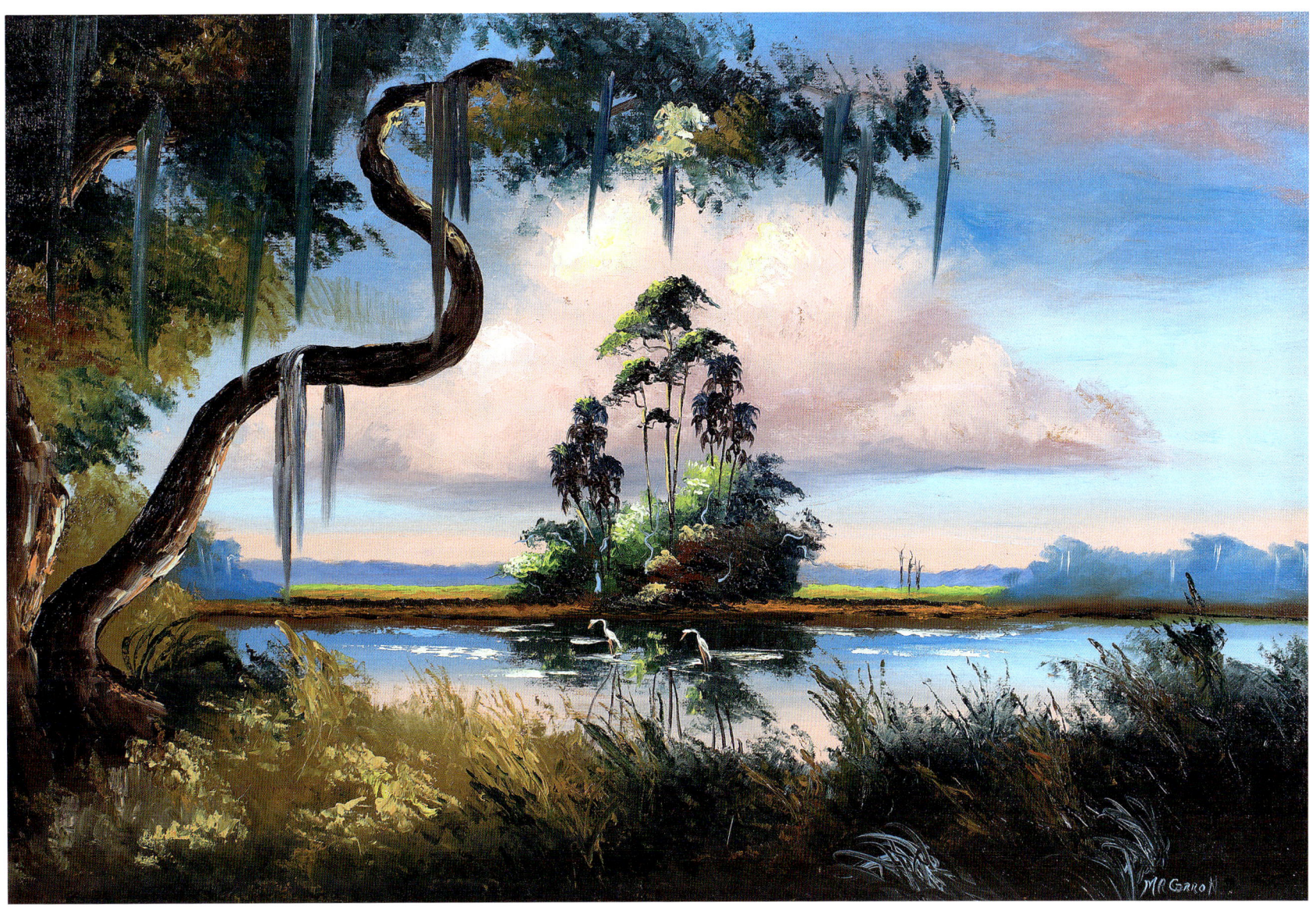

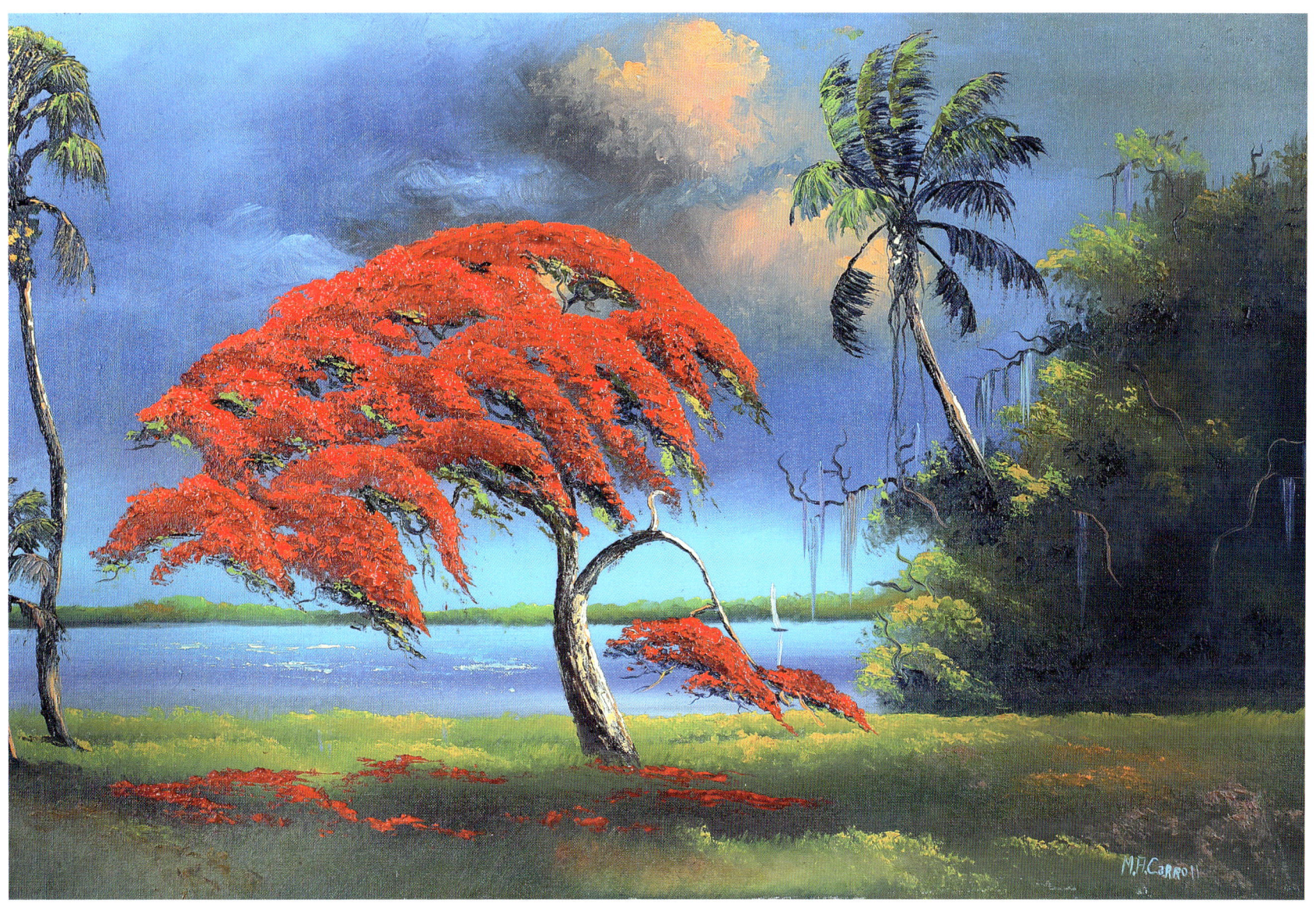

M.A.Carroll

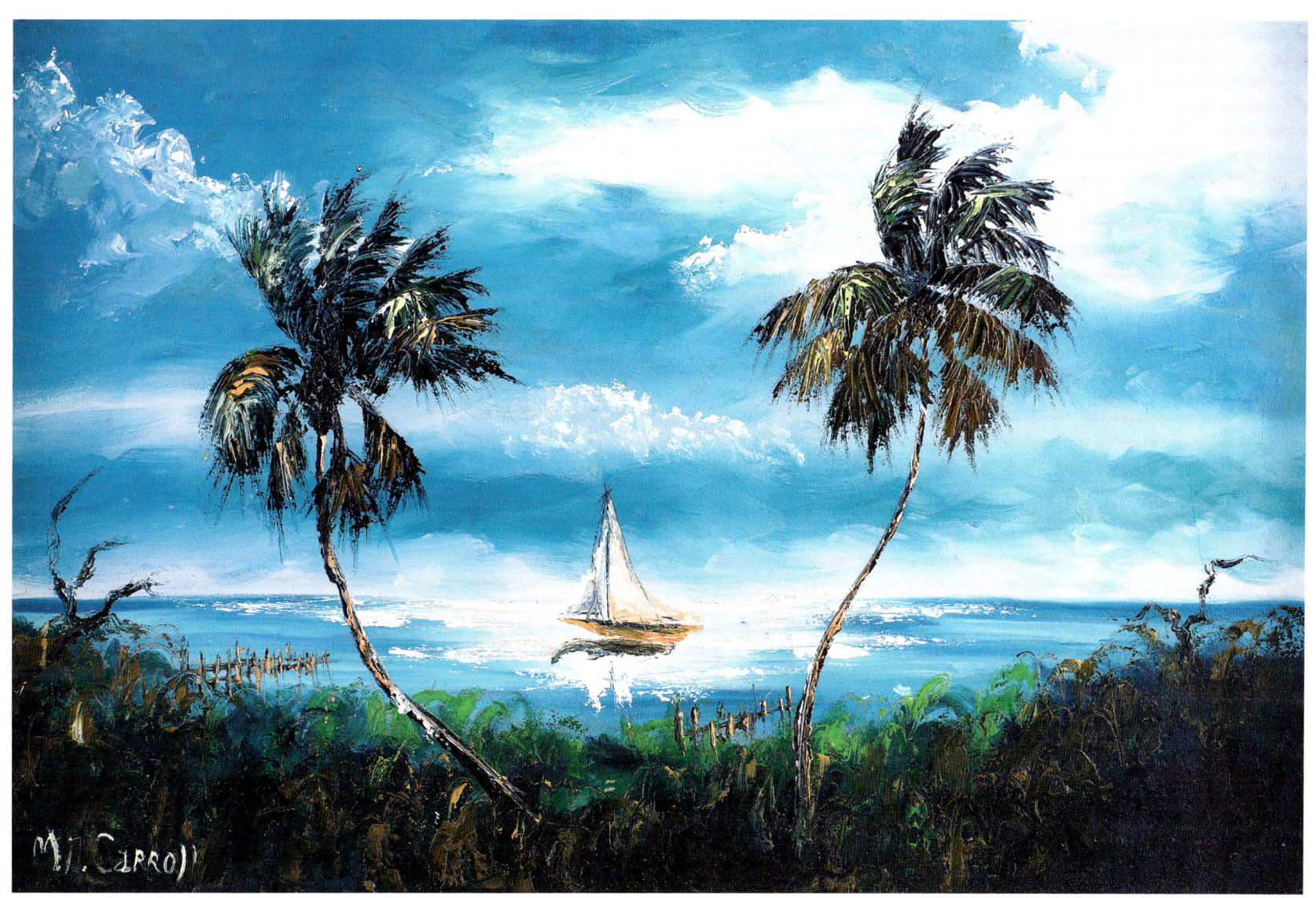

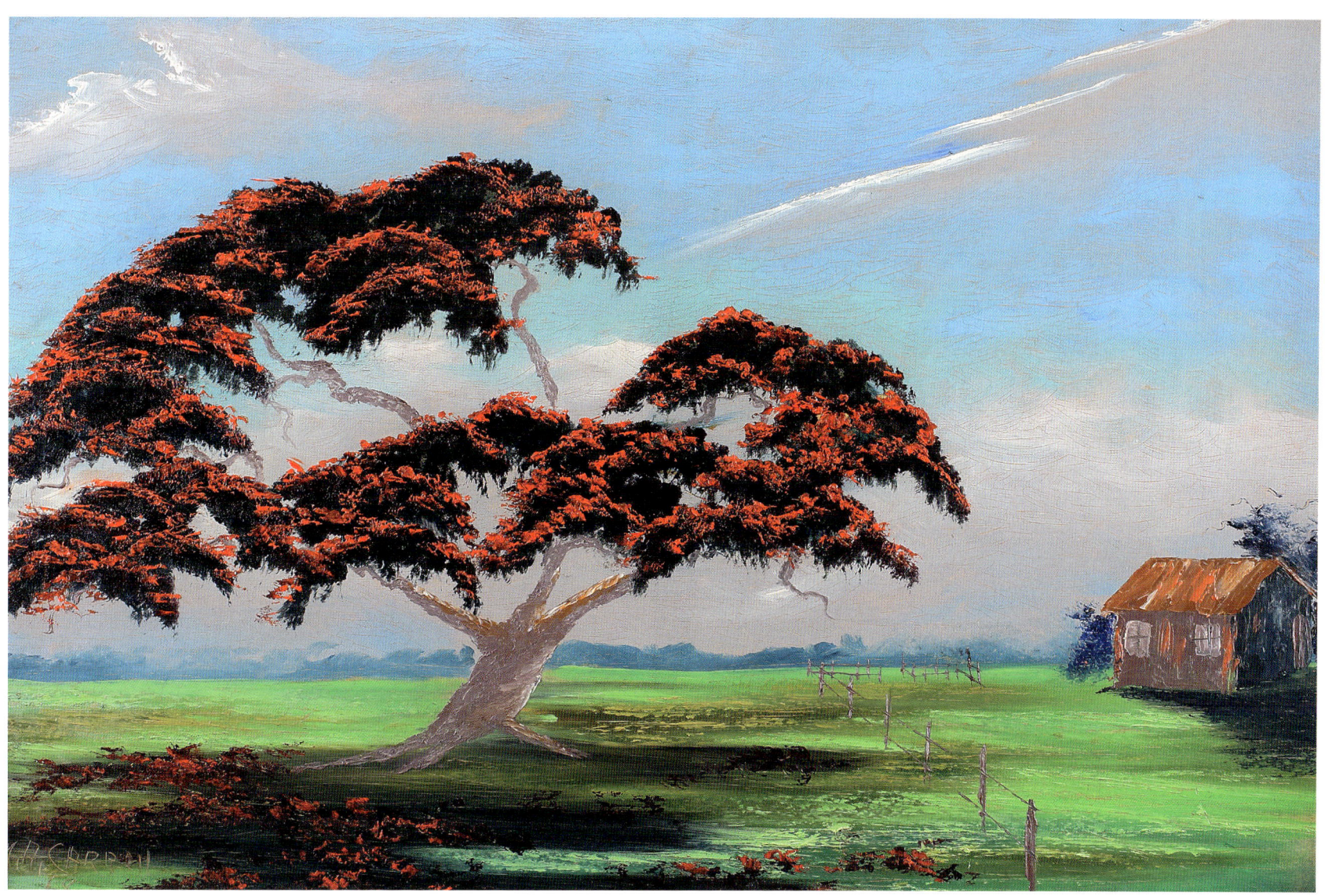

114

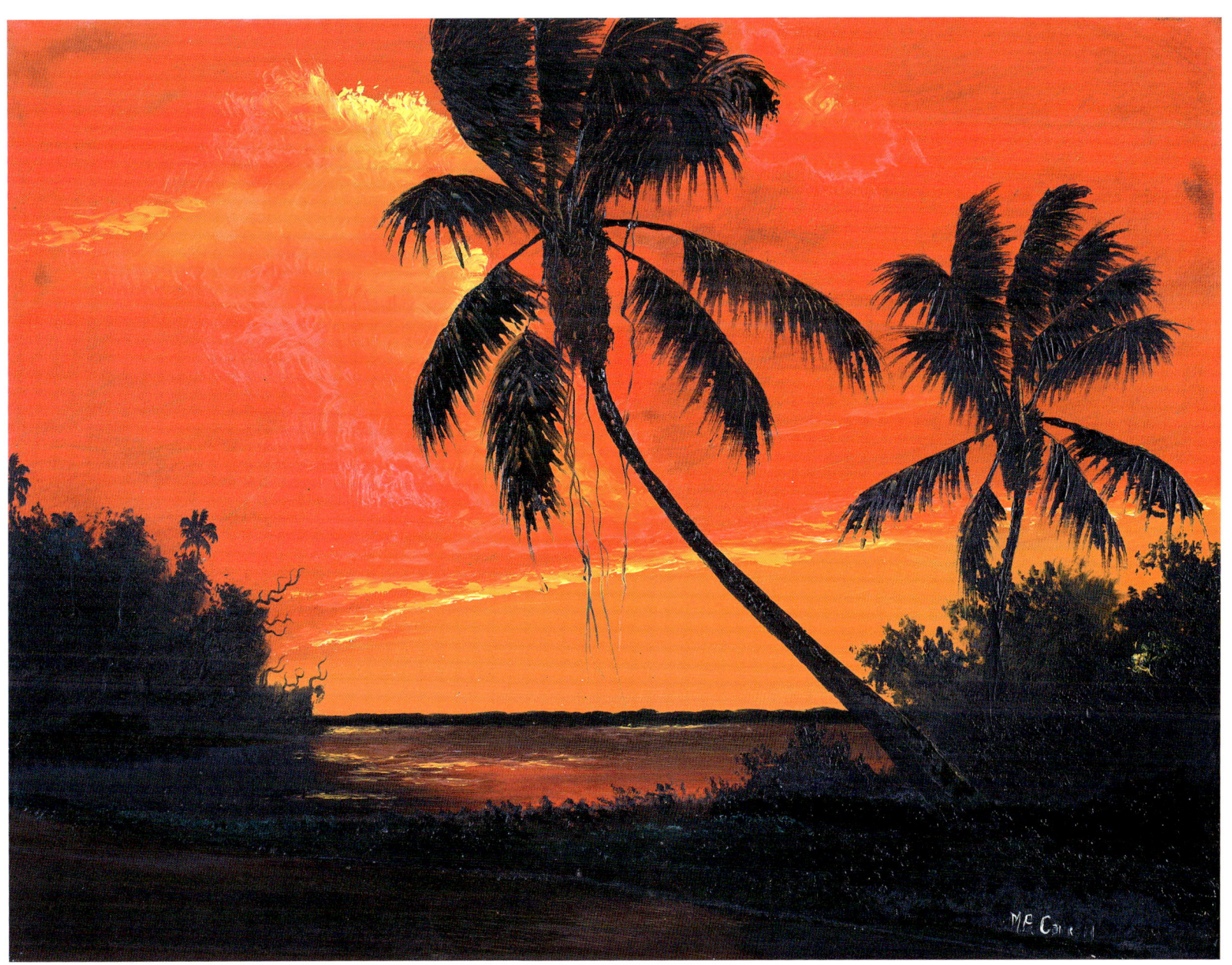

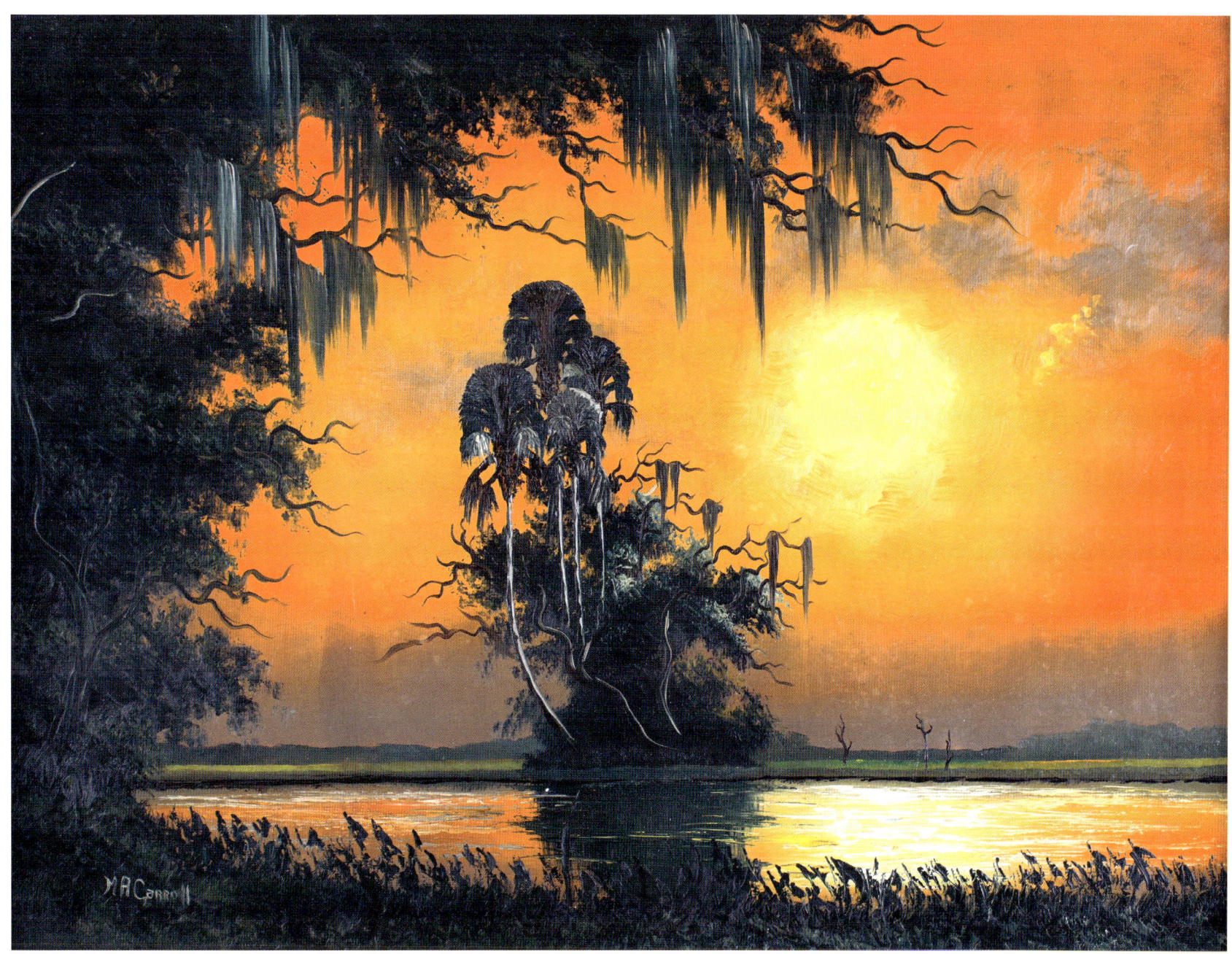

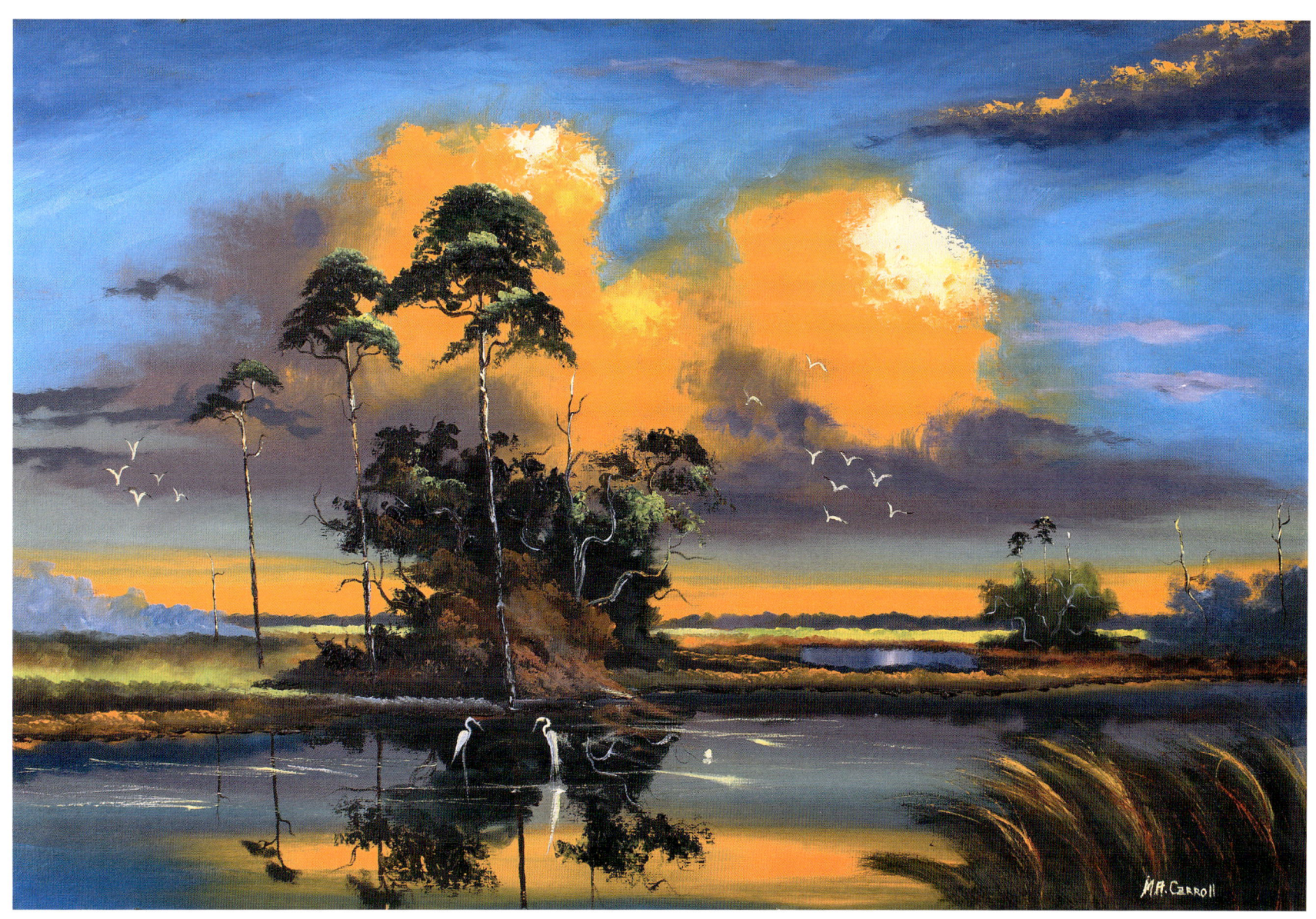

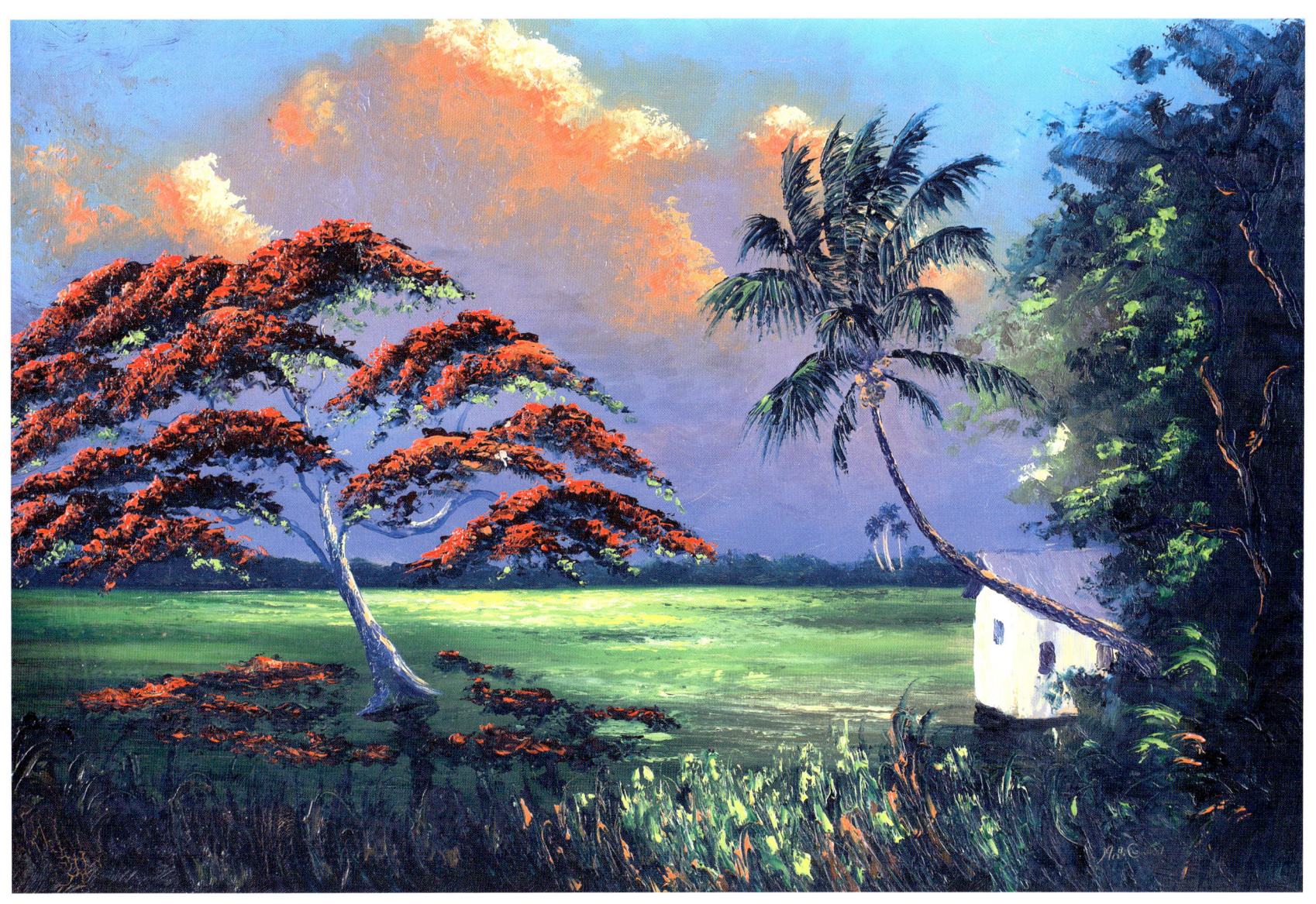

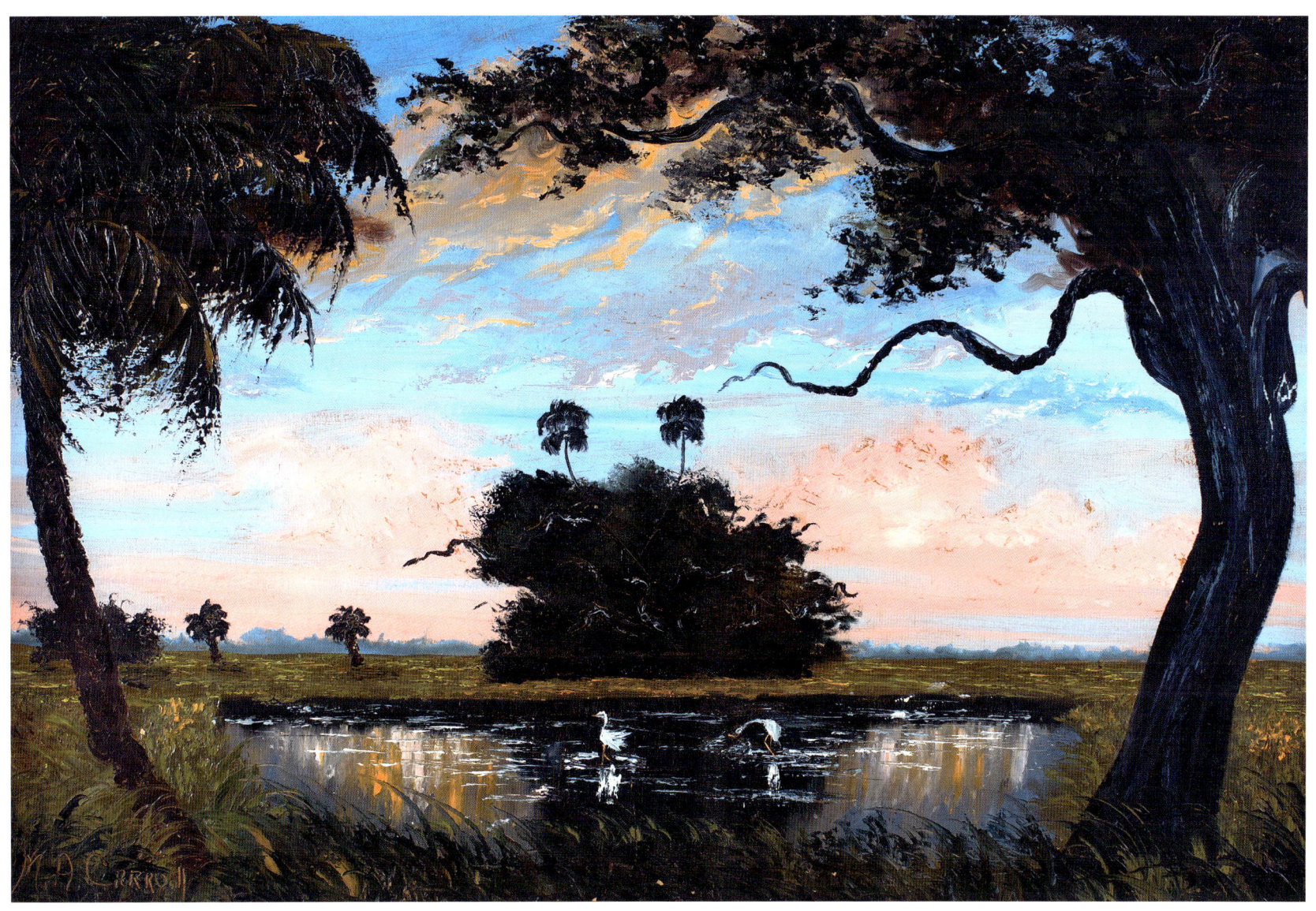

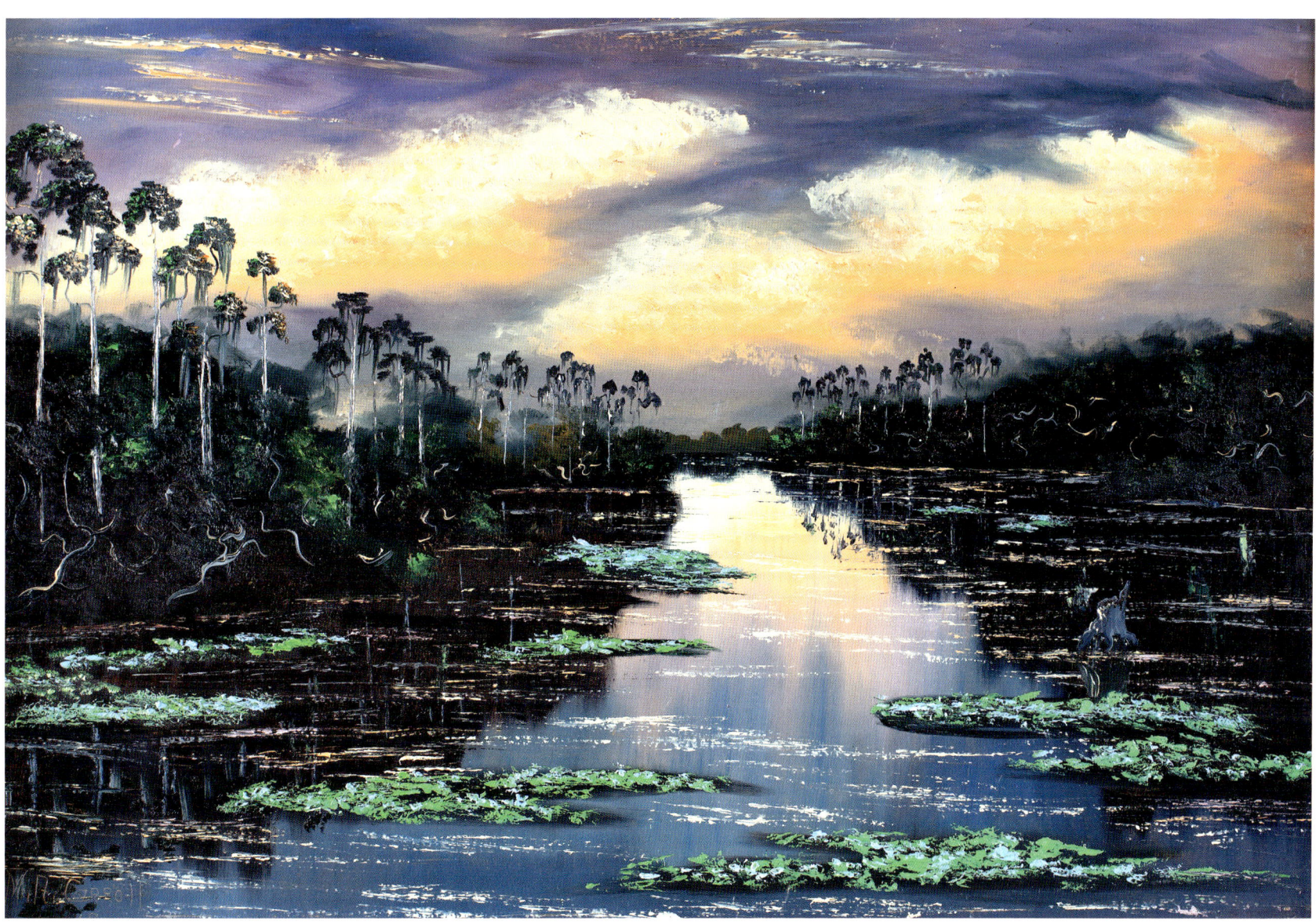

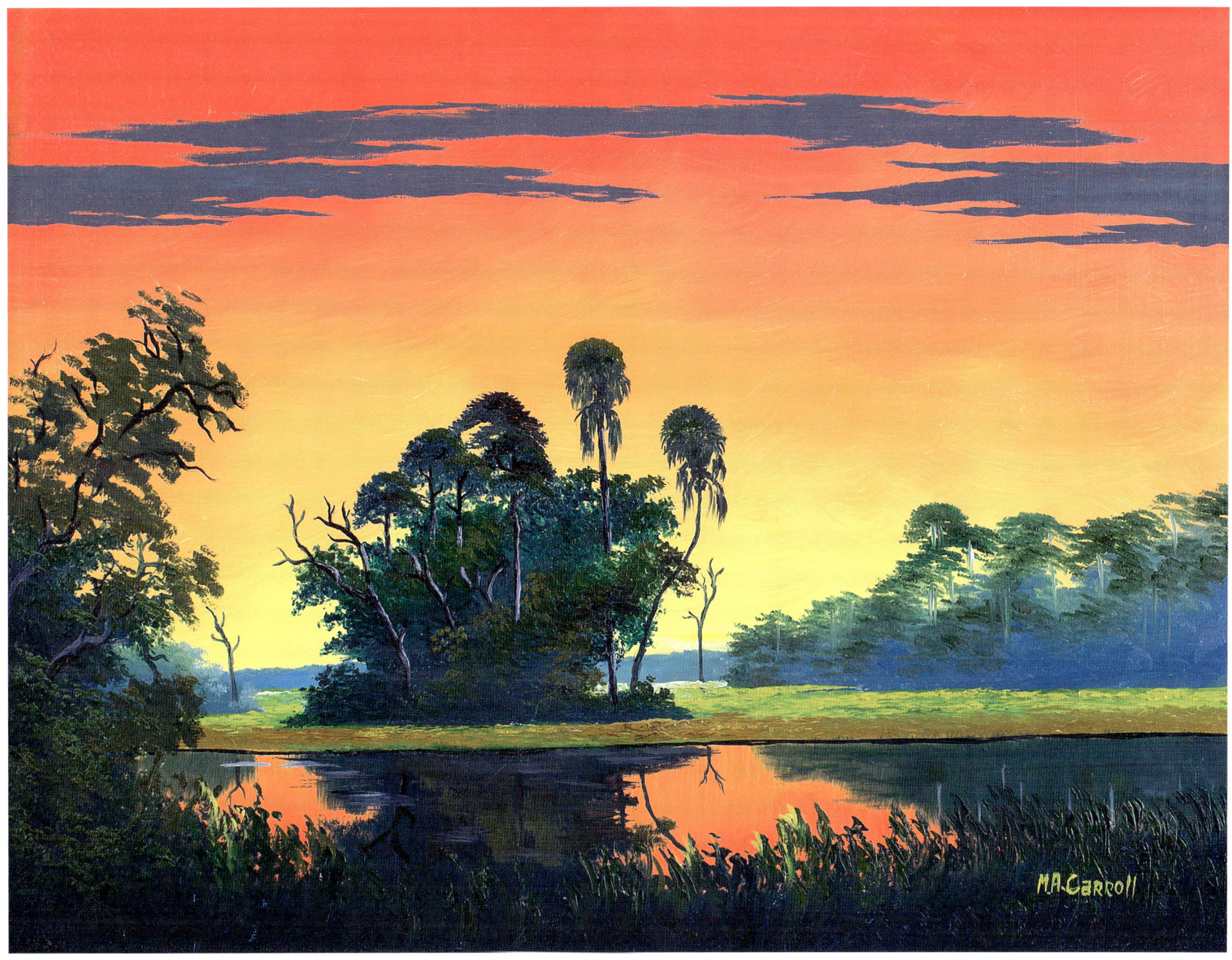

M.A.Carroll

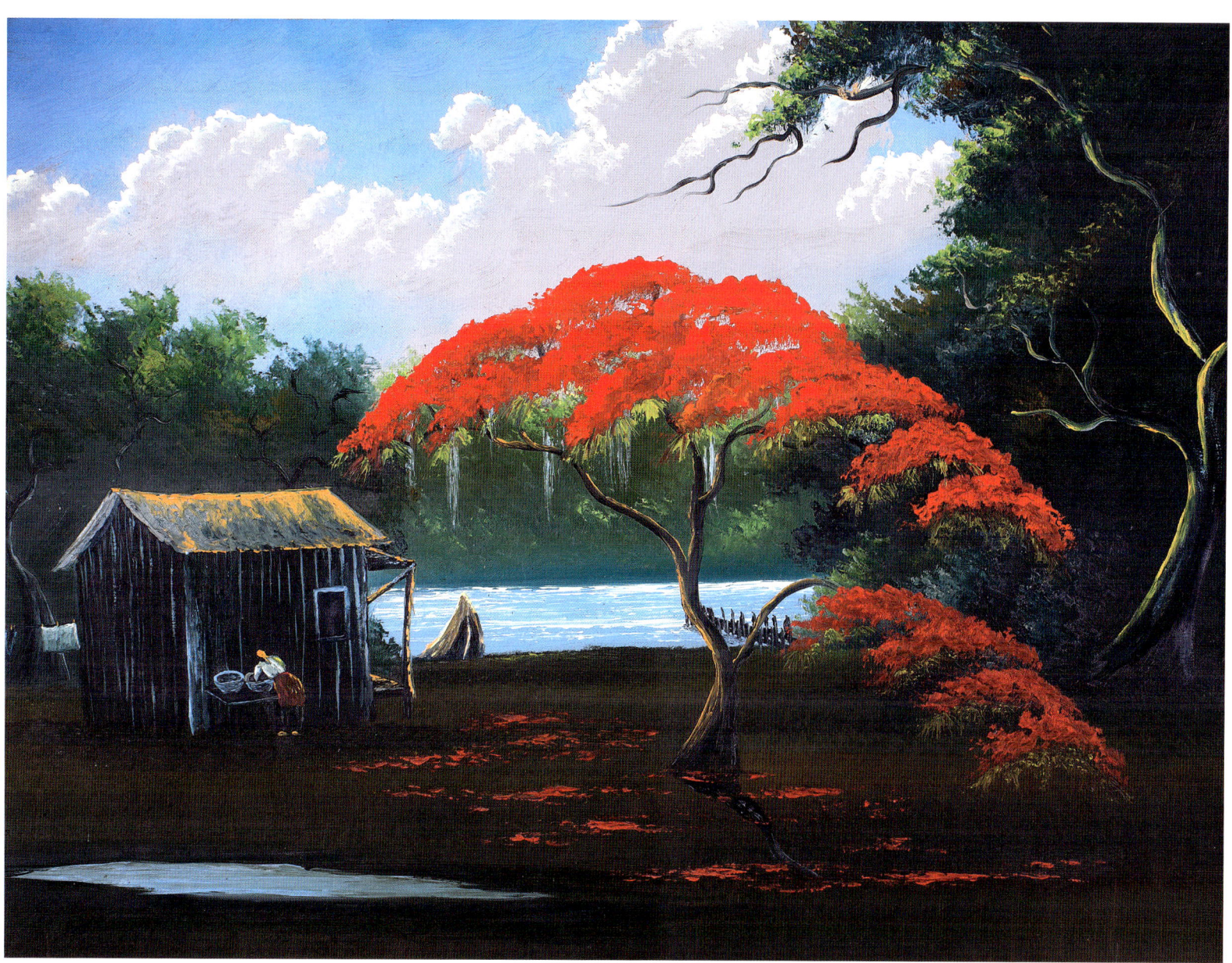

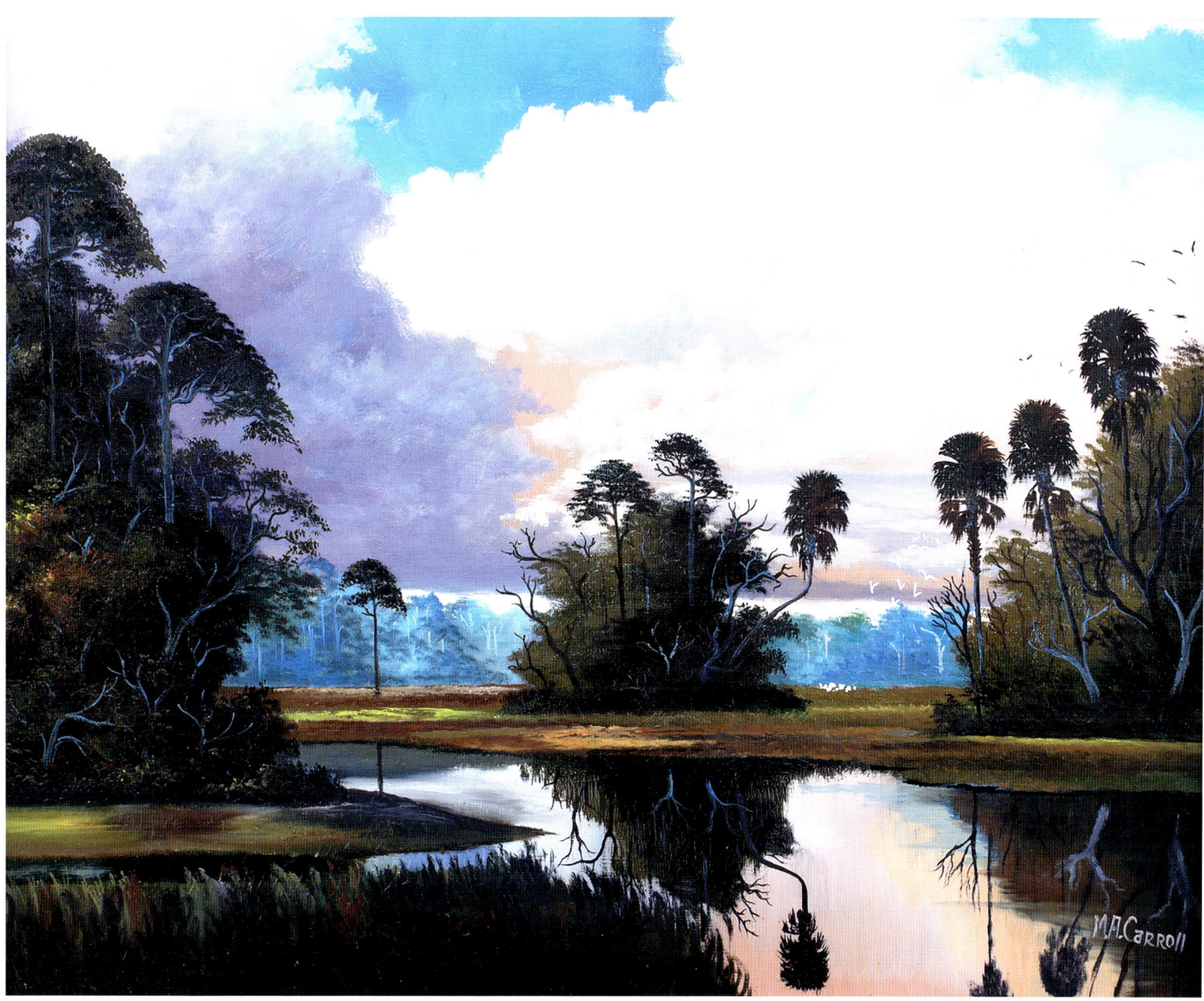

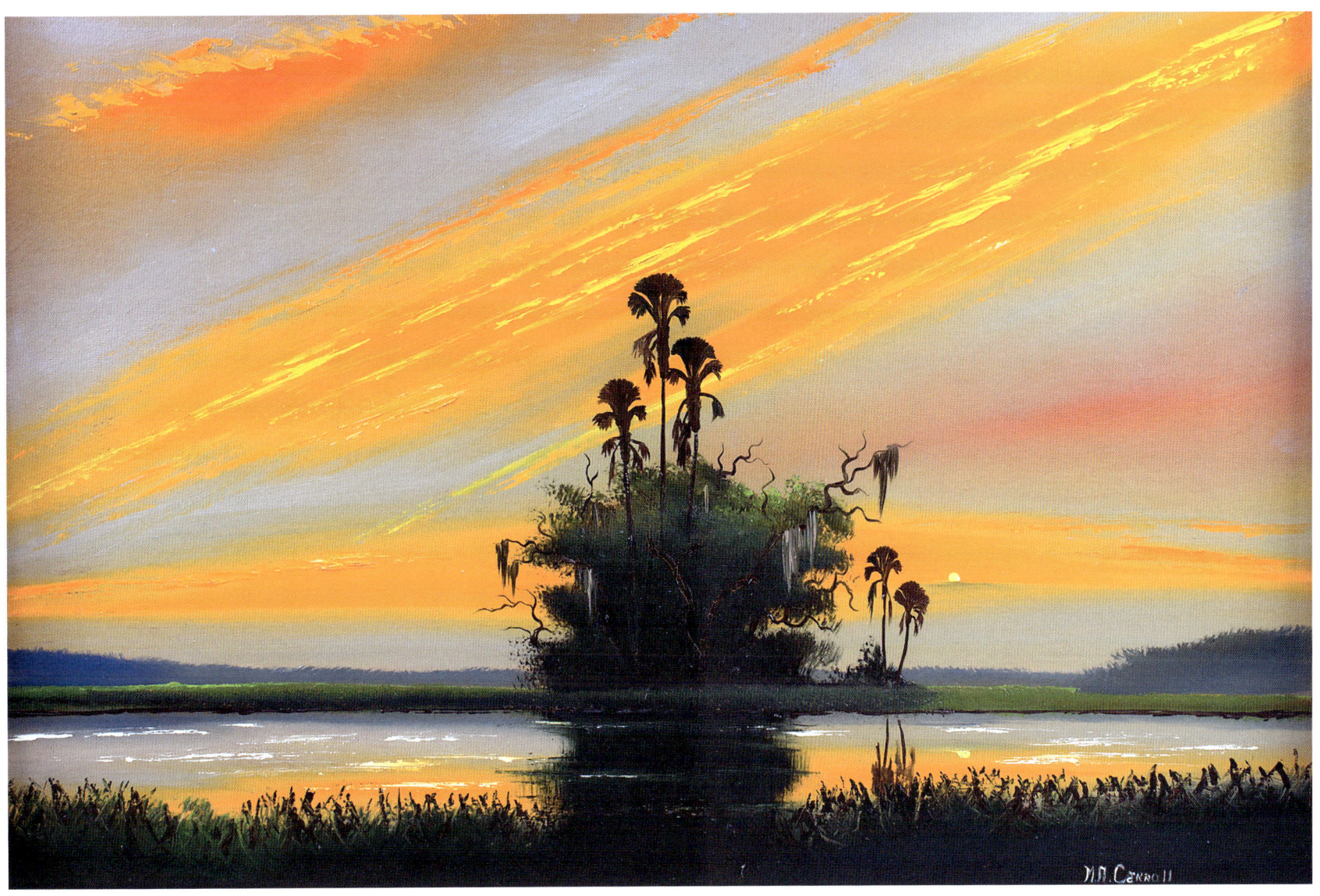

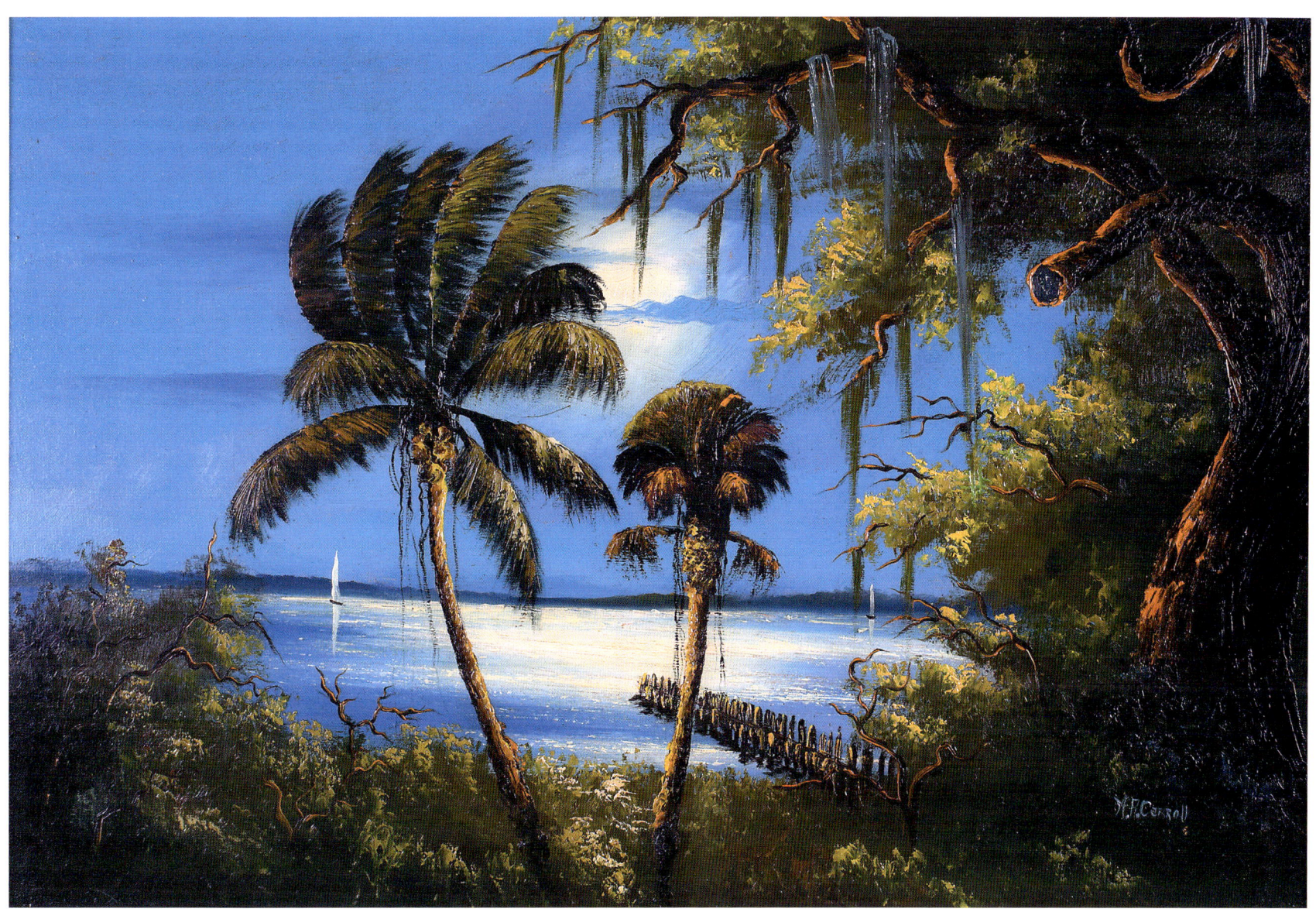

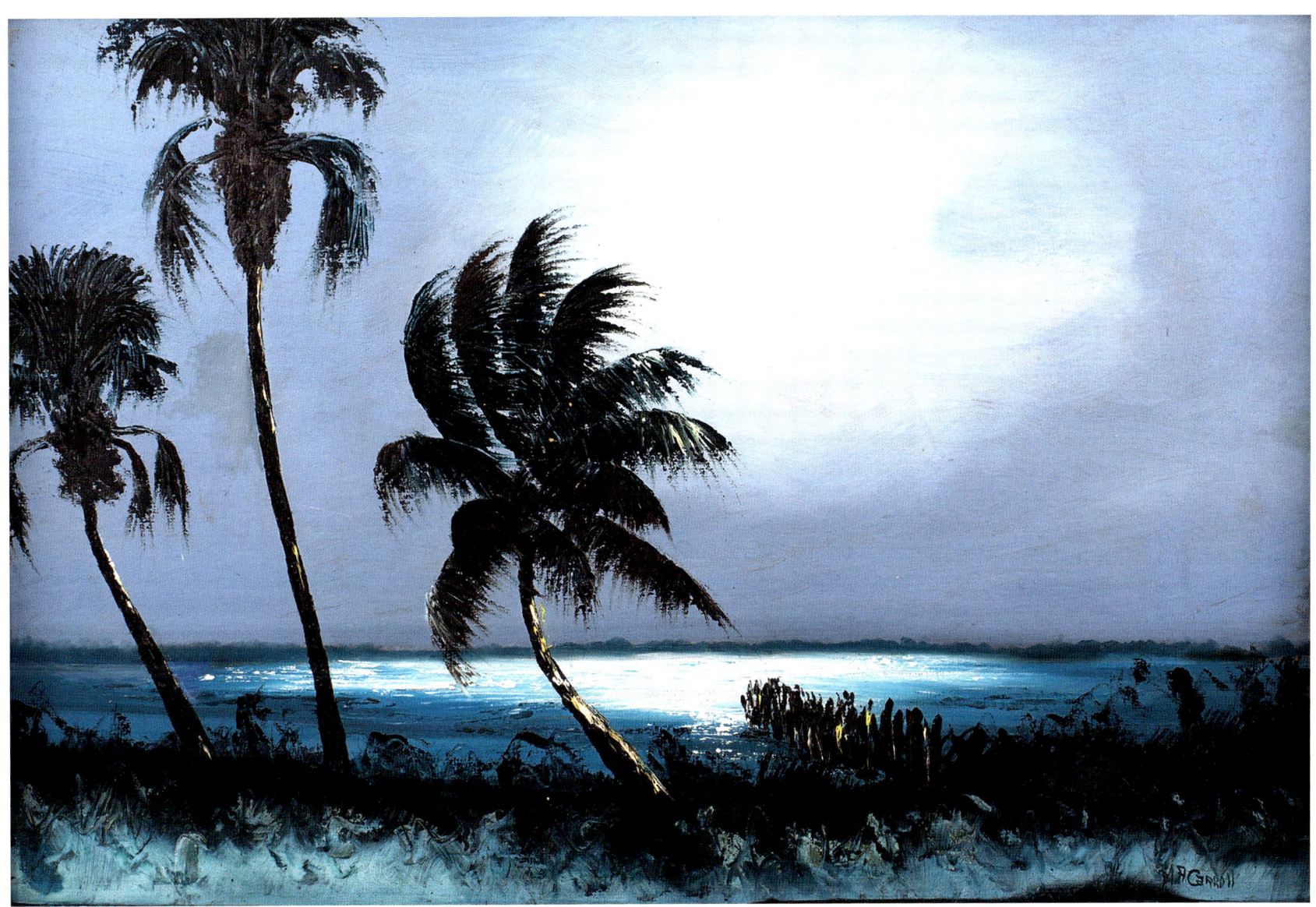

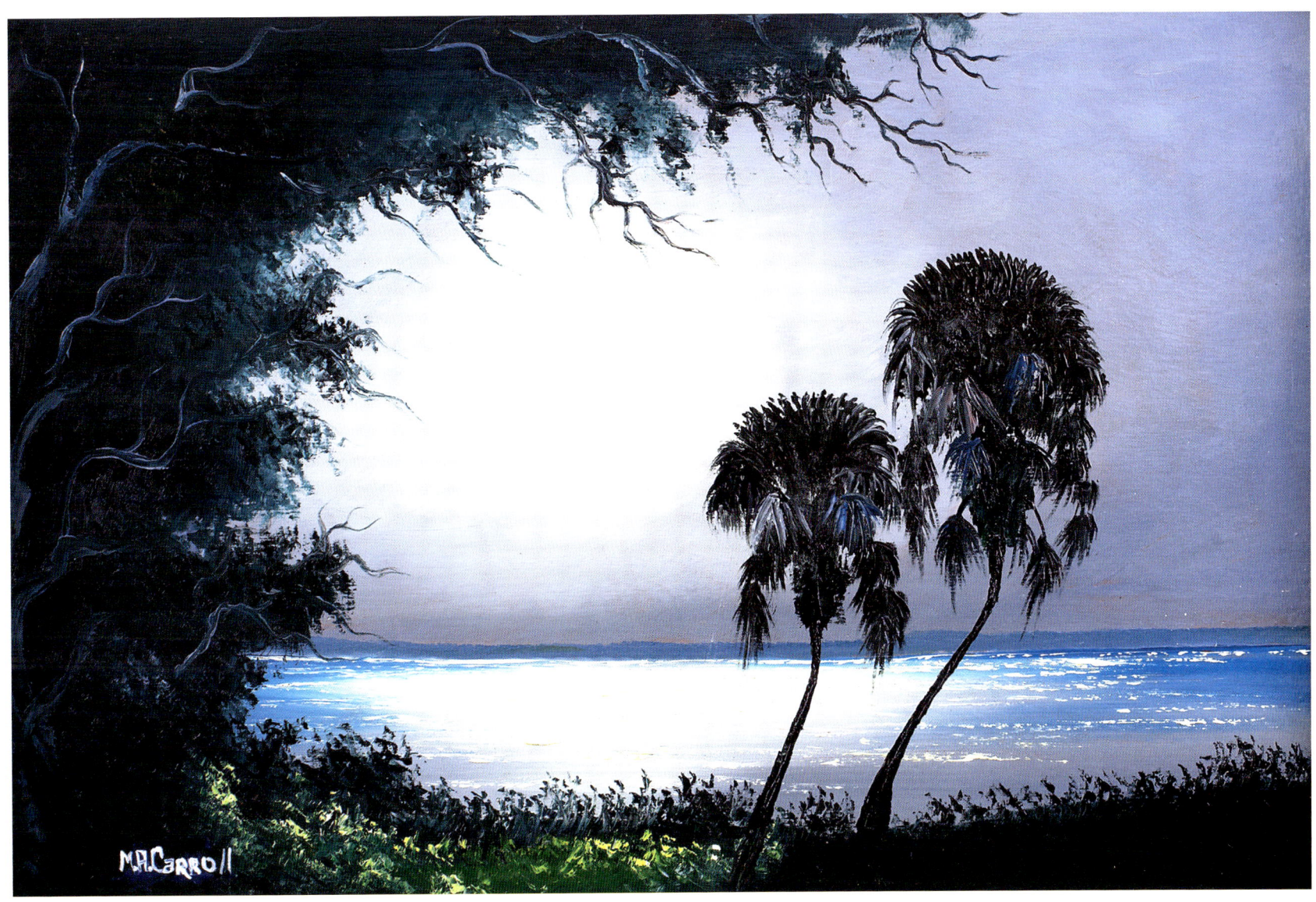

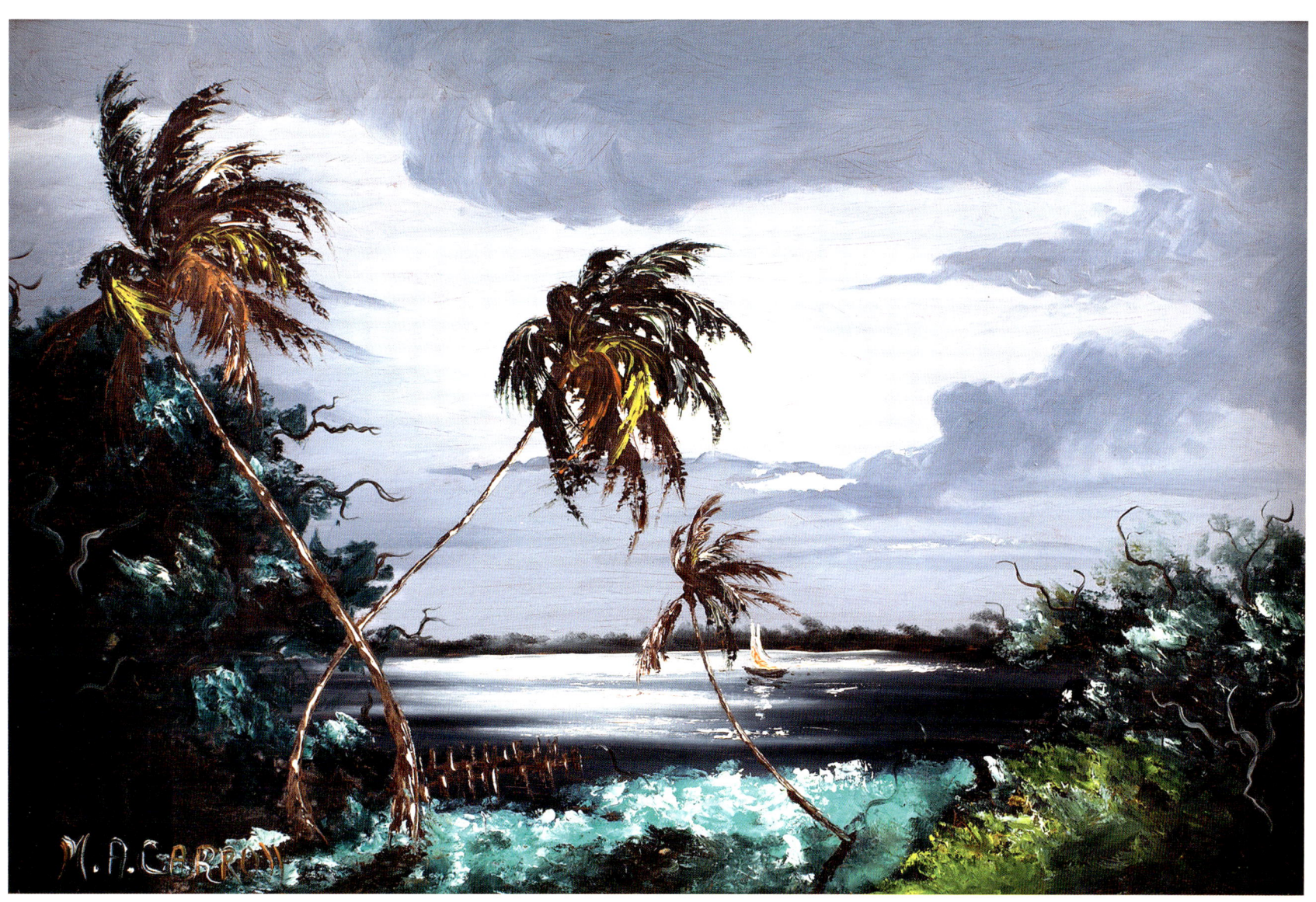

142

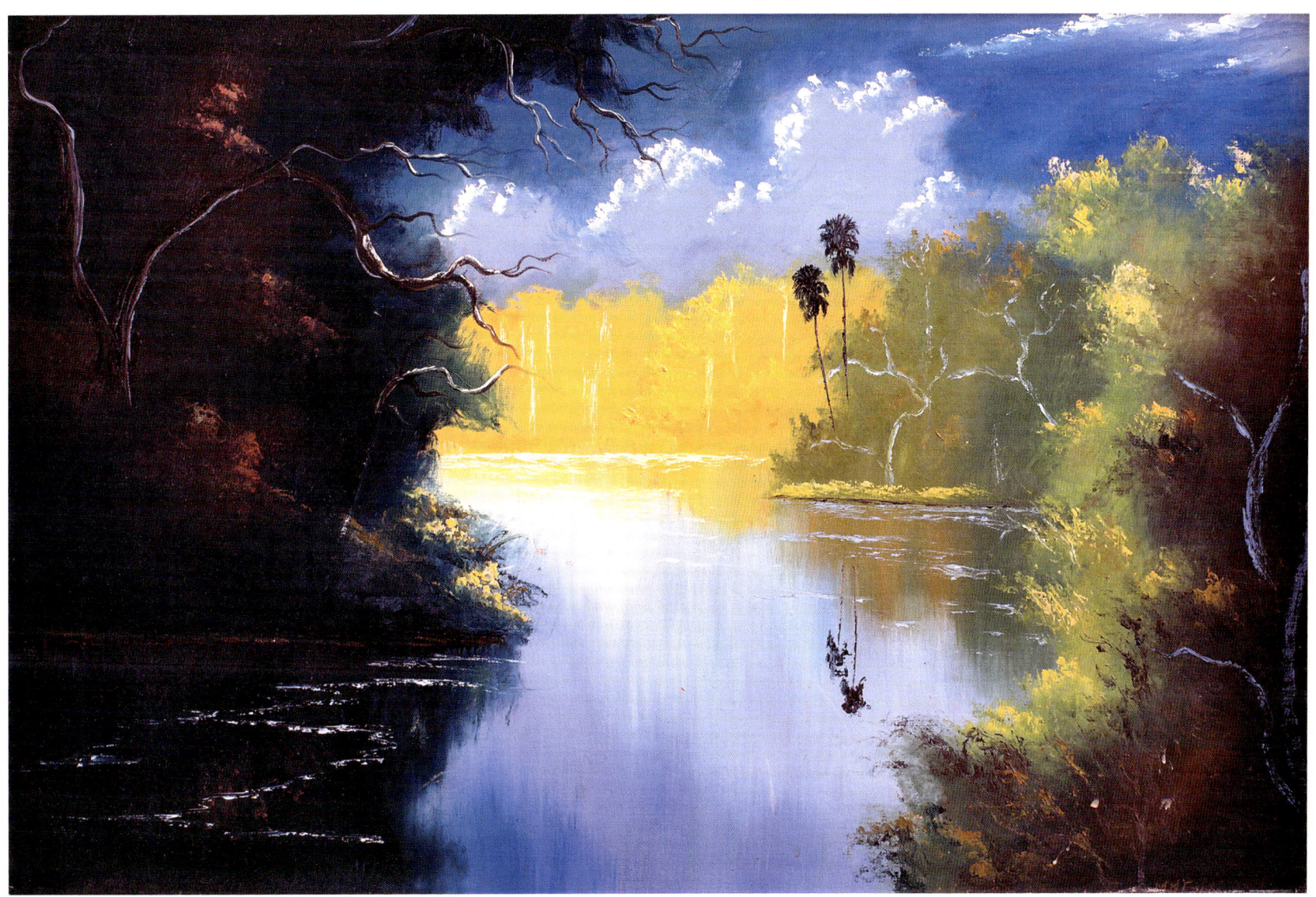

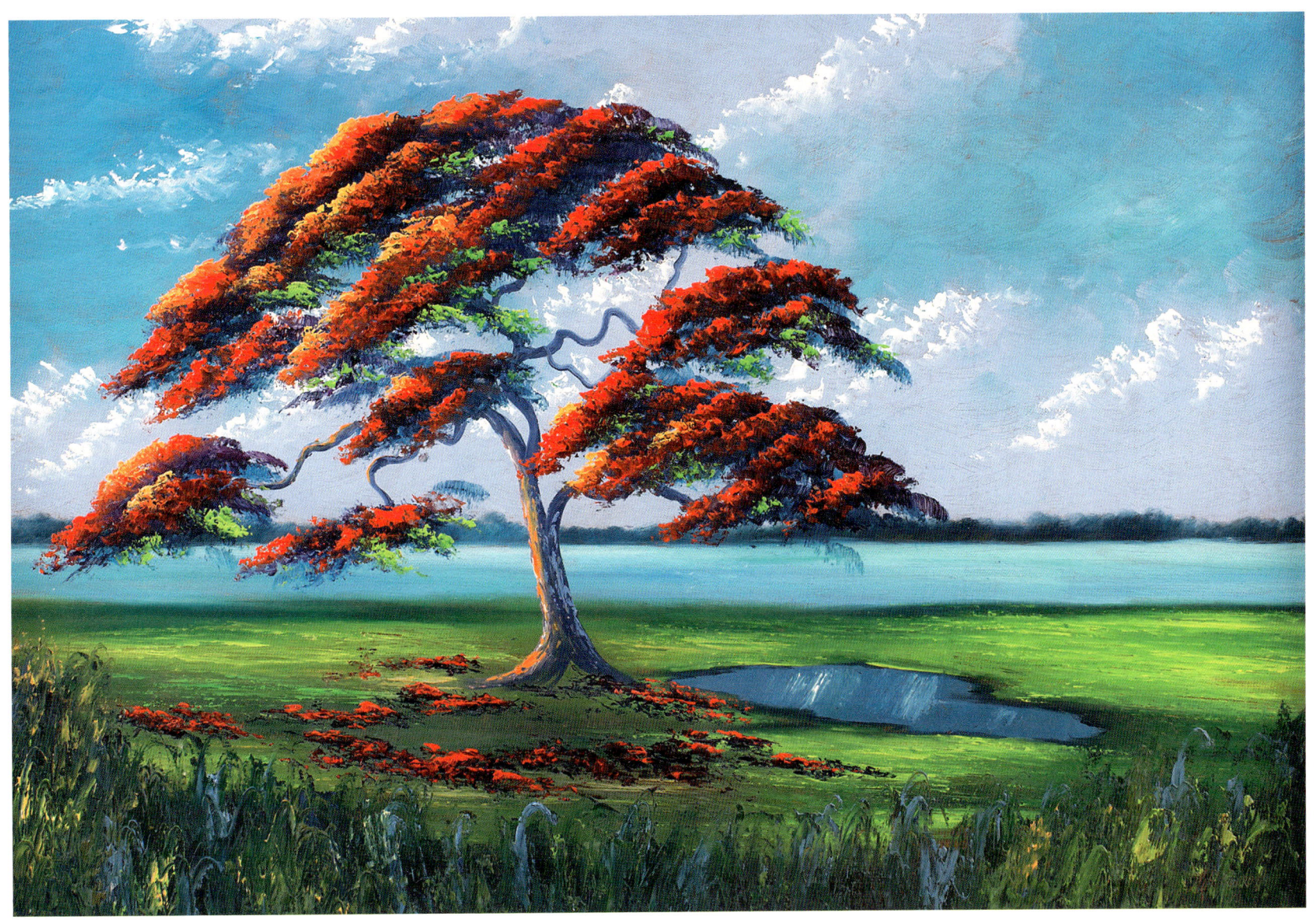

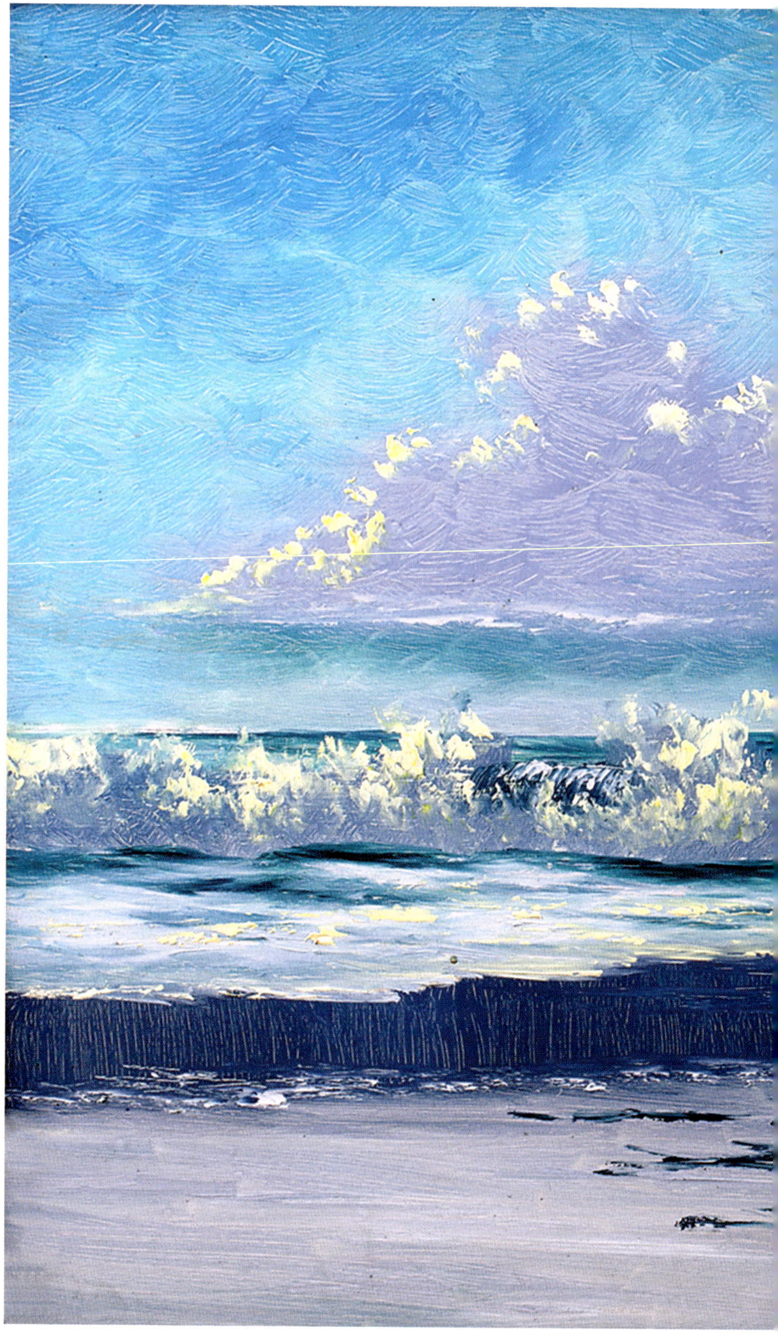

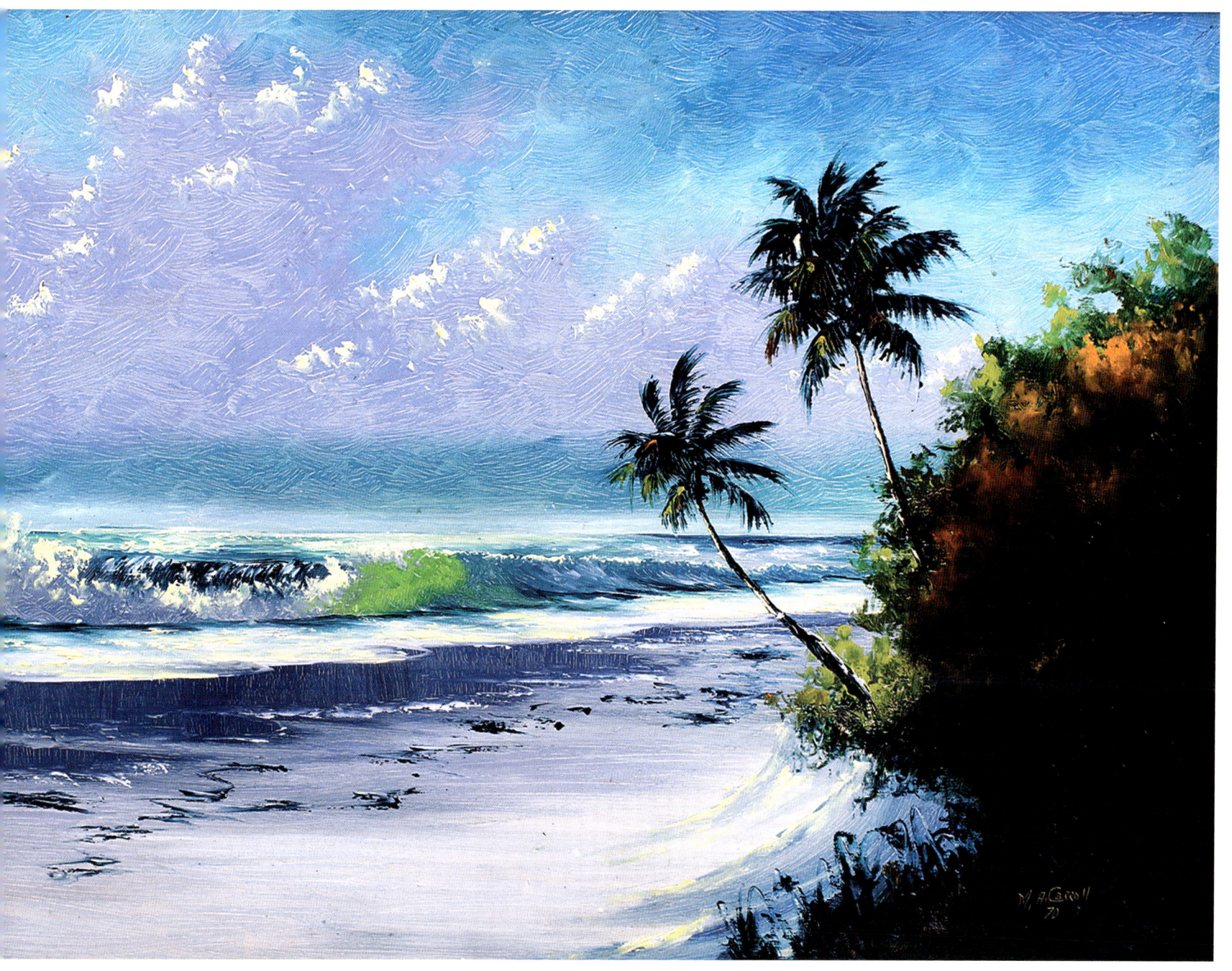

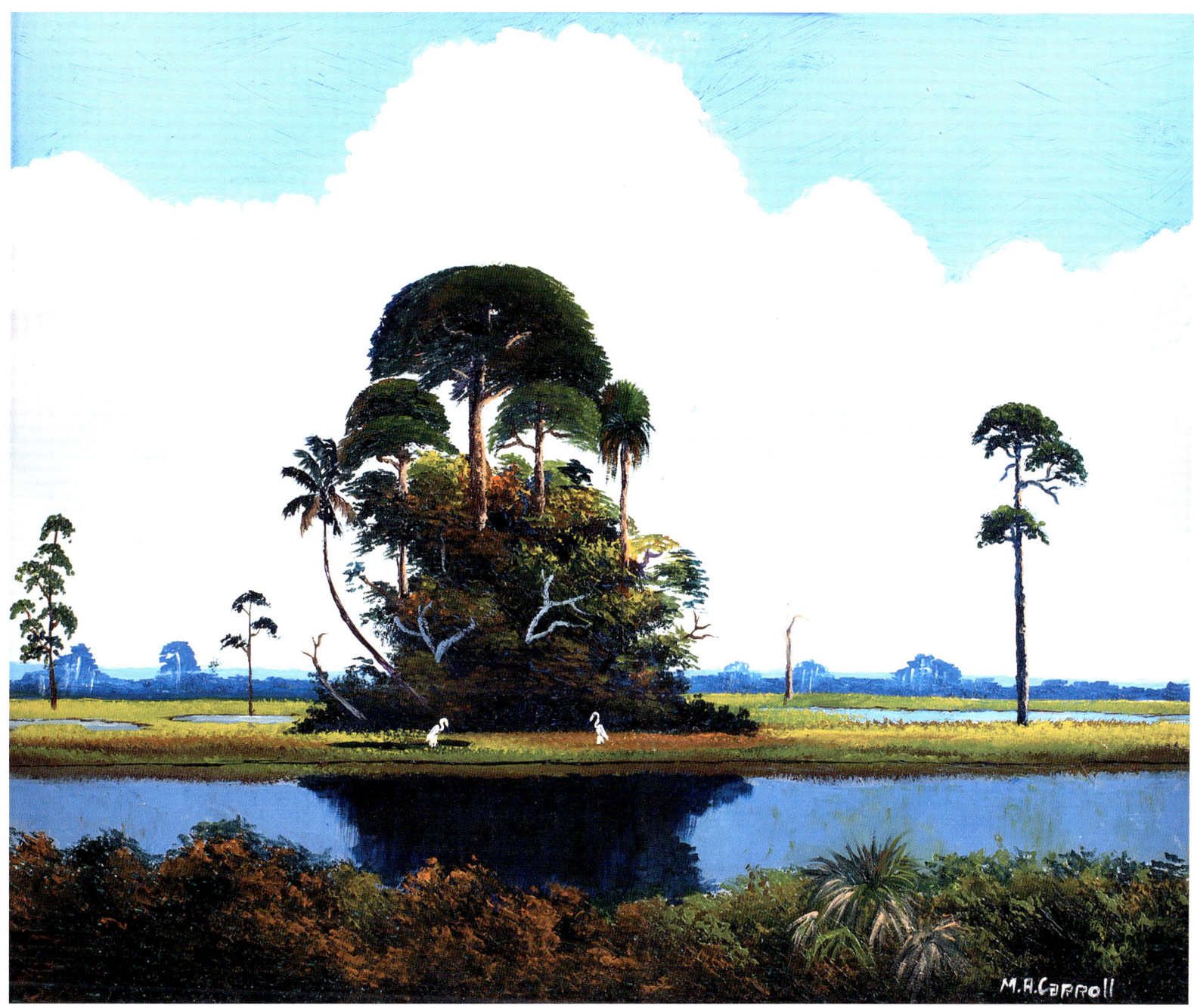

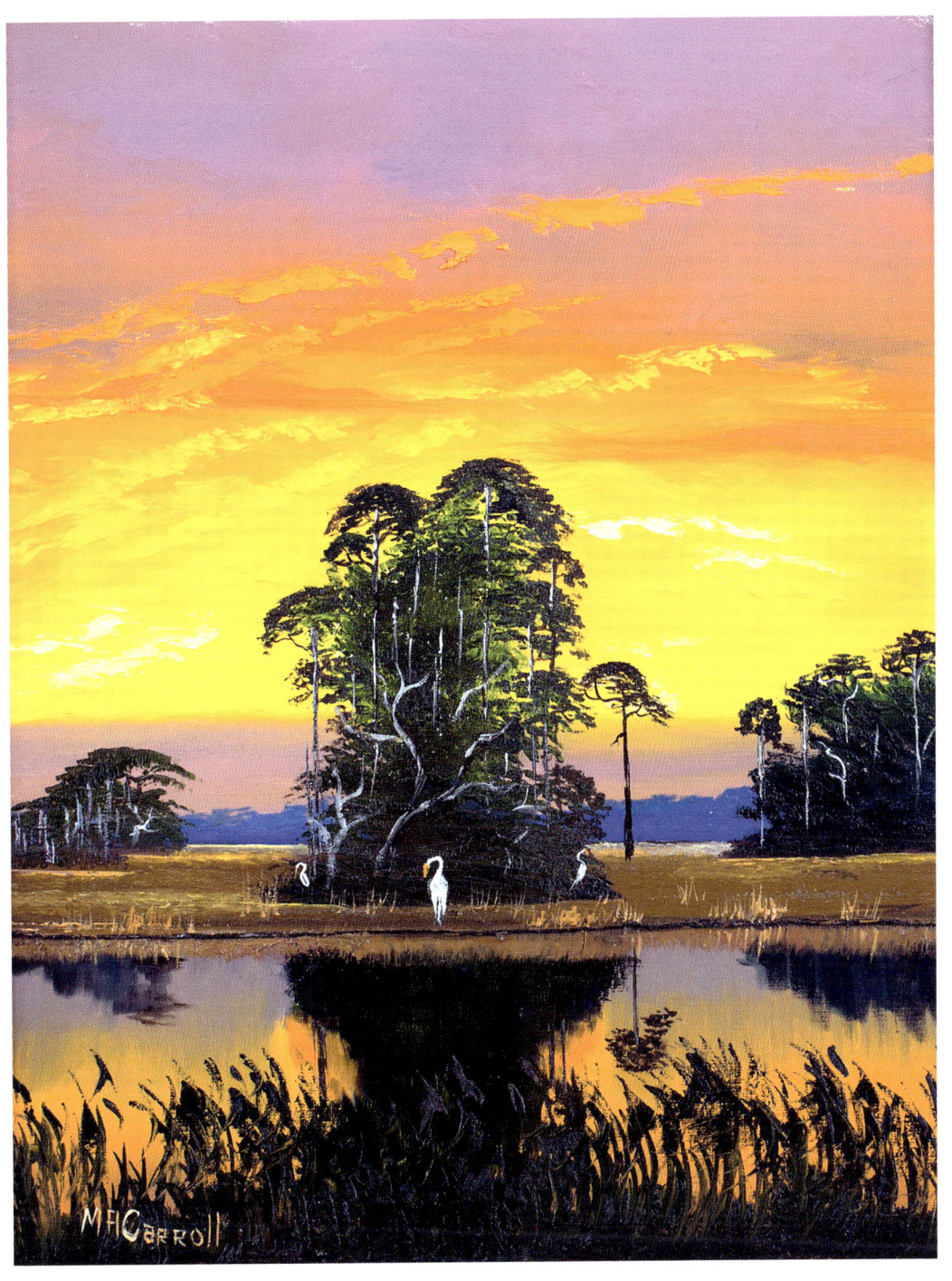

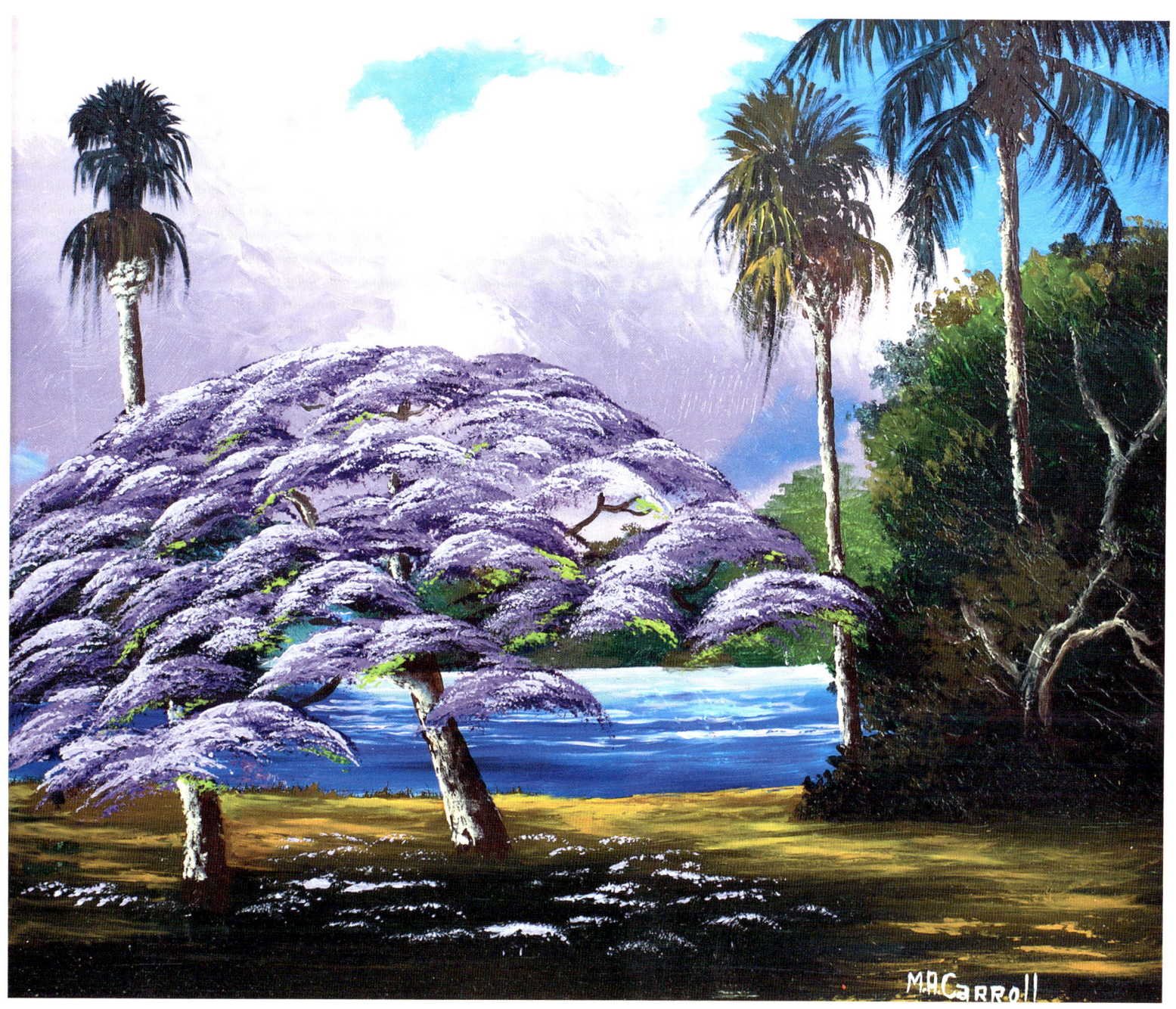

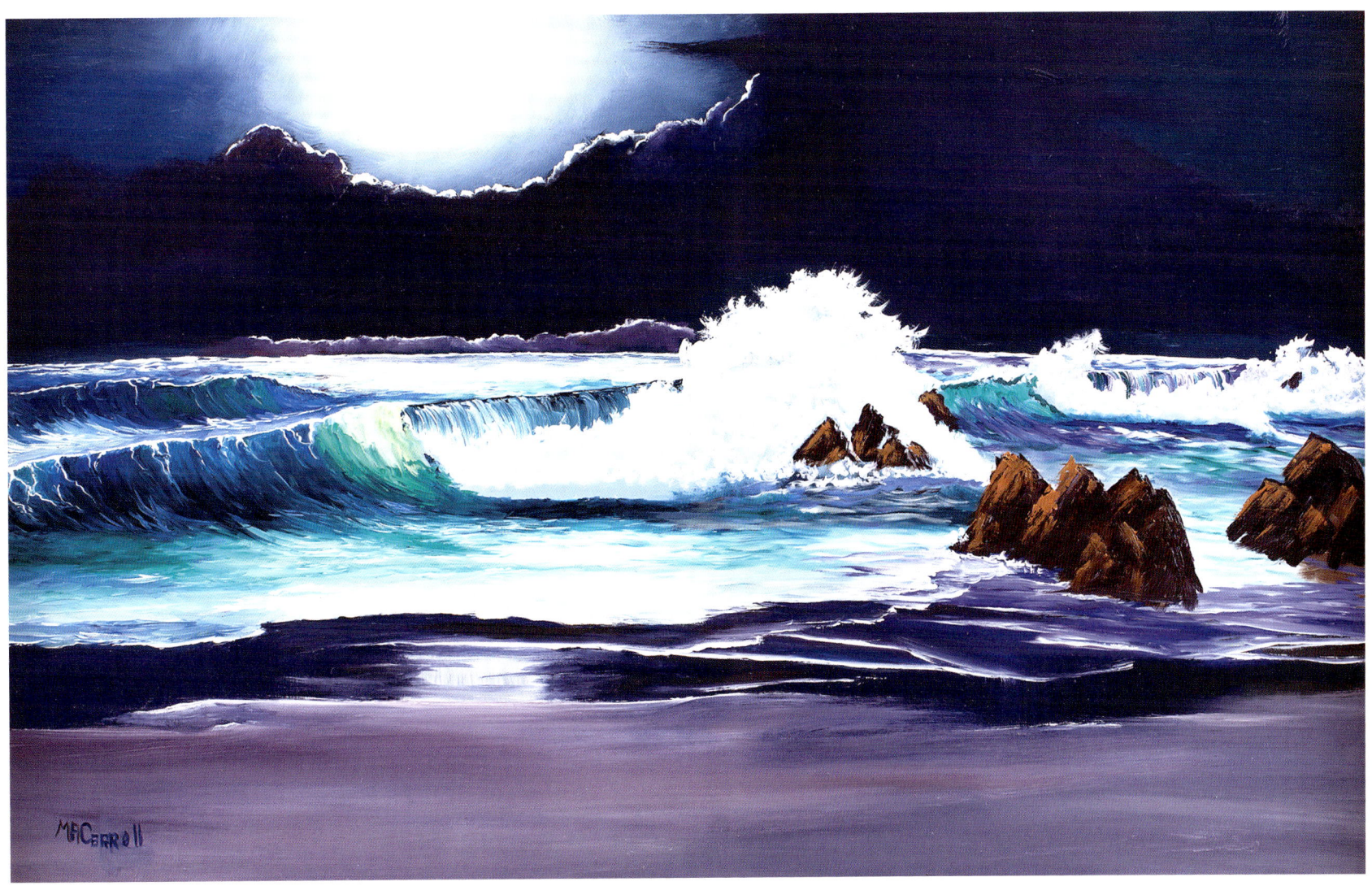

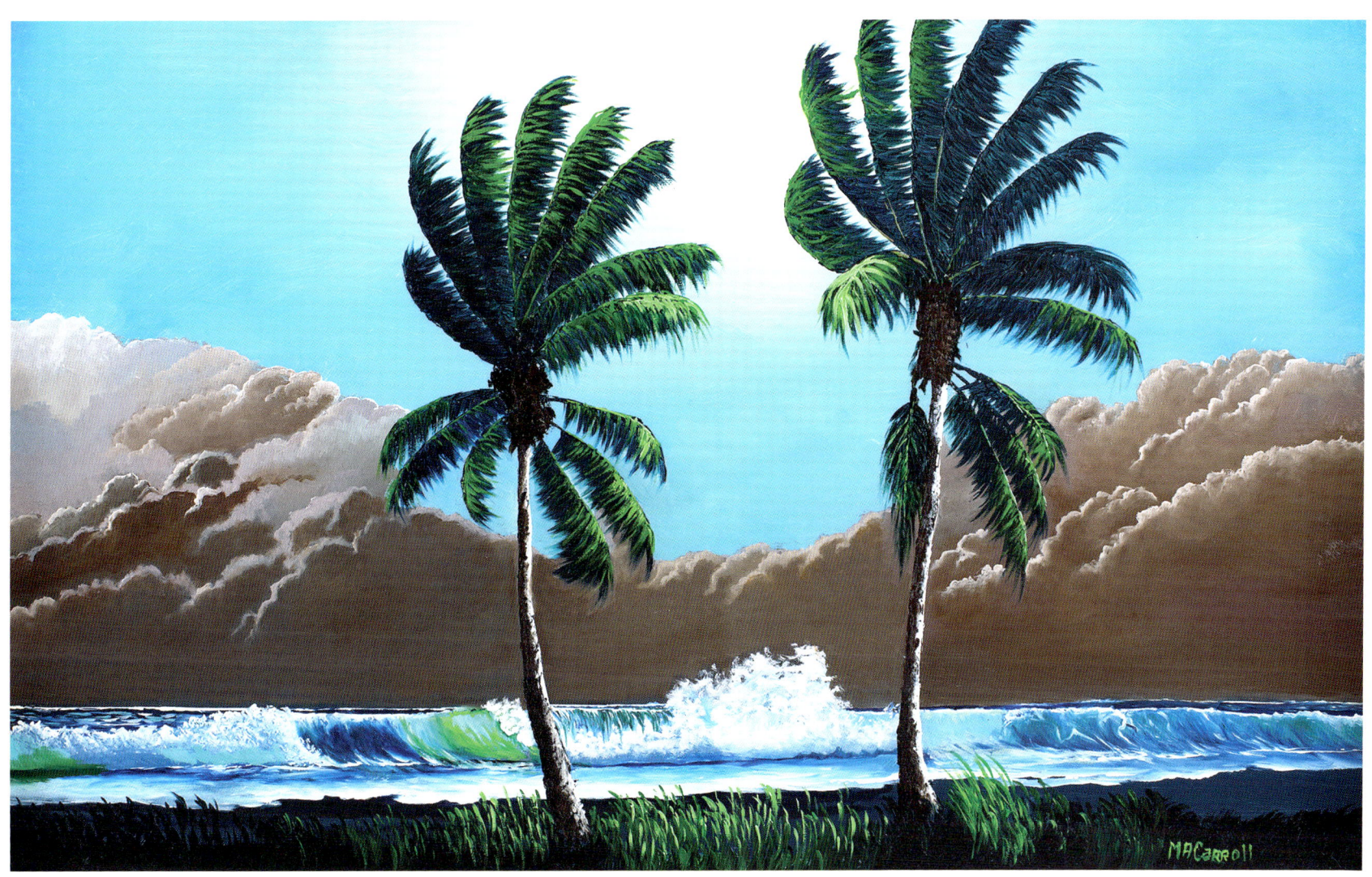

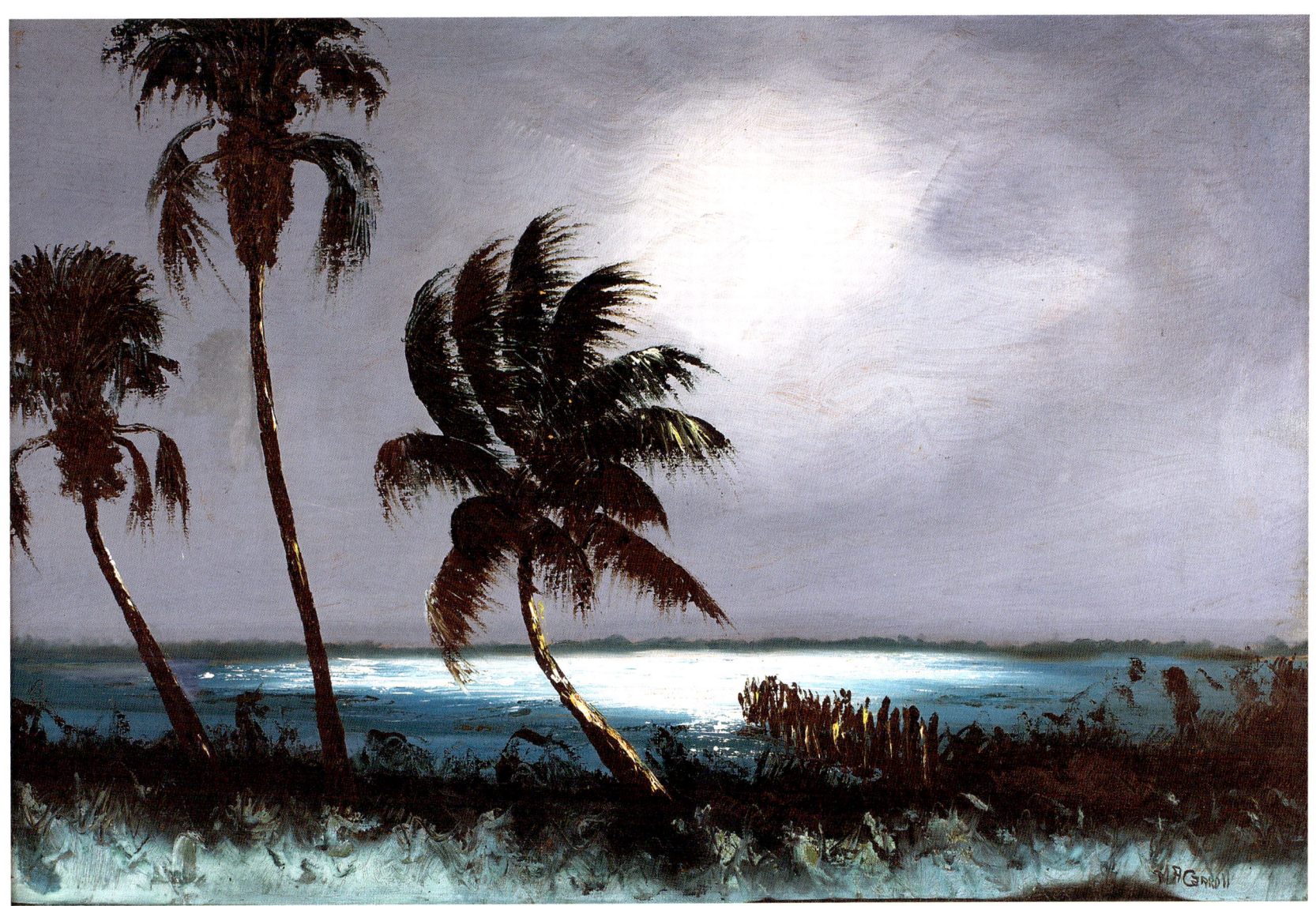

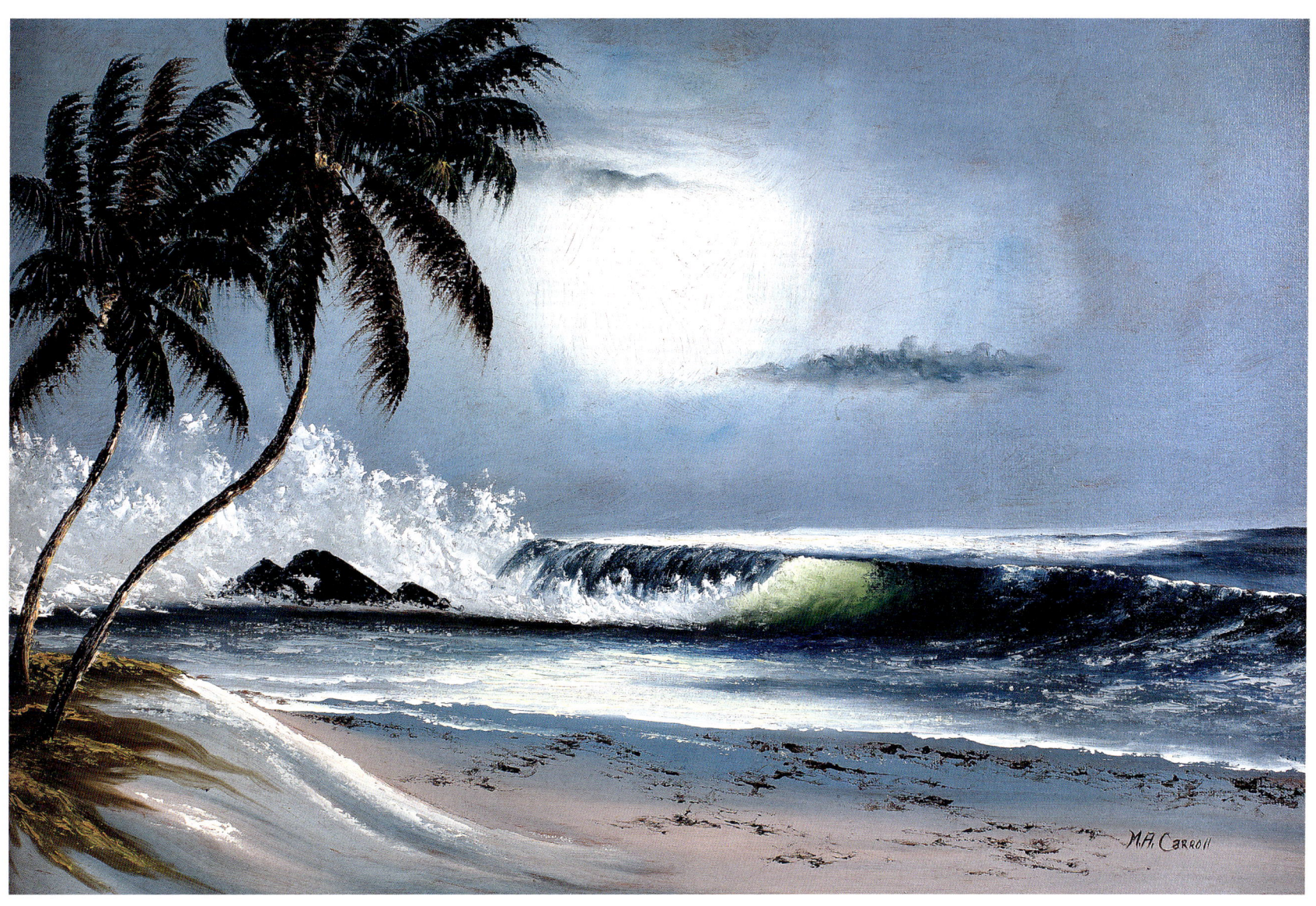

M.A. Carroll

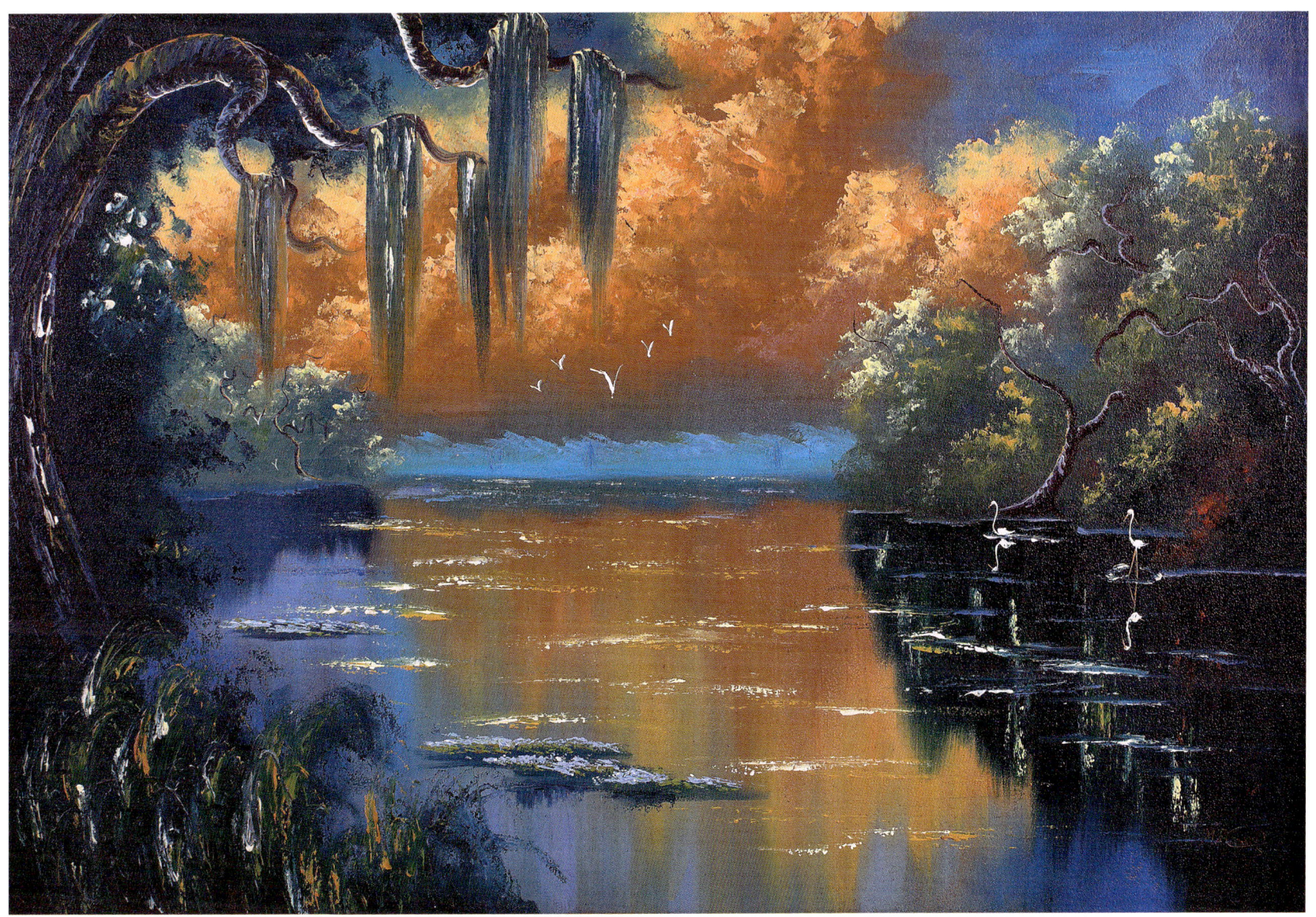

164

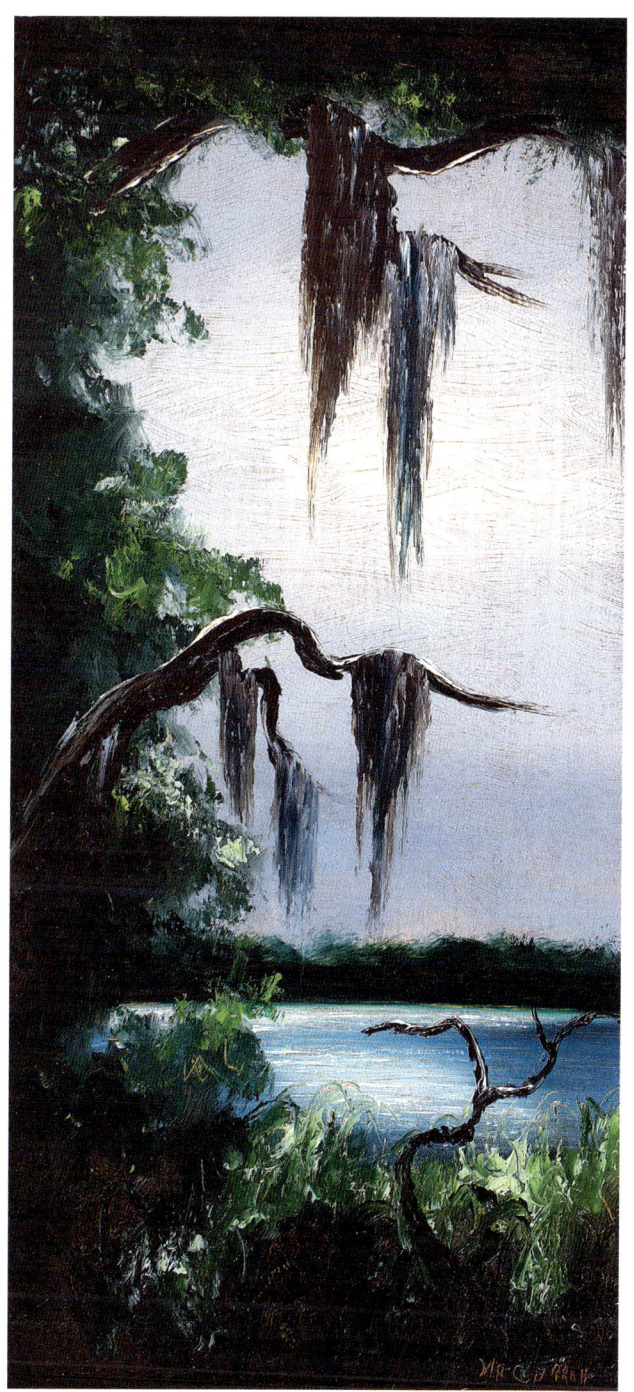
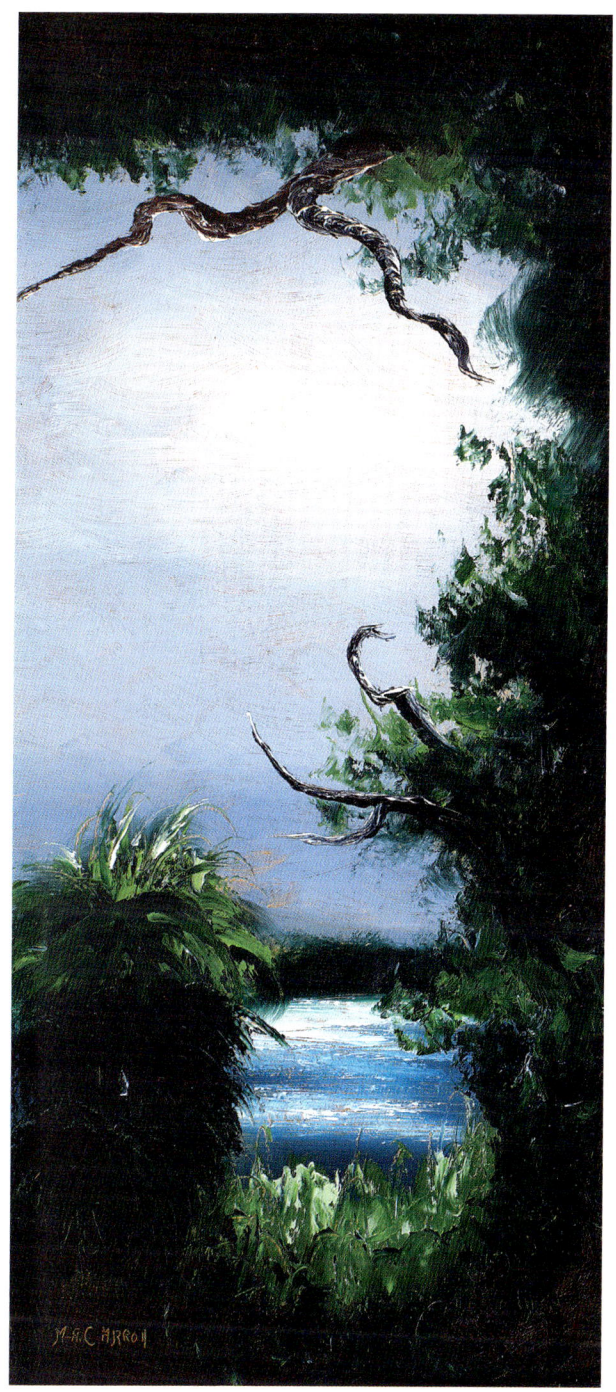

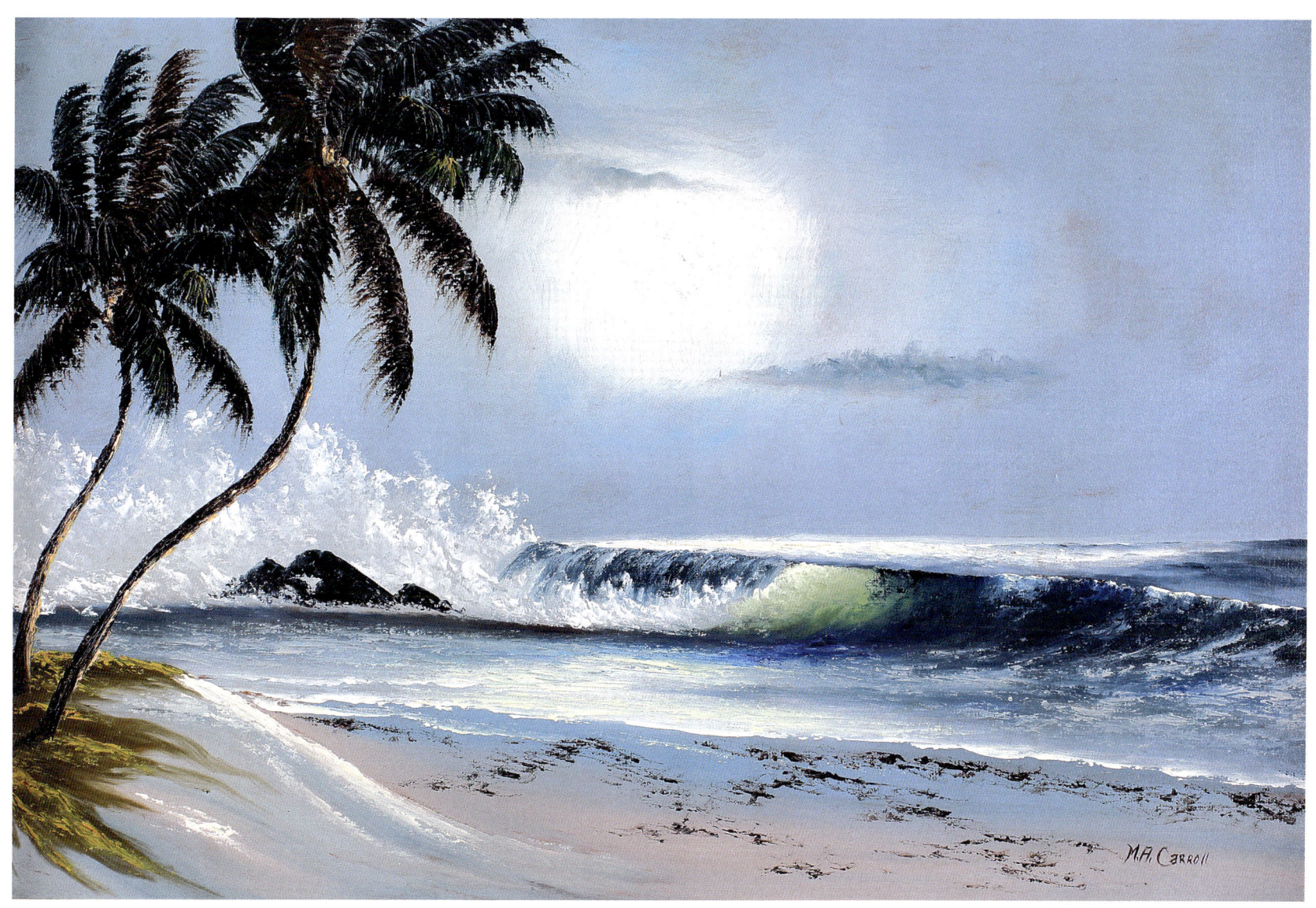

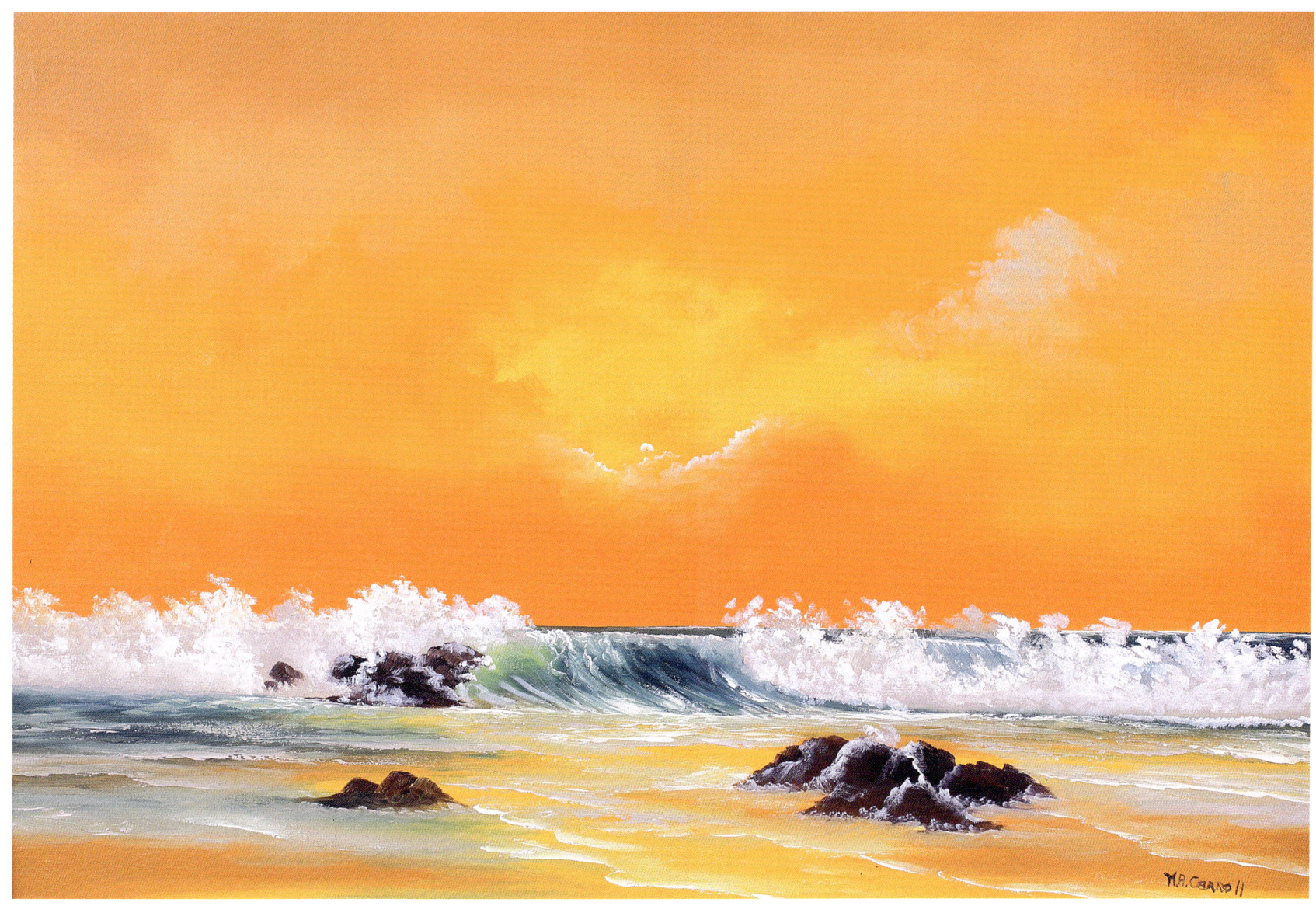

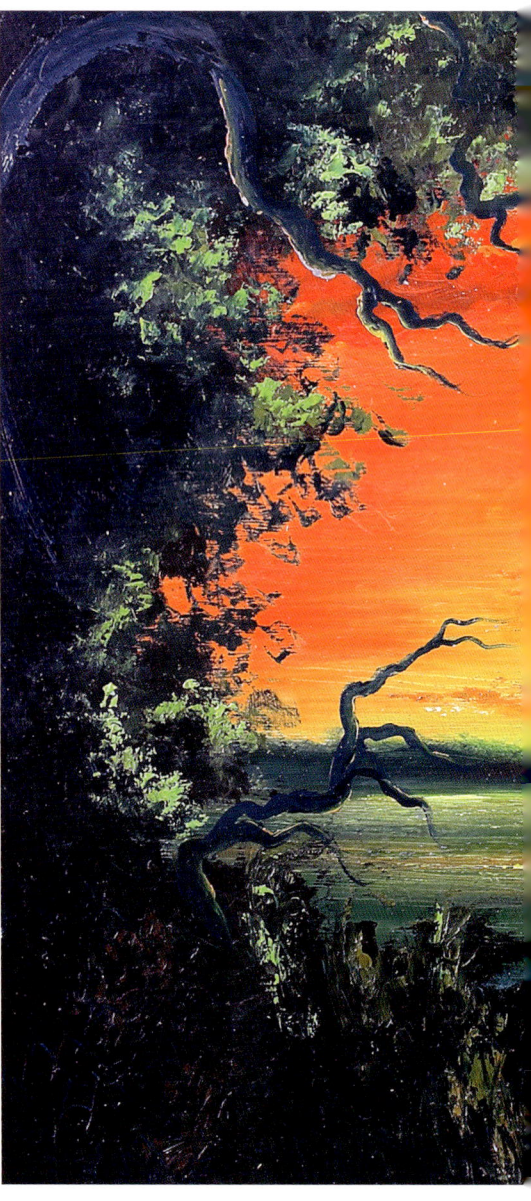

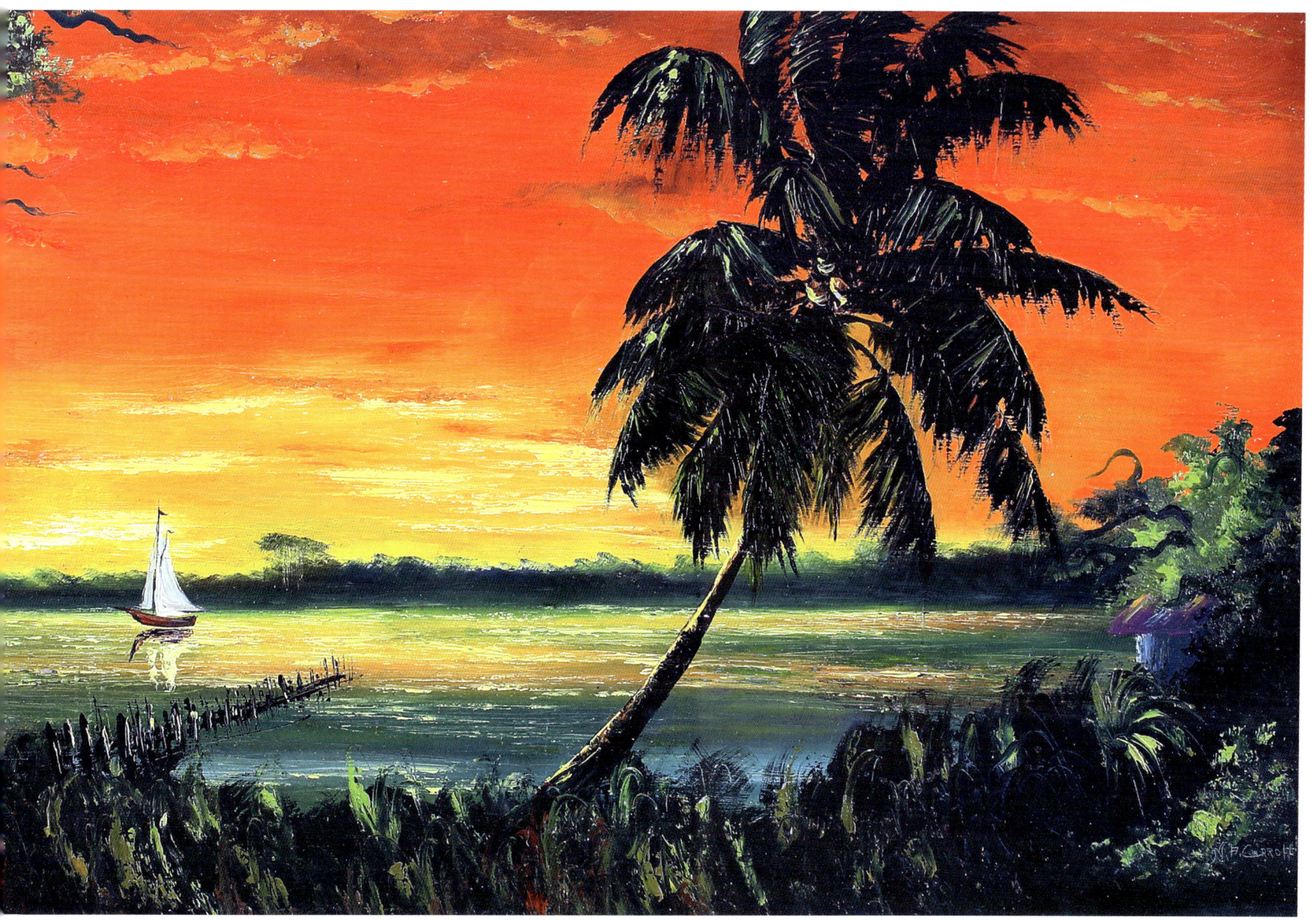

Acknowledgments

As always, my editor Margie Miller kept me and my prose in line and on track, and she never tired or faltered in the process. She's heaven-sent. I thank her and her husband Mel for their friendship and support.

I also appreciate Fort Pierce residents Linda Hudson and Jean Ellen Wilson for their knowledge of the city's history, their commitment to the city's civic betterment, and their fine reading and editorial input to the manuscript. In fact, Jean Ellen's observations compelled me to make significant improvements to both form and content. Similarly, Pam Cooper, supervisor of the Archive Center and Genealogy Department at Vero Beach's Indian River County Library, assisted me with zeal, as she has done before. A young scholar, Kristen Stone, read the manuscript when it was supposedly finished; she brought important literary and social insights to it and to me.

With the remarkable experiences I had unearthing and telling the stories of artists in a triptych of Highwaymen books, I thought I was done with this chapter of my life. When John Byram, University Press of Florida's editor in chief at the time, asked me to consider writing a book on Mary Ann Carroll, I was back to my life as a freewheeling noncommercial photographer. I was now rejuvenated and, as I recall, was off to Poland. So I said no at that time. Very soon thereafter Mary Ann asked me to write a book about her. I don't think she knew the magnitude of the request, but then, with John and her looking to me to tell her story, I could not say no again, for each of them had given me more than I had given them—trust.

Meredith Babb, director of University Press of Florida, has long had faith in me, and for this I am forever grateful. Her recommending Virginia Lynn Moylan to write the foreword to this book was excellent advice. I'm glad that Lynn's insight and knowledge accent these pages. I've admired her writing and her dedication, and I'm glad that I got to know her. Again I had the pleasure of working with the press's excellent copy editor Ann Marlowe, and again she further refined my ideas and words. Project editor Nevil Parker and I tweaked the text before it was etched in stone, and, at that point, it was both a relief and joy.

I am indebted, too, to the people who welcomed me into their homes to talk with me, each of whom is referenced in this essay. I enjoyed writing the book because it allowed me to know Mary Ann and the era in which the Highwaymen painted even better than I had before.

Some advanced collectors of Highwaymen painting have stayed by my side and have had my back at times. I'm grateful for the friendships I've forged with them. Tim Jacobs, Scott Schlesinger, Henry Bosma, Frank Mannino, Rich Kerchner, Ralph Oko, Omar and Elizabeth Castillo, and Roger Lightle are among those whose views have encouraged me. For this book especially, the assistance of Tim, Rich, and Roger, along with Omar and Elizabeth, was especially meaningful. These four people are really moving and shaking the Highwaymen scene these days. Ginger Baldwin, a selfless cultural impresario, has long supported my efforts. I'm also grateful for the friendship and support of Jim Fitch, who coined the name Highwaymen, and to Jeff Klinkenberg, Florida's premier journalist who focuses on our state's culture. These friends' excitement and understanding of the Highwaymen remains invaluable.

Above all, my wife Teresa Gurucharri Monroe should receive a medal of honor for standing by me and my work for so many years, and so do our children, Mathew and Jessica. More than simple acknowledgment, they deserve praise.

GARY MONROE, retired professor of fine arts and photography at Daytona State College, is a leading voice about Florida self-taught and vernacular art. Monroe is the author of numerous books, including *The Highwaymen: Florida's African-American Landscape Painters* and *Extraordinary Interpretations: Florida's Self-Taught Artists*. He has lectured and written widely about this realm of art and has served museums as a guest curator. Monroe's primary involvement is as a noncommercial photographer. In 2023 Emory University acquired his life's work for their Stuart A. Rose Manuscript, Archives, and Rare Book Library.